Freedom Will Conquer Racism
And Sexism

The 'Civil Rights Act' is damaging *everyone* in our country... especially blacks and women.

By J. Edward Pawlick

Mustard Seeds, Inc.
P.O. Box 812844
Wellesley, MA 02181-0026

E-Mail: freedom@mustardseeds.com
Web Site: www.mustardseeds.com

Copyright © 1998 by J. Edward Pawlick

All rights reserved. No part of this book may be reproduced in any form or by an electronic or mechanical means, including information storage and retrieval systems, without permission in writing from the publisher.

1 2 3 4 5 6 7 8 9

First Edition

ISBN 0-9662949-0-4

Dedication
To My Grandchildren

This book is dedicated to some of my grandchildren. They will not be welcomed anywhere in America if our society continues the way we are headed.

I am not concerned about my daughter or her future husband, who is black. But I am very concerned about their children.

They will not be welcomed by the "haters" among the blacks because they will not be "black" enough. The haters among the whites will not welcome them either. The only way that they *should* be welcomed is as "people," not by the color of the skin. The blood under their skin will be Italian, Jewish, German, Irish, Belgian, and Black. That is a recipe for the perfect American unless the race-haters have their way.

And what will be those grandchildren's status *under the law* as compared to their white cousins? Will they be special for some reason? If so, why?

I am sure that the direction of our country will change because the majority of our people are of good will. They may not understand what is happening now; but they're beginning to understand and when they do, they will call for change.

CONTENTS

	Page
Section I – How We Got Here	1
Chapter 1 – Born In Violence	2
Chapter 2 – We Wanted a Bill ... *Now!*	12
Chapter 3 – Who Added S-E-X?	26
Section II – The Betrayal	37
Chapter 4 – Who Was First To Betray Us?	44
Chapter 5 – The Supreme Court Disobeys The Law	53
Chapter 6 – The U.S. Government Attacks Our Businesses	6˙
Chapter 7 – The Supreme Court Makes It Worse	76
Chapter 8 – Were the "Elite" Surprised by the Supreme Court?	83
Section III – The Civil Rights Act Hasn't Helped Blacks ... It's Hurt	89
Chapter 9 – Freedom Was the Answer	91
Chapter 10 – The Civil Rights Act Hasn't Helped	100
Chapter 11 – Most Blacks Agree	113
Chapter 12 – There Was A better Way in 1964 – More Freedom	123
Chapter 13 – What Would Solomon Northrup Do?	133
Section IV – It Hasn't Helped Women	143
Chapter 14 – It Was Time For A Change	146
Chapter 15 – Who's Led The Change?	153
Chapter 16 – Do Women Need Special Treatment?	169
Chapter 17 – It's A Conflict Among Women — Not Men	179
Chapter 18 – "Sexual Harassment" Law Has Changed Our Morals and Damaged Women	186

	Page
Chapter 19 – The "Glass Ceiling" Is Women's Choice	201
Chapter 20 – No More Hate From Feminists	205

Section V – It's A Serious Threat to Our Freedom — 215
    Chapter 21 – Censorship Of A University — 216
    Chapter 22 – Civil Rights Activists: Where Are You? — 229
    Chapter 23 – Who Is Getting Too Much? — 233

Section VI – Much of Our Industry Is Rusting ... Everyone's Afraid To Talk About The Cause — 237
    Chapter 24 – Why Do We Insist On Driving Our Businesses Overseas? — 238
    Chapter 25 – We're *Punishing* Our Businesses — 253
    Chapter 26 – Another Small Business Is Harassed By The U.S. Government — 259

Section VII – How Can We Conquer Racism & Sexism? — 265
    Chapter 27 – Too Important For Lawyers And Judges — 267
    Chapter 28 – What Do You Think? — 272

Epilogue — 285

Appendix — 287
    Women's Organizations Which Disagree with NOW — 287
    Who Wrote This Book? or What Was It Really Like In 'The Good Old Days?' — 290

Endnotes — 303

VISIT OUR WEBSITE

For more information about

Conquering Racism and Sexism Through Freedom

visit our website at www.mustardseeds.com

Section I

HOW WE GOT HERE

Why has the Civil Rights Act failed?

Let's take a short look at how, and why, the "Civil Rights Act" was supported by a vast majority of American people in 1964.

We'll see that all of the leaders agreed and promised the American people (over and over again) that persuasion and cooperation were what we needed to correct any racial problems.

More liberty and freedom were promised. Instead, we have seen less freedom and an Orwellian nightmare of intrusive government that has enveloped our society. But we don't know how to change it because we don't know quite how it happened.

What we approved with enthusiasm in 1964 has been changed *very quietly* by the "elite." It has been taken apart, piece by piece, paragraph by paragraph, and changed while the American people were looking the other way.

1

BORN IN VIOLENCE

> "[We must be most careful about] liberty when the Government's purposes are beneficent. Men born to freedom are naturally alert to repel invasion of their liberty by evil-minded rulers. The greatest dangers to liberty lurk in insidious encroachment by men of zeal, well-meaning but without understanding."
>
> Justice Louis Brandeis. Quoted by Sen. Norris Cotton (R-NH) in his individual report from the Senate Commerce Committee in 1964.

In January, 1963, President John F. Kennedy was *not* in the lead in the writing of a Civil Rights Act.[1]

That is important because we must realize that it was not just liberal Democrats who were behind this Act. It was the entire country. Over 70% of the American people supported it when it finally came time for passage.[2]

In the spring of 1963, the Republicans in Congress had been chiding Kennedy for two years to take the leadership. He finally had to be pressured into supporting a bill.[3] It was a conservative Republican who kept pushing for a bill that spring.

When the Act was finally passed, the House rose in a rare standing ovation, a tribute to the leadership of that Congressman, William McCulloch, a conservative Republican from a small town in Ohio who had steered the Civil Rights Act through the treacherous cross-currents of Congress.[4]

BORN IN VIOLENCE

That is hard to believe, but it is essential that we understand it if we are to understand this Act. Nobody disputes those facts. The only thing that is disputed is how we should interpret those facts.

Came From A Conservative Republican

John Kennedy was elected President by the black voters of America. Richard Nixon got 51% of the *white* vote, but Kennedy won 68% of the *black* vote. It was that black vote which carried Kennedy to the presidency by a little over 100,000 votes, the closest presidential race in the entire century.[5]

But it was not President Kennedy who introduced a Civil Rights bill in January 1963. The blacks who had voted for him expected that President Kennedy would repay them, but they were disappointed.

Both 1961 and 1962 went by without any legislation on this subject being introduced by JFK.

When a tough Civil Rights bill was presented to Congress in January, 1963, it came from Congressman McCulloch.[6] The number of black voters in Bill McCulloch's rural district of Ohio was so small that they would practically fit into a telephone booth, but McCulloch wasn't looking for votes.

The entire spring of that year went by without the heavily Democratic Congress moving at all on Civil Rights. The chairman of the House Judiciary Committee was in charge, liberal Democrat Emanuel Celler from Brooklyn. But he still hadn't even scheduled a hearing on any Civil Rights bill.

What finally turned President Kennedy around and made him take a leadership role for a Civil Rights Act?

It was the violent reaction to the protests that occurred in the South that year.

Protests and Riots

When the nation watched the news one evening in May, 1963, it was shocked.[7]

There on their television screens, they saw black children, most of them teenagers but some no more than six years old, being blasted by high-pressure fire hoses in the streets of Birmingham, Alabama.

Little girls in starched dresses were among them. They fell to the ground and lay bleeding.

FREEDOM WILL CONQUER RACISM (AND SEXISM)

Within days, the name and face of Eugene "Bull" Connor, who headed the police and firemen in Birmingham, a tough steel town, became famous not only in America, but across the entire world.

A bad part of America had been illuminated by a bright arc for the entire world to see.

This press coverage was not an accident. Dr. Martin Luther King, Jr., had counted on the power of the press and particularly that new medium, television, to show the world how hard it was to be a black person in the South. His organization "was making a deliberate effort to provoke a violent response to its nonviolent demonstrations, and thereby force President Kennedy to act."[8]

When King came to Birmingham in the spring of 1963, he had not been invited by anyone, white or black. He came uninvited because it was his belief that Bull Connor would react in a violent manner, receive a lot of press coverage and cause shock around the country. And he was right.[9]

But many in Birmingham did not want King there because Bull Connor had just been rejected by the voters and would soon be replaced in office by a much more moderate man.[10] To many Birmingham blacks, King's actions inflamed the tensions of the city just at the point when they seemed to be making progress.

Complained one black lawyer, "The new administration should have been given a chance to confer with the various groups interested in change." Said a white Jesuit priest who was Alabama's chairman of the U. S. Civil Rights Commission, "These demonstrations are poorly timed and misdirected."[11]

Attorney General Robert F. Kennedy said that King had "just grievances" but "the timing of the present demonstrations is open to question." Even more questionable, said Bobby, is the use of children as troops.

"Schoolchildren participating in street demonstrations is a dangerous business. An injured, maimed or dead child is a price that none of us can afford to pay."[12]

But regardless of what the demonstrations did for the city of Birmingham, Martin Luther King was correct. The actions of Bull Connor outraged the country and its President.

How could anyone not be shocked by what was happening before their eyes?

How could anyone not want to reach out and help the victims of this terrible sickness that suddenly became evident in our society? So the nation came to favor a new law to end this crazy business.

JFK Assumes Leadership

In June, 1963, President Kennedy finally acted. When he did decide to act, this issue became very important to him. On June 1, he met with some of his closest advisers.[13] On June 11, he made a television speech to the nation[14] and on June 19 he sent a Civil Rights Act to Congress.[15] But even then, his bill was mainly concerned with opening up lunch counters and hotels. There was *nothing* in his bill about rights to a job. He sent a separate bill to deal with that problem.[16]

The President met with 100 top executives of chain stores operating in the South to get their support. He still did not want a law about employment. Said one of the businessmen, "He kept stressing that voluntary action by businessmen was far more effective—and preferred by him—instead of forcing integration through new laws."[17]

Regardless of whether you approve of JFK or not, everyone agrees that he was finally moved by the demonstrations of Martin Luther King.

Even his official biographer agrees. Harvard Professor Arthur Schlesinger says that after the protests and the violence began in 1963, "Kennedy now responded to the Negro revolution by seeking to assume its leadership."[18]

Martin Luther King later said approvingly of Kennedy that the President responded to "creative pressure.... He [Kennedy] frankly acknowledged that he was responding to mass demands and did so because he thought it was right to do so."[19]

And JFK did assume that leadership in a strong and forceful manner. So much so that former President Eisenhower, who had had trouble with many Democrats when he had been promoting civil rights bills, wondered about the sudden conversion, saying, "To Republicans, 'the rights of men' is a living doctrine. To our opponents, it is a campaign catch-phrase, a political gimmick ...."[20]

Whatever the reason, the Civil Rights Act started to become the biggest domestic issue in 1963.

FREEDOM WILL CONQUER RACISM (AND SEXISM)

All through the summer of 1963, the Civil Rights Act was news as the Judiciary Committee in the House continued to hold hearings on the bill. The stories of violence continued to come in from the South.

Year of the Lunch Counters

This was the year of the "lunch counter". In 1963 blacks merely tried to get a hamburger or a cup of coffee in the South. And they usually tried a lunch counter in a nationwide chain such as Woolworth's.[21]

The head of the NAACP, Roy Wilkins, stated it very eloquently:

"For millions of Americans, this is vacation time. Families load their automobiles and trek across country. I invite the members of this committee to imagine themselves darker in color and to plan an auto trip from Norfolk, Va., to the Gulf Coast of Mississippi. How far do you drive each day? Where and under what conditions can you and your family eat? Can you stop after a reasonable day behind the wheel, or must you drive until you reach a city where relatives or friends will accommodate you for the night? Will your children be denied a soft drink or an ice cream cone because they are not white? When you travel through what we call hostile territory, you take your chances. You drive and drive and drive."[22]

And the blacks were showing America just how true that was. All across the South, the country was writhing with peaceful—and violent—demonstrations.

In Jackson, Mississippi, for example, a group of sit-in demonstrators sat at a lunch counter in a five-and-ten store, while whites ridiculed and insulted them, then poured ketchup, mustard and sugar on them. Finally, enraged by the stoic silence, a white dragged a black off the stool and kicked him in the face again and again. The black was sent to the hospital and was then arrested for disturbing the peace.[23]

In Cambridge, Maryland, more than a dozen white toughs were waiting in a lunchroom when the demonstrators arrived. They locked the door behind the blacks and then commenced to beat them while angry blacks outside heard the screams and groans and pounded on the locked door.[24]

If that weren't enough, this tension excited the real kooks. In June, a father of three, a World War II veteran, college graduate, varsity football player, and head of the NAACP in Mississippi, was shot in the back and killed as he entered his home. He was Medgar Evers. His killer turned out to be a "troubled" man who had come from old Southern stock.[25]

In September came two bombings in Birmingham. The home of a black attorney was blasted by dynamite. And then on Sunday, September 15, more than 10 sticks of dynamite exploded in a black church. Four little girls were buried and killed in the debris. The church's minister told the gathering crowds, "Please go home. The Lord is our shepherd and we shall not want." Another pleaded: "Go home and pray for the men who did this evil deed. We must have love in our hearts for these men."[26]

But, as the police arrived, some began to throw rocks at them and the police rolled up their riot tank. Before that day ended, two more blacks lay dead (one of them killed by white 16-year-olds).

Violence on Both Sides

But the racism and violence were not limited to white people. The people with hate in their hearts were active among both whites and blacks.

The head of the NAACP in Philadelphia said, "My basic strength is those 300,000 lower- class guys who are ready to mob, rob, steal and kill."[27]

And at the NAACP convention in Chicago, the first black man to be admitted to the University of Mississippi, James Meredith (who had gone through tremendous emotional pressure, in September, 1962, with $4.5 million spent to protect him and with two lives lost in rioting) was reduced to tears of frustration. "[I] shed my first tears since I was a child" over the "intolerance and bigotry" he found at the NAACP.[28]

At the same convention, the head of the largest black church in America, the National Baptist Convention, U.S.A., spoke against a mass march on Washington. But he received thunderous boos and was unable to speak. A crowd of about 50 gathered around him, shouting "Kill him, kill him." He was pinned against the platform until finally rescued by ushers.[29]

During the same week, black people in Harlem threw eggs at Martin Luther King.[30]

The head of the NAACP, Roy Wilkins, said, "The Negro citizen has come to the point where he is not afraid of violence. He no longer shrinks back. He will assert himself, and if violence comes, so be it."[31]

Actually, the NAACP, which had always done its fighting for black rights in the courts and in Congress, found itself on the defensive during this period as King sought to become the new leader[32] with a new venue, the streets, as he brought the young, black militants into the streets for action.*

As riot followed riot, many in the country became weary of the violence.

Even President Kennedy warned in July, "I'm concerned about these demonstrations. I think they go beyond information, beyond protest, and they get into a very bad situation where you get violence, and I think the cause of advancing equal opportunities only loses. So I have warned against demonstrations which could lead to bloodshed, and I warn now against them."[33]

Violence Was Only By A Few

But the violence was limited to only a few people in both the black and white communities. Most people wanted to live in peace with their neighbors, no matter what their color.

The only problem was that one crazy person with a few sticks of dynamite would get massive press coverage and scores of television cameras, photographers and reporters. But thousands of good people could work without anyone hearing about it.

Most of the opposition from white leaders was coming only from Alabama and Mississippi. In Spartanburg, South Carolina, most downtown restaurants quietly opened their businesses to all. In North Carolina, the mayors of Winston-Salem, Durham and Charlotte announced that dozens of restaurants had done likewise.[35]

---

* One of King's lieutenants, Andrew Young, was to write later, in 1996, "There were many, including Thurgood Marshall, the author of the NAACP's legal strategy [and later a justice on the U.S. Supreme Court], who greatly resented Martin and [his organization's] willingness to break the law, even unjust laws. They had crafted a decades-long strategy of promoting civil rights through obedience to the law and [King and his people] seemed poised to undermine that carefully nurtured strategy." Andrew Young, *An Easy Burden: The Civil Rights Movement and the Transformation of America* (Harper Audio, 1996).

BORN IN VIOLENCE

In Raleigh, a biracial committee announced that it was desegregated "on a citywide basis," and thirty-five of Richmond's better restaurants did the same.[35] Even in Mississippi, Cleve McDowell peacefully entered the law school at the University of Mississippi where only nine months previously two men died and dozens were injured when James Meredith enrolled there.[36]

The head of the NAACP, Roy Wilkins, said, "White people are like colored. They are glad and sad. They know poverty and trouble and divorce and sickness. I may be an incurable optimist, but I believe there are more people who want to do good than do evil. The Negro couldn't have made it without the help of some white people."[37]

Time magazine made Martin Luther King its "Man of the Year" and said, "After 1963, with the help of Martin Luther King Jr., the Negro will never again be where or what he was."[38]

And it was true.*

Of course, the racism on both sides did not disappear overnight. But the whole attitude was changing.**

The biggest victory during that year came in August and was called the "March on Washington for Jobs and Freedom."

Many people did not want such a march. In a year of violence and racism, they were justifiably afraid of what might happen if thousands of people gathered on a hot summer day.

---

* Wilkins also said that the blacks must realize that life would not be soft after the Act was passed. He said:

"The back of segregation is broken; a whole new era is before us. This will be a period when the Negro will have to make readjustments. We must counsel our Negro population on induction into an integrated society, teach them that you can't blame all disabilities on race, because this is self- defeating. A great number of Negroes are ready for all their rights now. A great number are not fully aware of the competition and responsibility which await them in an unsegregated world."

"There's going to be beer, and doubleheaders with the Yankees, and ice cream and mortgages and taxes, and all the things that whites have in their world, and tedium too. It's not going to be heaven." *Time,* August 30, 1963.

** American racial attitudes had been growing more egalitarian, particularly since World War II. Whereas only 2% of southern and 42% of northern whites favored integrated schools in 1942, by 1972 70% of southern and 90% of northern whites did. The year 1964 probably marked the high point of American public opinion's belief in and hope for racial equality. Graham, *Civil Rights Era,* pp. 455-56.

FREEDOM WILL CONQUER RACISM (AND SEXISM)

President Kennedy was among them.[39]

It was rumored that blacks would throw themselves in front of buses, trains and airplanes. A sit-in at the Capitol was discussed. But it was feared among the leaders that this would be counter-productive.

But since a march was inevitable, Kennedy knew he had to support it in order to maintain his leadership.

The March on Washington was a great success. Over 200,000 persons (about 85% black) gathered peacefully in front of the Lincoln Memorial. Martin Luther King came to the end of his prepared text but the audience would not let him stop.

"I have a dream," he cried.

"I have a dream that one day on the red hills of Georgia the sons of former slaves and the sons of former slave owners will be able to sit down together at the table of brotherhood."

The crowd, which was always directly involved in a Martin Luther King speech, was cheering but became silent as he continued.

"I have a dream that even the state of Mississippi, a state sweltering with people's injustices, sweltering with the heat of oppression, will be transformed into an oasis of freedom and justice." Applause and cheers almost drowned him out.

"I have a dream that my four little children will one day live in a nation where they will not be judged by the color of their skin but by the content of their character."

After the event was over *Time* magazine said, "No one who saw the proceedings could come to any other conclusion than that those scores of thousands of marching Negroes were able to accept the responsibilities of first-class citizenship."[40]

Meanwhile ... Back At Congress

Meanwhile, back at Congress, the less exciting, but much more important work was going on steadily. President Kennedy knew that he had to have the help of the Republicans. So he had agreed to a deal with Bill McCulloch (the congressman from Ohio):

- JFK wouldn't allow the Democratic Senate to gut the bill as it had done in prior years. It would be a strong bill or nothing at all.
- JFK would see that the Republicans got equal credit for passage of the bill.[41]

McCulloch became very angry in October, 1963, when it looked as though the Democrat in charge, Congressman Celler, was breaking the agreement. It took President Kennedy's personal intervention to keep the process on track, and meetings were held in the White House itself.[42]

Although nothing had been included in the President's bill about rights in *employment*, it was included in the bill that was hammered out in the White House. (JFK had told the black leaders after the March on Washington that an inclusion of this would be the one sure thing that would kill any bill.[43])

It was said that President Kennedy could never understand why the Republicans cooperated with him on a bill that could only hurt them.[44] The solid South that always went Democratic was just starting to be broken, with a few Republicans being elected here and there. But the Civil Rights Act would critically hurt any Republican chances of picking up many new white supporters in the South and winning the election in 1964.

"They couldn't understand," said the Republican leader in the House, Charlie Halleck, "that once in a while a guy does something because it's right.... Hell, I didn't do it for political advantage. The colored votes in my district didn't amount to a bottle of cold pee."[45]

But gone was any hope of getting a bill passed in 1963. By the time a bill was finally reported out of the Judiciary Committee in the House, it was already midway through November.[46] Most people forget that President Kennedy had a very disappointing record in getting laws passed by Congress.[47]

There was a question whether the public was behind the Civil Rights bill. One Democrat Congressman began to believe there would not be a bill under Kennedy. "There just wasn't that kind of movement behind it. It was running out of gas again."[48]

But President Kennedy was on his way to Texas, where he would appear in a parade in Dallas.

2

WE WANTED A BILL ... *NOW!*

<u>Friday, November 22, 1963.</u>   President John F. Kennedy was shot in a parade in Dallas.

<u>Monday, three days later.</u>   Lyndon Johnson walked slowly behind Mrs. Kennedy and the horse-drawn caisson that carried the body of the late President to the slopes of Arlington Cemetery, just across the Potomac from the White House.

<u>Wednesday, only two days later.</u>   President Johnson talked to the entire nation via television when he addressed a jam-packed session at the Capitol building.

    Seldom has a president ever had the full attention of the nation as President Johnson did on Wednesday, November 27, 1963.
    The Capitol was crowded with Senators, Congressmen, the Supreme Court, the Cabinet, the Joint Chiefs of Staff, and all of the ambassadors and other diplomats.
    The President began, slowly and softly, "All I have, I would have given gladly, not to be standing here today."[1]
    As America riveted its attention on the TV screen and hung on his every word, the tall Texan went on to declare that there was a fitting memorial that the nation could give to its fallen leader.
    Pass a strong civil rights bill.

WE WANTED A BILL ... NOW!

"No memorial oration or eulogy," the President said, "could more eloquently honor President Kennedy's memory than the earliest passage of the civil rights bill for which he fought so long. We have talked long enough in this country about equal rights. We have talked for one hundred years or more. It is time now to write the next chapter, and to write it in the books of law."

The President stopped and looked at the jammed chamber.

"I urge you again, as I did in 1957 and again in 1960, to enact a civil rights law so that we can move forward to eliminate from this Nation any trace of discrimination and oppression that is based upon race or color. There could be no greater source of strength to this Nation both at home and abroad."

And so the challenge was presented to a shocked nation. If you really want to honor your fallen President, you will pass a civil rights act.

This was to be the "Kennedy Memorial."

Almost everyone agrees that Lyndon Johnson sincerely wanted a bill, but they also agree that this was in his best personal, political interest. He was a farm boy from Texas with a conservative, Southern bias who had never gotten much respect from the many Harvard men with their three-button suits who had surrounded the late President. Johnson told a biographer later:

"I knew that if I didn't get out in front on this issue, [the liberals] would get me. They'd throw up my background against me, they'd use it to prove that I was incapable of bringing unity to the land I love so much....I couldn't let that happen. I had to produce a civil rights bill that was even stronger than the one they'd have gotten if Kennedy had lived. Without it, I'd be dead before I could even begin."[2]

The Mood Was Different

When the Congressmen and Senators went home for Christmas a few weeks later, they found that the President's message had been heard. The people of America wanted a bill and they blamed the old men who were chairmen of the committees in Congress for frustrating JFK and not giving them one.[3]

America had become like a big Town Meeting where the people had heard enough of the debating. They wanted a vote ... *now*. They wanted to do something about those lunch counters where black people couldn't even get a cup of coffee. They wanted to stop all those racists who were trying to prevent black people from entering kindergarten or a state college.

An overwhelming 70 percent favored the bill.[4] They were tired of the delay. *And they were not interested in details.*

The popular feeling was that the only ones who were against the bill were "racists." Who else *could* be against it?

And this was correct, almost. Most of the people who did speak out against the bill were Southerners. And these Southerners did a disservice to the country cause by making it politically impossible for anyone else to have a rational discussion.

Even the churches joined in for the bill. The leaders of the civil rights groups met with Jewish, Catholic and Protestant leaders to put pressure on the Congressmen and Senators from those states where there were no labor unions or black voters. In these states, the local clergy and their parishioners met with their congressmen. This was new for church groups, to engage in purely political lobbying. A trio of Jewish, Protestant, and Catholic seminarians were to begin a 24-hour vigil in front of the Lincoln Memorial.[5]

It appeared that anyone who quarreled with *any* portion of this *particular* Act, was (1) not only a "racist" but was (2) against God. The *specific* wording in this specific bill had received the blessing of God. There was to be no further debate.

Now it was the "good guys" against the "racists." There was no in-between.

Success In The House

It took the House of Representatives only a week to debate and pass the bill by an overwhelming vote on February 10, 1964. Outside of members from the solid South, only 34 of the 420 Congressmen opposed it.

Although it was quickly passed by the House, there had been some concern that the federal government would be able to tell an employer whom it could hire. Or that a certain "quota" of blacks must be hired.

This concern had been expressed in a Minority Report from the Judiciary Committee by Southern members. But that concern was quickly handled by the leadership of Congress.

WE WANTED A BILL ... NOW!

When Congressman Celler rose to introduce the bill on January 31, he had swiftly laid that fear to rest. Many in Congress were assured by his remarks because they knew that when the sponsor of a bill makes any statement on the floor of Congress, it becomes part of the "legislative history" of the bill. All of the courts in the U. S., *including the Supreme Court,* look at this when they come to interpret a bill.

Celler told the Congress that the opponents of the Act were not telling the truth, and he was going to set the record straight. He continued:

"Specifically, the charge has been made that the [federal bureaucracy] would have the power to prevent a business from employing and promoting the people it wished, and that a 'federal inspector' could then order the hiring and promotion only of employees of certain races or religious groups."[6]

But the bald, 75-year-old from Brooklyn knew that this was incorrect.

"This description of the bill is entirely wrong," he told the assembled crowd of Congress and others.

And then he went on to further allay any fears by pointing out that the government would always have to *prove* that a business had discriminated.

"[The government] would be required to prove in the court that the particular employer involved had, in fact, discriminated against one or more of his employees..."

Even a judge could not favor one race over another.

"The court could not order that any preference be given to any particular race, religion or other group, but would be limited to ordering an end to discrimination. The statement that a Federal inspector could order the employment and promotion only of members of a specific racial or religious group is therefore patently erroneous."

We could publish a series of books filled with assurances of this type that were proclaimed with great authority by Congressman after Congressman during the debate. Pages and pages of this are in the Congressional Record. Thereafter, the House went on to overwhelmingly approve the bill.

The "record" was crystal clear for any court which would later interpret the Act.

FREEDOM WILL CONQUER RACISM (AND SEXISM)

Democrats Try to Renege

There was one point of high drama in the debate. On the seventh day, Congressman McCulloch was in the restroom when the Democrat Majority Whip, Hale Boggs of Louisiana, who was a good friend of Lyndon Johnson, rose to support an amendment which would drastically weaken one section of the bill.

When McCulloch learned of this, he became furious because he could see a last minute effort by the Democrats to compromise with their Southern members in order to avoid a very embarrassing, party-breaking filibuster in the Senate. It was to be 1957 all over again when Majority Leader Lyndon Johnson had agreed to weaken that bill.

"Look!" McCulloch's wife, Mabel, whispered to Roy Wilkins, who was sitting next to her in the gallery. "Bill's face is red. He's mad!"[7]

McCulloch reached for the microphone.

"If we pick up this old provision...," he announced angrily, "I regret to say that my individual support of the legislation will come to an end."

The House was shocked. but McCulloch was tired of being repeatedly betrayed every time he thought that he and the Democrats had an agreement. And his colleagues could see that he meant it. The amendment went down to defeat, 80 for and 206 against, *despite the support of the Democratic leader.*

On To The Senate

And so on to the U. S. Senate went this bill which had now become so popular. But it would surely suffer a more hostile audience there. The Senate had either killed or watered-down every civil rights bill that had ever been presented to it. This was accomplished by the use of the filibuster, where teams of Senators would talk for hours and days on end and not allow a measure to come to a vote.

In addition, a full-page advertisement had been placed in 200 newspapers by opponents of the bill. The opponents called themselves the "Coordinating Committee for Fundamental American Freedoms." It was chaired by William Loeb, publisher of the Union Leader newspaper in New Hampshire, and it had a former president of the American Bar Association from Mississippi as its Secretary. Actually, it was a terrible ad. It looked home-made, it had many exaggerations and it turned out to be financed almost exclusively by the state of Mississippi. Although it raised many legitimate concerns, it placed these legitimate concerns "off limits" because it made it appear that they were being raised only by racists. Therefore, it made any legitimate debate impossible.

But the ad did worry many persons across the country, and the newspapers and Senators reported that their mail against the bill was becoming more heavy after the ad was published.

Debate Begins

Debate started in the Senate on Monday, March 9, 1964. But the filibustering by Southern Democrats began immediately; and it wasn't until June 10 that the Senate was able to stop the filibuster by obtaining a vote of two-thirds of the Senators, a feat which few had thought would be accomplished.

During the filibuster, the concern about "quotas" was raised again and again but the leaders of the Senate kept saying that this was a ridiculous claim. They said this was a "red herring" to confuse the citizens.

It's true that the concern about quotas was being raised almost exclusively by Southerners. The sponsor of the bill, Senator Humphrey, was most troubled by Senator Robertson of Virginia (the father of Pat Robertson, a presidential candidate in 1988 and later the leader of the Christian Coalition). A few days after the debate started, Robertson was rambling on:

"The passage of this [portion of the Act which refers to employment] will be a severe blow to the free enterprise system which has helped make America great. An employer will not be free to make selections as to individuals he prefers to hire. This [Act] suggests that hiring should be done on some percentage basis in order that racial imbalance will be overcome."[8]

Hubert Humphrey was concerned when he heard more about this quota business. Robertson went on to give an example: "It is contemplated by this [portion of the Act concerning employment] that the percentage of colored and white population in a community shall be in similar percentages in every business establishment that employs over 25 persons. Thus, if there were 10,000 colored persons in a city and 15,000 whites, an employer with 25 employees would, in order to overcome racial imbalance be required to have 10 colored personnel and 15 white. And if by chance that employer had 20 colored employees, he would have to fire 10 of them in order to rectify the situation. Of course, this works the other way around where whites would be fired. The impracticality and unworkability of this [portion of the Act] seem self-evident."

At which point, Senator Humphrey felt he had no choice but to intervene.

"The bill does not require that at all. If it did, I would vote against it."

But the Senator from Virginia was not to be stilled. "Did the Senator ever hear about the camel that got into the tent. Did the camel come all the way into the tent the first time?"

"I have heard that story," Humphrey replied.

"That is an old maxim," continued Robertson. "In other words, let us start by getting in a little way first." But Humphrey was something of a country boy himself and could match a tale with a tale.

"I am asking the Senator not to put up his own tent and then bring in his own trained camel. The Senator is putting up his own little tent and bringing in his camel. As a matter of fact, there is no tent and there is no camel. Also, there is no magic. We are saying that under the commerce clause of the Constitution there shall be a program of equal employment opportunity."

"Is there anything in the woodpile?" Robertson queried.

"No; there is not; neither is there a chipmunk. The bill has been given the Virginia treatment. It means that it has had refined legislative processing."

Humphrey Reassures

The bill was not officially introduced until the last day of March, and as the chief sponsor of the bill, Senator Humphrey talked for 2 ½ hours. He again replied to the persons who were saying that Title VII, the portion of the bill dealing with employment, would require a quota system. He gave some time to this subject.

"Contrary to the allegations of some opponents of this title, there is nothing in it that will give any power to the Commission or to any court to require hiring, firing, or promotion of employees in order to meet a racial 'quota' or to achieve a certain racial balance.

"That bugaboo has been brought up a dozen times; but it is nonexistent. In fact, the very opposite is true. Title VII prohibits discrimination. In effect, it says that race, religion and national origin are not to be used as the basis for hiring and firing. Title VII is designed to encourage hiring on the basis of ability and qualifications, not race or religion."[9]

Senator Humphrey's successful strategy was to treat all of his opponents with extreme courtesy and never to question the sincerity of anyone. But even he could not be perfect and as he concluded, he noted that the opposition was coming from bigots:

"This bill cannot be attacked on its merits. Instead, bogeymen and hobgoblins have been raised to frighten well meaning Americans."

An Historic Event in Birmingham

That Easter Sunday a remarkable event took place.

Some 35,000 people gathered in the tough city of Birmingham, which had been visible as the epitome of racial hatred less than a year earlier during Bull Connor's reign. The 35,000 participants were almost equally divided between blacks and whites. They came together in a city-owned, football field for the largest integrated gathering in Alabama history.

They came to hear Evangelist Billy Graham, who proclaimed, "What a moment and what an hour in Birmingham." The majority of the city at last had a chance to exhibit their goodwill as opposed to the extremists. However, their effort received only a tiny fraction of the worldwide headlines that the extremists had received.

Said a local newspaper publisher, "It is the greatest thing that has happened to Birmingham."[10]

More History for the Judges

What was happening outside the Capitol in Washington became important to all of the American people. CBS News assigned Roger Mudd to permanent duty on the Capitol steps. Five times every day, Mudd reported to the American people on exactly what was happening at that hour to the civil rights bill inside the Senate.

And inside the Capitol more "legislative history" was being made for the judges. To make sure that the intent of the bill was clear, the two floor managers of Title VII, Democrat Senator Clark and Republican Case, prepared a written Memorandum so that all the Senators would understand the bill more clearly. In that memo, they again rebutted that old chestnut about "quotas."

"There is no requirement in title VII that an employer maintain a racial balance in his work force," the Memorandum stated.[11]

"On the contrary, any deliberate attempt to maintain a racial balance, whatever such a balance may be, would involve a violation of title VII because maintaining such a balance would require an employer to hire or to refuse to hire on the basis of race. It must be emphasized that discrimination is prohibited as to any individual. While the presence or absence of other members of the same minority group in the work force may be a relevant factor in determining whether in a given case a decision to hire or to refuse to hire was based on race, color, etc., it is only one factor, and the question in each case would be whether that individual was discriminated against."

But there had been a disturbing new development in Illinois. A state agency had held that the Motorola radio company could not ask a black man, who was applying for a job, to take an IQ test.[12] This, of course, led to concerns that any business would be forbidden under the proposed federal law from using IQ or similar psychological tests. But the memorandum to the Senators was clear:[13]

"There is no requirement in title VII that employers abandon bona fide qualification tests where, because of differences in background and education, members of some groups are able to perform better on these tests than members of other groups. An employer may set his qualifications as high as he likes, he may test to determine which applicants have these qualifications, and he may hire, assign, and promote on the basis of test performance."

After introducing that Memorandum, Senator Clark looked around him and saw that he was speaking to an empty Senate. But he wanted to answer the objections that were being raised. So he introduced another document, that gave the "official" answers to a number of "objections" that had been made by Senators:

"Objection: Many employers will lean over backwards to avoid discrimination, and as a result will discriminate against other employees.

"Answer: [T]he Commission [which is being established by the Act] has a clear mandate not to discriminate against whites.

"Objection: The bill would make it unlawful for an employer to use qualification tests based upon verbal skills and other factors which may relate to the environmental conditioning of the applicant.

In other words, all applicants must be treated as if they came from low-income, deprived communities in order to equate environmental inequalities of the culturally deprived group.

"**Answer:** The employer may set his qualifications as high as he likes, and may hire, assign, and promote on the basis of test performance.

"**Objection:** If the employer discharges a Negro, he must prove that the dismissal has nothing to do with race. When an employer promotes or increases the pay of a white employee, he must show that he was not biased against the Negro worker who was not promoted.

"**Answer:** The Commission must prove ... that the discharge or other personnel action was because of race.

"**Objection:** The bill would require employers to establish quotas for nonwhites in proportion to the percentage of nonwhites in the labor market area.

"**Answer:** Quotas are themselves discriminatory."[14]

Even More History for the Judges

Senator Robertson came back to haunt Senator Humphrey on a lazy Thursday in April. He forced Humphrey to write some more "legislative history" by getting him to put more "on the record" and say:

"But I feel sure that the Senator from Virginia is not going to suggest or intimate that under this title of the bill there would be such a thing as a quota or a required percentage."[15]

Robertson shot back. "Not only am I going to intimate it, I am going to charge it; and I am also going to point it out in detail."

Finally, after ten minutes of this badgering, even the calm Senator Humphrey became exasperated and burst out:

"The Senator from Virginia is off on a rabbit hunt again, and I am not going to follow him through the sagebrush. But I would like to make an offer to him. If the Senator can find in title VII ... any language which provides that an employer will have to hire on the basis of percentage or quota related to color, race, religion, or national origin, I will start eating the pages one after another, because it is not in there."[16]

It was not difficult to see why Humphrey was exasperated. The advertisements that had been placed by the Mississippi group were still having their effect. Even though the House was no longer involved, Congressman Bill McCulloch felt he had to answer them. He prepared a long list of answers to the advertisement and then the conservative Ohio Republican closed with a final promise and reassurance to his constituents and the other citizens of America who might still be troubled.

"For the Americans who do not discriminate against their fellow citizens because of race, color or religion, the Federal Civil Rights Bill will have no effect on their daily lives."[17]

Passes Senate

Senator Humphrey wanted to get the bill moving while public opinion was still in favor because black extremists were back at work. A stall-in was planned for the opening day of the World's Fair in New York; others threatened to leave their water faucets open. This could cause a backlash against the bill.[18] And young hoodlums were still at work. In New York City, people were becoming afraid to ride on the subways because gangs of young black toughs were robbing and knifing anyone they found. After a young black man helped rescue a white man, he told police, "I'm scared of my life up here in New York. It's safer in Mississippi."[19] And whites pelted an NAACP float in Boston's St. Patrick's Parade with rocks, eggs and beer cans.[20] Humphrey was forced to warn that "Civil wrongs do not bring civil rights. Civil disobedience does not bring equal protection under the laws."[21] Even President Johnson was forced to make a statement: "We do not condone violence or taking the law into your own hands, or threatening the health or safety of our people."[22]

Those full-page advertisements again forced Senator Humphrey to state his case because of what he called the "well-financed drive by certain opponents to confuse and mislead the American people." He said on the Senate floor:

"The title does not provide that any preferential treatment in employment shall be given to Negroes or to any other persons or groups. It does not provide that any quota systems may be established to maintain racial balance in employment. In fact, the title would prohibit preferential treatment for any particular group, and any person, whether or not a member of any minority group would be permitted to file a complaint of discriminatory employment practices."[23]

And so on June 19 the bill passed the Senate by a vote of 73-27. Every Senator voted for it except the solid-South and Goldwater of

Arizona, Hickenlooper of Iowa, Cotton of New Hampshire, Mechem of New Mexico, Tower of Texas, and Simpson of Wyoming.

Amendments Had Been Added By Senators

When the bill went back to the House on July 2, it was a totally re-written bill, known as the Dirksen Bill, named after the Republican leader in the Senate, who had changed it in many areas. But everything was satisfactory to Bill McCulloch and the other leaders in the House because the Democratic leadership in the Senate had followed their agreement with McCulloch and had changed nothing without the Congressman's approval.

Many amendments had been added to make it more clear. One of the amendments made it clear that there would be no quotas: "Nothing ...shall be interpreted to require any employer...to grant preferential treatment to any individual or to any group...on account of an imbalance which may exist with respect to ... any race."[24]

This amendment was perfectly satisfactory to everyone because it didn't change the bill in any way. It was what everyone had known all along. It just made it more clear.

Senator Humphrey told the Senate: "[We] have carefully stated on numerous occasions that [this bill] does not require an employer to achieve any sort of racial balance in his work force by giving preferential treatment to any individual or group. Since doubts have persisted, [this amendment] is added to state this point expressly. [It] does not represent any change in the substance of the [bill]."[25]

Another amendment added the word "intentionally" to make it crystal clear that a business had to "intend" to discriminate in order for it to be unlawful. Senator Humphrey again made it clear that this amendment did not change the Act; it just made it more clear:

"[T]he proposed change does not involve any substantial change in the title. The expressed requirement of intent is designed to make it wholly clear that inadvertent or accidental discrimination will not violate the title or result in entry of court orders. It simply means the [business] must have intended to discriminate."[26]

Back to the House

And so back to the House went the Dirksen bill where it was approved without any changes.

FREEDOM WILL CONQUER RACISM (AND SEXISM)

In encouraging his colleagues to pass the measure, Congressman Lindsay once again felt compelled to allay any fears:

"[W]e wish to emphasize also that this bill does not require quotas, racial balance, or any of the other things that the opponents have been saying about it."[27]

And on the day of the final vote, Congressman McCulloch once again arose to assure the members. Said he:

"Much inaccurate information has been circulated about the legislation both as it left the House [after being approved in February 1964 and sent to the Senate] and as it is now before the House [for final approval]. In view thereof, I wish to negate only a few of the most glaring inaccuracies that have had such wide dissemination....

"Fourth. The bill does not permit the Federal Government to require an employer or union to hire or accept for membership a quota of persons from any particular minority group."[28]

Barry Goldwater Is Vilified

Barry Goldwater, who became the Republican presidential candidate that year, was vilified for his vote. He explained his vote on the Senate floor and most agreed that his stand was on conviction, letting the political chips fall where they may.

His vote was cruelly used against him in the presidential campaign that fall.

This is epitomized by an editorial in *The New York Times* on the morning of his expected nomination for President. "[N]o matter how much Senator Goldwater may disavow it, this will be a victory less of reasonable conservatives of the right than of extremists of the right. What a travesty it is for the 'party of Lincoln,' in this year 1964, to be so unrepresentative of the Negro as to nominate the man who stood almost alone among Republicans in Congress against the Civil Rights Act."[29]

On the day after his nomination the *Times* said: "[Goldwater's nomination will attract voters] who choose in this way to express their resentment against the civil rights advances of the Negro....[His nomination] will represent a viewpoint that the party of Lincoln must in honor and honesty reject. The nomination of Barry Goldwater and the adoption of a Goldwater platform threaten to reduce a once great party to the status of an ugly, angry frustrated faction."[30]

However, the *Times* chief political correspondent, James Reston, had a much different viewpoint in his column on the same page, right next to the editorial; but his moderate voice was in vain. He said:

"A great deal has been written about the 'extremists' in the Senator's camp, but there is in this party, and much more widely in this country, a very large group of moderate, responsible people who are profoundly disturbed about the moral, social, economic and political condition of our national life, and no matter what some of us think about the moral ambiguity of Goldwater's racial and foreign policies, he has become a symbol of protest for these people."

Ever since that election in 1964 when Goldwater was soundly defeated, almost all Congressmen and Senators have been afraid to vote against any bill that has "Civil Rights" *anywhere* in its title.*

Signed In White House

On the same day that it was passed, July 2, 1964, the bill was carried over to the White House; and at 6 o'clock that evening almost the entire Senate and a large part of the house gathered in the East Room to watch President Johnson use over 70 pens to sign copies of it.

In the glare of the television lights, the President told America,

"We believe that all men are entitled to the blessings of liberty. Yet millions are deprived of those blessings -- not because of their own failures, but because of the color of their skin."[31]

But we had made a giant step towards removing all discrimination.

And a solemn contract had been made with the American people that all of us would henceforth have equal opportunities ... regardless of our race or color.

---

*   Years later, in 1988, Sen. Orrin G. Hatch said it clearly, "People are just scared to death to vote against a civil rights bill, no matter how bad it is." *Congressional Quarterly,* March 26, 1988, p. 774. When President Bush vetoed the Civil Rights Act of 1990 he told Congress, "I deeply regret having to take this action with respect to a bill bearing such a title..." 137 *Congressional Record,* p. S 16457.

3

WHO ADDED S-E-X?

> *Many readers will find it difficult to believe how "sex" became a part of the "Civil Rights Bill of 1964." But this is a true and accurate report, difficult though it may be to believe.*

Was there a mistake at the end of the last chapter? Did the printer get it wrong?

Lyndon Johnson is quoted as saying, "[M]illions are deprived...because of the color of their skin."

Shouldn't it read: "Because of the color of their skin <u>*or*</u> because of their sex"? What's going on here? We'd better take a closer look at what Lyndon Johnson said with much of America watching as he stared into those television cameras on July 2nd, 1964:

"I am about to sign into law the Civil Rights Act of 1964. "I want to take this occasion to talk to you about what the law means to every American. We believe that all men are created equal. Yet many are denied equal treatment. We believe that all men have certain unalienable rights. Yet many Americans do not enjoy these rights. We believe that all men are entitled to the blessings of liberty.

"Yet millions are being deprived of those blessings, not because of their own failures—but because of the color of their skin."[1]

We had it printed right. Johnson is talking only about the rights of black people. In his 1,000 word address to the nation, he never once mentioned or alluded to the word "sex" or the rights of women.

WHO ADDED S-E-X?

What's going on? We know that President Johnson was a consummate politician. If he had a chance to score some points with a political group, he wouldn't miss the opportunity. Why doesn't he mention "women" anywhere in his entire speech?

A Saturday Afternoon in Congress

You will not believe what happened in Congress *in less than two hours* on a Saturday afternoon, February 8, 1964. You will think that I made this up. But this is exactly what took place.

The leader of the Southern Democrats in the House of Representatives, Howard W. (Judge) Smith, was worried that the Civil Rights Act was going to pass.

He was facing sure defeat and he knew it. The debate had started only a week before, but it was obvious that it would pass with a large majority and very soon. Things did not look good for the Southerners.

Congressman Smith was an 80-year-old Virginian. He had been in Congress when Franklin Roosevelt was first sworn in as President back in 1932. For years he had been feared as the most powerful person in the House. Crafty and shrewd, he knew every trick in the book.

So when he rose to his feet that Saturday before a bored group of lawmakers, a few looked up expectantly in the hope that something more lively might happen now.

Seven years earlier in 1957, Smith had delayed a Civil Rights bill that President Eisenhower was supporting because Smith said he had to go back to his farm in Virginia to inspect a barn that had just burned down. This caused House Speaker Sam Rayburn to quip, "I knew Howard Smith would do most anything to block a Civil Rights bill, but I never knew he would resort to arson."[2]

But that was 1957. This was 1964. Did the old man still have the power?

"Mr. Chairman, I offer an amendment," the Judge called out.[3]

He then ambled slowly up to the front of the House to a clerk and handed him a sheet of paper. The clerk started to read from the Judge's amendment:

"Amendment offered by Mr. Smith of Virginia: On page 68, line 23, after the word 'religion', insert the word 'sex.'"

"On page 69, line 10, after the word 'religion', insert the word 'sex.'"

FREEDOM WILL CONQUER RACISM (AND SEXISM)

As the clerk droned on with more places where the word "sex" was being added to Title VII, the judge moved over to the well of the House where the microphone was, enjoying the confusion and pandemonium that he was creating. If he couldn't defeat this bill any other way, he would surely do so by putting "women's rights" in the middle of the bill. Surely this would arouse and confuse everyone and cause havoc to the bill.

"Mr. Chairman," Judge Smith spoke when the House had quieted down somewhat,

"This amendment is offered to the fair employment practices title of this bill to include within our desire to prevent discrimination against another minority group, the women—but a very essential minority group—in the absence of which the majority group would not be here today."

As the House began to wake up on this dull Saturday afternoon, it broke into laughter at the Judge's last remark. So he had to caution them in his mirthful way:

"Now, I am very serious about this amendment." The judge then went on to read a letter he had received from a woman in his district as to why "sex" must be included in this Civil Rights bill:

"I suggest," the letter said, "that you might also favor an amendment or a bill to correct the present 'imbalance' which exists between males and females." But the Judge had to stop again and warn all of the members of Congress, "This is serious," before he went on with the letter as follows:

"The census of 1960 shows that we had 88,331,000 males living in this country, and 90,992,000 females, which leaves the country with an 'imbalance' of 2,661,000 females. Just why the Creator would set up such an imbalance of spinsters, shutting off the 'right' of every female to have a husband of her own, is, of course, known only to nature. But I am sure you will agree that this is a grave injustice." And the Judge did agree with the letter writer as he looked up to make sure that the import of his words wasn't being missed.

"And I do agree, and I am reading you the letter because I want all the rest of you to agree, you of the majority." And he went on reading.

"But I am sure you will agree that this is a grave injustice to womankind and something the Congress and President Johnson should take immediate steps to correct . . ."

WHO ADDED S-E-X?

But the laughter became too great at this point, and Congressman Smith had to stop.

"And you interrupted me just now before I could finish reading the sentence which continues on,

"Immediate steps to correct, especially in this election year."

The Judge read some more from the letter and finished with: "What harm will this do to the condition of the bill," at which time the Chairman announced that his time had expired.

When Congressman Celler, who was handling the bill for the Democrats in the House, arose in opposition to the amendment, Judge Smith exclaimed in mock horror:

"Oh, no."

Tenor of Debate

This ludicrous beginning set the tone of the whole debate on "sex" and women's rights as a part of the Civil Rights Act of 1964.

When a piece of legislation is considered by Congress, there are many people who come to testify before the various committees and give their opinions about the strengths and weaknesses of the bill. Congress doesn't pass a bill without giving it very careful and deliberate thought to make sure that everything has been considered. This amendment was one of the most far-reaching laws that Congress has ever passed in its history. It would quickly penetrate American society and American business to unparalleled depths.

Yet, incredibly, there were no *hearings* whatsoever on this amendment! The only *debate* that took place lasted less than two hours on that Saturday. Most of it sounded like a meeting about a Women's Auxiliary of a fraternal lodge.

The Republican members were anxious to leave town because they all had speaking engagements on Lincoln's Birthday. They were even ready to work the next day, Sunday, and wrap it up, so they could leave.

Of the eleven Congressmen who spoke in favor of the amendment, all eleven were Southerners who would later vote against the bill itself. They were only trying to confuse things.

The five "responsible" Congressman who spoke against the amendment were liberal leaders from both parties.

FREEDOM WILL CONQUER RACISM (AND SEXISM)

Of the five women who spoke, four were in favor and one was against.

When the amendment came to a vote less than two hours after Judge Smith first rose to present it, it passed by a vote of 168 for the amendment and 133 against.[4] Therefore, 119 Congressman didn't even bother to vote on this amendment.

An attempt was made later on to get a roll call vote so that every member would have to say how he or she voted. But the House didn't want this vote to be recorded. So we have no record of who voted for this amendment, who voted against it, or who sat on their hands.

We must agree, however, that all Southerners were obviously alerted to this amendment before it was presented and were present therefore at the vote. If this is true and you could take away the 96 Southerners who were voting for the amendment just as a way of killing the entire bill, the amendment lost by a very large margin. Only 72 (other than the Southerners) voted for it and 133 were against it.

This means that, except for the Southerners, the amendment on "sex" was actually *defeated* by a vast majority on that Saturday afternoon.

We have "sex" in the Civil Rights Act of 1964 only because a small group of arch-conservative Southerners put it there. The "responsible" members of Congress voted against it.

The "Auxiliary" Meets

How did this Amendment pass? What was the debate that took place after Judge Smith sat down and the Chamber became quiet again?

The leadership tried to get control. Poor Bill McCulloch saw an entire year of excruciating, difficult work going down the drain. How hard he had labored to bring all of these groups together! And now it was about to be lost. He didn't say a word. . . .

The 75-year-old Congressman Celler rose and attempted to set the tone of the debate but he was unsuccessful. He first reminded the House that a President's "Commission on the Status of Women," which was chaired by Eleanor Roosevelt, had recommended against such an amendment. He also noted that the far-reaching "Equal Pay Act" had just been passed the year before and it required that women get the same pay as men.[5]

WHO ADDED S-E-X?

But Judge Smith did not want this to be a serious discussion, so he would interrupt from time to time.

"I wanted to ask the gentleman to clarify what he said. I did not exactly get what he stated about Negroes. He said he was surprised."[6] To which Celler responded.

"I was a little surprised at your offering the amendment."

"About what?"

The Congressman from Brooklyn tried to regain control of the debate.

"Because I think the amendment seems illogical, ill timed, ill placed, and improper. I was of that opinion, the amendment coming from the astute and very wise gentleman from Virginia."

But Judge Smith would have none of it. If he could keep the House laughing and off guard, he might just pass this pesky amendment.

"Your surprise at my offering the amendment does not nearly approach my surprise, amazement, and sorrow at your opposition to it."

The 75-year-old liberal Democrat was no match for the 80-year-old Virginian, and instead of keeping things on a serious level, Celler joined in the banter:

"As long as there is a little levity here, let me repeat what I heard some years ago, which runs as follows:

"Lives there a man with hide so tough
  Who says, Two sexes are not enough."

The Congressman from Brooklyn tried to get back to a serious discussion by repeating what the President's Commission had recommended:

"The Commission says, wait until mature studies have been made."

But he was unable to keep control. He was next accosted by a Congressman from Texas who asked whether a letter which Celler had read from the Labor Department was from a man or a woman. Celler reported it was from a man, apparently not noticing that the man was merely transmitting a statement from a woman who was Assistant Secretary of Labor. The Congressman from Texas went on:

"I had an idea that would be true, the letter from the Women's Bureau of the Department of Labor opposing this equal rights for women amendment was signed by a man. I think there is no need for me to say more." No one bothered to correct him and tell the Texan that he was misrepresenting the facts.[7]

FREEDOM WILL CONQUER RACISM (AND SEXISM)

A woman, Congresswoman Frances Bolton, then rose in support of the amendment and cited the fact that America's women athletes had just done well in the Winter Olympics at Innsbruck.[8] She finished with the following:

"Even your bones harden long before our bones do. We live longer, we have more endurance."

At this point Mrs. Griffiths of Michigan attempted a serious discussion in favor of the amendment by making it clear that the bill without the amendment would allow black women to sue but would not allow white women to if they thought they were treated unfairly. She talked on for fifteen minutes.[9] She ended her debate with:

"Mr. Chairman, a vote against this amendment today by a white man is a vote against his wife, or his widow, or his daughter, or his sister."[10]

Katherine St. George of New York added this:

"We are entitled to this little crumb of equality. The addition of that little, terrifying word 's-e-x' will not hurt this legislation in any way. In fact, it will improve it. It will make it comprehensive. It will make it logical. It will make it right."[11]

And then rose Edith Green.

She was the only woman to speak against the amendment, pointing out that she had to bow to no one as a crusader for the rights of women. She had been the author of the Equal Pay Act for women which had just passed the year before. However, The Civil Rights Act of 1964 was about rights for blacks, not for women.

"I do not believe this is the time or place for this amendment," she said.[12] And she went on to tell why:

"For every discrimination that has been made against a woman in this country there has been 10 times as much discrimination against the Negro of this country.

"There has been 10 times—maybe 100 times—as much humiliation for the Negro woman, for the Negro man and for the Negro child. Yes; and for the Negro baby who is born into a world of discrimination."

And the Congresswoman went on to point out that there had not been one single bit of testimony in the committees on this subject. Also, not one organization from the entire country nor even one Congressman had petitioned a committee to add this type of amendment. In other words, sex had never been seriously considered.

WHO ADDED S-E-X?

She closed with a caution that this would cause great problems for the businesses of America:

"There will be new problems for business, for managers, for industrial concerns. These should be taken into consideration before any vote is made in favor of this amendment without any hearings at all on the legislation."[13]

Four other liberal leaders of Congress arose in opposition to the amendment: Roosevelt from California, the son of Franklin D. Roosevelt; Thompson from New Jersey, of the Committee on Education and Labor; Lindsay of New York; and Mathias of Maryland.

But as we said, the amendment of Judge Smith passed in less than two hours, 168-133, with 96 Southerners giving it the margin of success.

Some of the debate in favor of it from Southerners ran as follows:

"Unless this amendment is adopted, the white women of this country would be drastically discriminated against in favor of a Negro woman."[14]

"[This amendment is] making it possible for the white Christian woman to receive the same consideration for employment as the colored woman."[15]

What Happened Then?

Hardly anyone in the nation seemed to notice what happened on that Saturday in February 1964. The entire Civil Rights Act passed the House two days later, on Monday, February 10.

Time magazine covered the story in three paragraphs with the headline "Tomfoolery" at the top, saying:

"[T]he ...diehard Democratic opponents knew they were fighting a lost cause. They therefore spent the last hours of debate engaging in tomfoolery. For example, Virginia's Judge Howard Smith ...offered an amendment that would ban discrimination by reason of gender as well as race ...

"Four other female House members rose to second the idea. But Oregon Democrat Edith Green went and spoiled all the fun. 'At the risk of being called an Aunt Jane, if not an Uncle Tom,' she said, 'let us not add any amendment that would get in the way of our primary objective.' Her logic failed to impress the House. It passed the amendment, 168-133, to the delight of a woman in the gallery, who shouted 'We made it. We made it. God bless America.' She was promptly ejected."[16]

And the American people never realized the serious implications of what was going to happen to them.

The *New York Times* included the amendment as only one of many amendments that were passed. On the following Tuesday, when it did a wrap-up of the passage of the entire Civil Rights Act, it had one little paragraph on page 33:

"On Saturday, the Southerners were able to add sex to the list of discriminations in employment to be banned, in addition to race, religion and national origin. Officials of the Justice Department had no great objection to this, although they said it would complicate administration of the program."[17]

So this radical change to American life was made with no one noticing.

When the Civil Rights Act was sent to the Senate, it never went to any committee for study or hearings. Neither was this particular amendment ever discussed on the floor of the Senate.

Two months *after* the words "sex" had been added by the House, Congressman McCulloch was still assuring the nation that anyone who does not discriminate because of "race, color or religion" need have no worry. There was no mention or thought of the word, "sex."

President Johnson told the nation six months later that this bill would end discrimination because of a person's color. Again, no mention or thought of the word, "sex."

And so the Southerners of Congress had added "sex" to the Civil Rights Act of 1964 as a scheme to kill the entire bill, but no one cared or noticed.*

---

* Some readers will say that the public was *not* against adding "sex" to the bill. Otherwise, the Senate would have removed it. In addition, those readers will say, the final bill was not passed by the House until five months later. There was "plenty of time" for the public to complain and have this removed if they so desired. But it is clear why the public didn't complain. They didn't complain because they didn't know it was in the bill. Even President Johnson did not mention it when he signed the bill. And the press was not reporting it. The fact that "sex" had been added was totally lost in the intense pressure to pass a bill, *any* bill.

WHO ADDED S-E-X?

Against the Law

It was now against the law to "discriminate" because of race or sex. But what does it mean to "discriminate?" Some Congressmen had tried to define the word, but their efforts were obscured in the drive to pass a law "now", not later.

It would be up to the bureaucracy in the buildings in Washington and it would be up to the judges in the courts of America to decide what this two hour session would mean to the fabric of our society.

Section II

THE BETRAYAL

When was America "betrayed?"

Is that too strong a word? We learned about the solemn pledges to the American people that the Civil Rights Act would be used to give blacks and whites an "equal opportunity." There would be no favoritism for whites anymore. They would be treated just the same as blacks.

We would have a "color-blind" society.

It would not matter what the color of your skin was.

The vast majority of Americans, both black and white, agreed with that. And they still do.

And so the promise was made that there would be no "balancing" of the races and no "quotas." And, as you have read, this promise was made over and *over* and <u>over</u> .... and over again.

In order to understand how we were betrayed, it will be helpful if you become a little "street-wise." You should understand the practical effects of how a law works. You must know what is known only by those lawyers who actually practice in a courtroom and not just in a walnut-paneled office or in a law school classroom.

FREEDOM WILL CONQUER RACISM (AND SEXISM)

Street-Wise Truth If the U.S. government sues you, it doesn't matter *to you* whether they call it "criminal" or "civil."

If the U.S. government sues you under the Civil Rights Act, with all of its power and lawyers, it really doesn't matter to you whether they call it a "criminal" or a "civil" suit, the effect is *exactly* the same to you. You won't know the difference.

It will not be a "civil" trial which is between two persons; it will be a "criminal" trial between you and the U.S. government.

You are being punished — and you are punished whether you win or lose. It's true that you can't be put in jail (unless you don't do exactly what the judge tells you), but very few criminals are put in jail either. You must hire lawyers, spend valuable time in court, and possibly pay a "fine" to the "injured party" that is usually much *larger* than would ever be required if you were a criminal defendant.

It would be much better for you if they did call it a "criminal" trial. Then you would receive the usual standards of fairness and due process that a robber or a murderer would. But because they label it a "civil" trial, you receive little of those protections. And you are often presumed to be guilty before the trial has even started.

If an individual person is suing you under the Civil Rights Act, you are being punished. But when the U.S. government is suing you, the power is awesome.

Street-Wise Truth A criminal law is invalid if it's too "vague."

A favorite defense of any criminal lawyer is to argue that a law is too "vague." How could the defendant obey the law? He didn't know what he was supposed to do.

The federal courts look with great favor on this argument. These judges have forced the attorneys for many cities and states to burn the midnight oil trying to write a law so that the federal judges can "understand" it.

For example, California wrote a law saying that a person who was loitering on the streets had to provide an identification that was "credible and reliable" when requested by a police officer. The U. S. Supreme Court said this was too "vague."[1] It wasn't clear what was "credible and reliable."[2]

But look at what the Civil Rights Act says:

"It shall be ...unlawful ... for an employer ... to ... discriminate against any individual...."[3]

Just think about that. "...*discriminate*..."

Do you know what "discriminate" means? Does a businessman or a lawyer? Or for that matter, did the Congress? Do the judges know? In most of the cases in this area, the judges *disagree* all the time.

That's all there is to guide a judge (or a businessman). A judge can literally decide that the law means *anything* he or she wants it to mean. A business can not—"*discriminate.*"

You do not need to be a lawyer or a judge to define this word. You can take your turn at defining the word, "discriminate." Any of us can do it. Should we allow nine people, the Supreme Court, to make this important decision as to what it means to discriminate?" Why didn't Congress tell us what it meant?*

Yet if a business, college or government doesn't follow the "law" (whatever it is finally determined to be), it can (1) be fined millions of dollars, (2) have employees forced upon it that it doesn't want, and (3) receive terrible publicity.

Are common criminals entitled to more protection under our laws than hardworking business people?

---

* Many members of Congress tried very hard to force a definition of the word. One of the many examples occurred in April of 1964 when Senator Robertson asked Senator Humphrey, "What does 'discrimination' mean? If it means what I think it does, and which it could mean, it means that a man could be required to have a quota or he would be discriminating. The question comes down to what is meant by 'discrimination' and the framers of the bill will not tell us."

FREEDOM WILL CONQUER RACISM (AND SEXISM)

Why hasn't the U.S. Supreme Court said that this statute is too "vague" to be enforced? That would be the only fair decision, as you will see.*

Street-Wise Truth   Too Many "Laws" Will Destroy a Society

While attending law school in the 1950s, we were taught that a successful society lives by its mores, i.e. its *unwritten* rules. If you hold a door for the person behind you, it is not because it is a "law." If you give your seat to a woman, it is not because it is a "law."

You do these things because this is gracious and a part of civilized living. You cannot write a "law" about every gracious act. It would destroy society to attempt to do so. The vast majority of citizens are very happy to follow the mores of their society.

In the law schools of today, they apparently teach just the opposite, i.e. every "slight" should be outlawed. And everyone must sue for every "slight."

This has led us to a very litigious society that wants to sue for every problem.

Street-Wise Truth   Lawsuits are "Violent"

A law suit is an act of violence, i.e., an act of war.

We forget that a lawyer is a mercenary, a "hired gun" who will represent the first person who approaches him or her. There's nothing wrong with that; but it is a fact. In a lawsuit, we use words instead of bullets, but they destroy just as much.

Many of the plain people in Pennsylvania, such as the River Brethren, Mennonites and Amish, will *never* bring a lawsuit for

---

* Some scholars have argued with me that it is very clear what "discriminate" means: They say the only trouble is that the courts have not followed the clear meaning of the word. But this begs the point because if these scholars and the courts disagree so strongly as to what it means, then its correct meaning is obviously not apparent. The Supreme Court used the vagueness of the concept to give it a meaning that none of its proponents publicly endorsed in 1964.

exactly that reason. They know that a lawsuit is an act of violence against a neighbor, and their religious beliefs will not allow it.

Most of us do not totally agree with the plain people. We believe that an act of violence, like war, is sometimes necessary in this world; but, nevertheless, most of the time we would like to "Think Peace."

Therefore, is it a good idea to be telling every person who has been discriminated against to always sue? It may be good for the legal business, but is it always good for the plaintiff, even if he or she wins? (And we lawyers know that whether or not he or she wins will depend largely upon who the attorneys and judge are, not necessarily upon the merits.)

I have seen many people involved in lawsuits in my lifetime, and there is no question that with most of them this becomes the most important part of their lives. Their "honor" is at stake, as in a duel. They have to win and it becomes an obsession. They start to look backward instead of where they are going.

When this happens, a person is in trouble because his or her career becomes secondary to winning.

Perhaps it is not good always to think of starting a suit even if you can win. Perhaps it is best just to get on with your life. We cannot take every problem in life to a federal court.

Most of us would agree there will undoubtedly be a time when something is so important that it will be necessary to sue.

But when we do, we had better remove the bumper sticker that says, "Think Peace," because we're going to war.

Street-Wise Truth The right to sue is the right to extort.

When a person has the power to sue someone, he or she has the power to *extort*.

That's true because the courts are so overcrowded. Almost no case goes to trial. Almost everything is settled before it gets to a judge or jury. Over 95% of all cases are settled.

Although a defendant may say, "I'll never pay that crook because this is a matter of principle," your attorney will say, "Settle."

If you don't agree to settle, you become known as a "nut;" and when your attorney talks with the judge or the other attorney, he or she always apologizes and says, "I have a client I can't control." This is true in any type of case, whether it results from an auto accident, a breach of contract or a discrimination suit. Although many people will think that I am exaggerating, I am not. Our entire judicial system today is structured to force a settlement of all cases.

This means that when "a class" of people is given the right to sue you, as in the Civil Rights Act, that class of people has been given the right to extort money from you. The only remaining question is *not* whether the business will pay but *how much* will it have to pay ... to "settle" the matter?

If you manage a business, you will learn this immediately, because when a Complaint is given to it when the suit is started, there will be attached a set of Interrogatories. This will consist of hundreds of detailed questions about the business. The completion of this form will take a valuable employee a week or more. It will drive the managers crazy when they have to waste their time in this manner. And that is exactly what it is meant to do. It is meant to force them to settle. It is just the beginning of the harassment that they will be subjected to as they fight this suit.

The object is to extort a sum of money.

Street-Wise Truth This debate is not about "Affirmative Action." It is about "Quotas."

This debate is not about "affirmative action."

"Affirmative action" is a wonderful thing. It's people-helping-people and it is warm and fuzzy. It is something that everyone wants to do; to help those people who need a hand to make their way up life's trail.

Everyone is for "affirmative action."

THE BETRAYAL

Affirmative action is, for example, publicizing your job openings so everyone can apply.

But "quotas" are something else. They are nothing but the *forcible* taking of something that belongs to one person and giving it to another. There is nothing good about quotas.

The "elite" have taken the good words, "affirmative action" and applied them universally to "quotas."

Every time someone debates the use of "quotas," the moderator or the newspaper labels the debate, "Is Affirmative Action Good or Bad?" And thus the battle has been decided before it's even started.

"Affirmative action" is voluntary; a compulsory requirement is a "quota."

Americans are against "quotas," not "affirmative action."

What Would You Have Done?

So, if you were a businessman in 1964, what would you have believed the Civil Rights Act required of you? Would you have been worried?

Remember the comforting words of Congressman Bill McCulloch. "For the Americans who do not discriminate against their fellow citizens because of race, color or religion, the Federal Civil Rights Bill will have no effect on their daily lives."[4]

4

WHO WAS FIRST TO BETRAY US?

Who do you believe was the first to betray America on this issue?

Senator Hubert Humphrey?   Was Hubert Humphrey telling falsehoods as he addressed the Senate as the floor leader of the Civil Rights Act? He was elected Vice President only a few months later, in November, 1964. Four years later he ran as the Democratic nominee for President. Since he was so close to power, many people would wonder.

Congressman Bill McCulloch?   Probably no one would accuse this man of misleading the American public on purpose. The worst sin that anyone could attribute to him would be that of naivete. He apparently trusted the "elite" with whom he was dealing. However, in his defense, it is true that he was making a good "legislative history" for the courts so that the judges would know the intent of Congress. It should also be noted that the U.S. Supreme Court, up until that time, had not yet embarked on rewriting the Constitution and the laws in its own image as they were to do with this and other laws and the Constitution in the ensuing years.

WHO WAS FIRST TO BETRAY US?

President Lyndon Johnson? We've already heard Lyndon Johnson tell a biographer much later that he had to "get out in front on this issue" or the liberals would get him. He had to prove to those Easterners with their three-button suits that he was just as liberal as they were. It was Lyndon Johnson who began the betrayal of America as he made an attempt to go down in history as a great President.

As the President, he was in charge of spending the billions of dollars that are necessary to buy everything that the government needs, from aircraft carriers to paper clips. He used this immense power, almost immediately after the Civil Rights Act was passed, to bypass it. He implemented a system that was totally the opposite of what Congress had approved.

In the same way that he lied to the American people about Vietnam and divided them so badly so that none were even debating the same subject, he did the same on civil rights.

Although his falsehoods about Vietnam have faded somewhat, we are still living with the disastrous results of the falsehoods about civil rights.

President Richard Nixon? Although Richard Nixon didn't *begin* the betrayal, he continued it enthusiastically although he could have stopped it. He was elected in 1968 by the "silent majority" who were already tired of the extreme liberalism of the '60's. But Nixon was more concerned about what the Easterners thought of him.

* * * *

The betrayal began in 1965 only a few months *after* the Act was passed. Johnson did not make any waves while Congress was still debating the Act and everyone was watching.

As the President, Johnson was in charge of everything that the government purchased, from postal trucks and aircraft carriers to pencils and computers. About a third of the businesses in America (about 250,000 of them) sold their products to the federal government (either directly or indirectly).[1]

In 1965, President Johnson quietly created a new "Office" in the Department of Labor.[2] He told it to issue "guidelines" to all the companies that did business with the government. (Its name was the Office of Federal Contract Compliance which was changed in 1978 to Office of Federal Contract Compliance Programs; in this book we shall call it OFCCP).

FREEDOM WILL CONQUER RACISM (AND SEXISM)

This is the Office that began the use of "quotas" in America.*

In 1967, in response to the ghetto riots that were sweeping the nation, Johnson told the OFCCP (even though he knew that the American public was solidly *behind* Civil Rights but just as solidly *against* quotas) to go to Cleveland (and later to Philadelphia) and tell the construction contractors that did business with the U. S. government that they had to have minorities in all the trades.[3] So these businesses "voluntarily" set numerical goals for their workforces.

This "voluntary" action was hailed by the "elite" as the enlightened way to achieve equal opportunity.

Violated the Civil Rights Act

But, wait a minute! Wouldn't such action by an American business violate the Civil Rights Act? They would be hiring people *because* of their race. Readers of this book have no doubt that they could not do that. But this plan of Johnson's was so popular among the "elite" that it was expanded.

This happened even though it's obvious to *anyone* that this violated the Civil Rights Act and the wishes of the American public, both black and white.

The person in charge of paying the federal government's bills, the Comptroller General saw what was happening. He said that he couldn't pay any contractors who used quotas because this would violate the Civil Rights Act.[4] By this time, Richard Nixon had become President. He remembered what had happened to Barry Goldwater.** And the "elite," led by *The New York Times,* were putting on the pressure. So Nixon had his Attorney General, John Mitchell, say the Comptroller General was wrong. And the program continued.

However, the Attorney General's announcement upset many Senators.

---

* In contrast, President Kennedy in 1961 had said that federal contractors should treat employees "without regard to their race, creed, color, or national origin," and they were required to open channels of communication with minority communities so that the minorities would know what jobs were available. See Exec. Order No 10, 925, 26 Fed. Reg. 1977.

* He also remembered what had happened to many of the Congressmen who voted "against civil rights" in 1964. One third of the Republicans who voted against the Civil Rights Act of 1964 lost their bid for reelection in 1964. 1964 *Congressional Quarterly Almanac*, p. 344.

WHO WAS FIRST TO BETRAY US?

They remembered what they had been told when they voted for the Act only five years earlier. Therefore, in December, 1969, when the Senate was considering a bill to pay some of the government's debts, they added an amendment. They knew that Nixon would have a hard time vetoing this appropriations bill even if they added an amendment that he didn't like. The amendment said that if the Comptroller found that a federal law (such as the Civil Rights Act) had been violated in any purchase made by the government, he did not have to pay the bill. The Senate voted 73 to 13 in favor of this amendment which would allow the Comptroller General to kill the quotas.[5]

That's when Nixon got angry.

He sent the Secretary of Labor, George Shultz (who later became Secretary of State under Reagan) and others to the House to stop it from also passing there. Nixon said the pending House vote was "an historic and critical civil rights vote." He threatened to veto the bill if the amendment were attached.

All this pressure was too much for House members to take. They also remembered what had happened to Barry Goldwater only five years earlier. They couldn't go back to their constituents at Christmas if the president was calling them "racists." The House voted against the amendment, with only 156 voting in favor and 208 against the amendment.

Then the Senate caved and also went along with the President. They too could remember what had happened to Barry Goldwater.

The vote this time was only 29 in favor of the amendment and 39 against.

The Senate had switched from 79 in favor of the Amendment to only 29 in favor. They did so because they were terrified that Nixon would call them "racists." Thirty-two Senators didn't vote at all, apparently because they were in favor of the amendment but were afraid to vote against President Nixon.[6]

Do you remember reading about that vote in the newspapers or seeing a mention of it on television?* I'm sure you don't. But that was a giant step in the betrayal.

---

* On its editorial page, *The New York Times* printed an editorial entitled, *Aid to Jim Crow,* in which it urged that the amendment be defeated because it was the unions and the "Southern segregationists" who were pushing the amendment. It

FREEDOM WILL CONQUER RACISM (AND SEXISM)

Then in 1970, the OFCCP started to talk about being "results oriented." In December, 1971, it made it clear what that meant. Quotas were required of *every* company doing any business with the federal government. Any employer without a sufficient number of minorities or women in its workforce was required to confess and to state what they were doing to correct that deficiency.[7]

George Shultz's assistant was Laurence Silberman. Is he proud of what he did?

Silberman says that he knew it was a terrible mistake within a year. "Once we got into the numbers game, it stopped being equal opportunity. It had to lead to efforts to impose more equal outcomes."[8] Has it been good?

"It's done enormous damage. I regard it as of transcendent importance that we get out of this mind-set."[9]

The President's OFCCP was very successful in forcing American businesses to use quotas. But the "elite" were still unhappy because only 35% of the businesses in the country were under the OFCCP's power, and it couldn't *sue* anyone.

Remember the "Federal Inspector"?

There was another bureaucracy which had power over *all* of America's businesses which had fifteen employees or more. This one had been established by the Civil Rights Act.

---

said, "It will be a disgrace if the feverish lobbying activities of organized labor frustrate a plan that is as desirable as it is just." December 22, 1969, p.32.

In its "news" columns, it printed a feature story, "Philadelphia Plan: How White House Engineered Major Victory," in which it glowingly described how liberal Republican Jacob Javitz told a White House staffer, "You see now what we can do up here when the President gives some leadership. We can practically accomplish miracles." And it said, "To some more skeptical folk, the victory was less a tribute to the President's skill than a reflection of the latent forces in Congress that are ready at any time to support meaningful civil rights legislation." December 26, 1969, p. 20.

And, therefore, this historic change in America's philosophy of freedom and civil rights took place as a simple "civil rights" issue, without anyone noticing the historic dimensions of the event.

The supporters of quotas will tell you that this vote meant that Congress *and you* approved the use of quotas. But the first vote was obviously the more accurate portrayal of Congress' feelings. In addition, the vote did not reflect the

WHO WAS FIRST TO BETRAY US?

It was the "Federal Inspector" that the Southern opponents of the Civil Rights Act had talked about during the debates. (The Southerners were inventing a "bogeyman," according to Sen. Humphrey). The "Federal Inspector" had been given a nice-sounding name, the Equal Employment Opportunity Commission (EEOC).

It *could* sue and it *did* have power over almost every business in the country.

Although you and I may not have been noticing what was going on in Washington, you can be sure that the EEOC was watching. It looked good to them. They saw how the OFCCP was expanding its power. They wanted to expand their power also.

However, their power had been limited by Congress. They could not interpret the law by writing "Rules" like most of the agencies are allowed to do.

Although most agencies have the power to write "Rules" and "interpret" the laws that are passed by Congress and to "flesh-out" all of the details as to what those laws really mean, the EEOC was not given this power. The other agencies, in effect, have the power to legislate, to write laws. In most of the laws that it writes nowadays, Congress is very vague and sets out only a broad outline. It gives most of the power to the agencies to actually write the law.*

---

feeling of the people because the press did not inform them about the true nature of the bill. The supporters of quotas are right about one thing. After 1969, there was nothing standing in the way of federal bureaucrats implementing quota systems all over the country.

    * This is done because it enables Congress to avoid all of the responsibility if a new law becomes unpopular. A General Counsel at the Office of Personnel Management stated it this way: "[T]he primary hidden agenda of the legislative process has been to permit Congress as an institution to avoid ultimate responsibility for the making of difficult or controversial decisions....Difficult public policy choices though nominally the province of Congress are in fact made in the Executive and Judicial Branches....The net effect is to insulate Congress, as an institution, from accountability for unpopular decisions, while preserving for Congress credit for choices that prove popular."

See J. Morris, "Clausewitz updated: Litigation as the continuation of policy making by other means," in R. Rector and M. Sanera, *Steering the Elephant: How Washington Works.* As cited by James C. Sharf in an address to the National Research Council, October 1, 1987, *Litigating Personnel Measurement Policy.*

But this power was specifically *not* given to the EEOC. The EEOC was given power only to write regulations about where a complaint would be filed, with how many copies, and other items of procedure.[10]

But this didn't bother the EEOC. It made the rules anyhow.*

To make matters worse, any agency which has the power to make rules must announce them well ahead of time so that everyone in the country will know about them and be able to make comments about them before they take effect. Because the EEOC didn't have the power to make any rules, it could just prepare them in secret without announcing them ahead of time for comment and criticism.

EEOC Outlaws Testing

In 1970, the EEOC issued a Rule which told the businesses of America, in effect, that if they used any test for hiring or promoting, this was "discrimination" unless an equal percentage of blacks passed as whites. That's correct, an I.Q. test, for example, was invalid unless an equal percent of blacks and whites pass the test. Or, unless the employer showed that there is no other way to hire or promote.[11]

But who was worried? It was clear what Congress had wanted. There was an excellent legislative history as to what Congress and the American people had decided when they passed Title VII. And our courts would make sure that the EEOC followed the law.

Remember, it was clearly in the legislative history (which all courts are required to read and follow) that, as a result of the Motorola case in Illinois, the Civil Rights Act had been carefully written so that it did not prohibit any testing that did not discriminate.[12]

The Courts Decide

The EEOC's Rule about "testing" was challenged by an electric power company in North Carolina. This company had discriminated

---

*   Alfred W. Blumrosen, the first Chief Conciliation officer for the EEOC, has revealed the ways in which the EEOC bureaucrats were able to get around the restrictive statutory language and legislative history of Title VII, engaging in "administrative creativity" and believing that "words develop meaning through use." Alfred W. Blumrosen, *Black Employment and the Law* (New Brunswick: Rutgers University Press, 1971), p. 52; Blumrosen, *Modern Law: The Law Transmission System and Equal Employment Opportunity* (Madison: University of Wisconsin Press, 1993), p. 102.

against blacks until 1965, when the Civil Rights Act went into effect, by employing them only in its "labor" department. Whites could work outside of the "labor" department if they were high school graduates, but blacks could not.

In 1965, the company changed its rule and said that blacks would be hired and promoted anywhere in the company exactly the same as anyone else. However, another requirement was added for anyone who wanted to work outside of the "labor" department. They had to pass an IQ test and a test for mechanical ability. This meant that everyone, both blacks and whites, would have to have a high school diploma and pass the tests if they worked outside of the "labor" department. In August, 1966, the first black was promoted out of the "labor" department.

But there was a problem. Not many blacks could meet these requirements. Whereas only 12% of black males in North Carolina had completed high school, 34% of white males had done so. So the company did two things. It offered to finance 2/3 of the tuition for any employee who wished to finish high school. And it said in September 1965 that present employees would not be required to finish high school if they passed the two standard tests for IQ and for mechanical ability. But there was another problem; the blacks did not do well on these tests either.

Of course, Congress had foreseen this *only a year previously* when it passed the Act.

For example, do you remember what Senators Clark and Case, the floor managers of the bill, put into their written Memorandum in response to the Illinois decision (so that there would be a good legislative history for the courts to follow)? They said:

"There is no requirement in title VII that employers abandon bona fide qualification tests where, because of differences in background and education, members of some groups are able to perform better on these tests than members of other groups. An employer may set his qualifications as high as he likes, he may test to determine which applicants have these qualifications, and he may hire, assign, and promote on the basis of test performance."[13]

It couldn't be any clearer than that.

FREEDOM WILL CONQUER RACISM (AND SEXISM)

But Senator John Tower of Texas had wanted to make sure it was absolutely crystal clear, so he had attached the following amendment to the text of the Act itself, that it would not be unlawful to use:

". . . any professionally developed ability test provided that such test . . . is not designed, intended or used to discriminate . . . ."[14]

So when a suit was started against the Duke Power Company in March 1966, the company was not worried. It was treating its employees equally. The company was moving to open up its new positions and promotions to blacks.

And so it wasn't surprised when a U. S. trial judge held in its favor and against the EEOC. And then the U. S. Court of Appeals did likewise. But this was to be an important test case, and so on to the U. S. Supreme Court went the EEOC with the case of *Griggs v. Duke Power Company*.[15]

5

THE SUPREME COURT
DISOBEYS THE LAW

The U. S. Supreme Court wilfully disobeyed the Civil Rights Act in 1971 in the case of *Griggs v. Duke Power Company.* There is no other way to describe its decision.*

It knowingly disregarded what Congress had written; and instead, it imposed its own views on the people of America.** Here is what happened.

---

* I have the utmost respect for the judges and the practicing lawyers of this country, particularly those in the small cities and towns who know their clients and their neighborhoods. They are truly the first line of defense against the corruption of a powerful government. While practicing for 12 years in a small city in the Pennsylvania Dutch area, I was extremely impressed with the law there. But the axiom that "power corrupts" applies to judges as well as other people. And there's no question that many of the judges of our country have usurped that kind of power many times in the last thirty years.

** Many lawyers will be upset by my statement; they will say it is "extreme." But there is no other way to describe the fact that the Court *totally* disregarded the intent of Congress and substituted its own. That is not a matter of opinion.

FREEDOM WILL CONQUER RACISM (AND SEXISM)

- All of the parties in the case agreed that Duke Power Company did not *intend* to discriminate.

But, said the Supreme Court, this may be true but it is *irrelevant*. But we must ask, "How could this be irrelevant when Congress had said it was highly relevant?"

When the Civil Rights Act passed the House of Representatives, there was nothing in it about "intent." However, when it got to the Senate, that body specifically amended the Act. It wrote that a court could punish a business *only* if the business had "intentionally" engaged in discrimination.

When this amendment came to the floor of the Senate, Sen. Humphrey said that the amendment didn't change the Act at all because everyone already knew that an employer had to have "intended" to discriminate. Therefore, the amendment was fine because it really wasn't changing anything. He said:

"[T]he proposed change does not involve any substantial change in the title. The expressed requirement of intent is designed to make it wholly clear that inadvertent or accidental discrimination will not violate the title or result in entry of court orders. It simply means the business must have intended to discriminate."[1]

Despite the fact that Sen. Humphrey had always assumed that "intent" was necessary and the Senate had added this amendment specifically requiring that "intent" be shown, the Supreme Court said:

"The Court of Appeals held that the Company had adopted the diploma and test requirements without any 'intention to discriminate against Negro employees.' ....We do not suggest that either the District Court or the Court of Appeals erred in examining the employer's intent; but good intent or absence of discriminatory intent does not redeem employment procedures or testing mechanisms that operate as 'built-in headwinds' for minority groups and are unrelated to measuring job capability."[2]

The Court gave us no citations to the Act to uphold this statement because it would be impossible to do so. There are none. Wasn't the

---

If you would like it stated in a more scholarly way, Prof. Richard A. Epstein, of the U. of Chicago Law School, says that the *Griggs* opinion is a "travesty of statutory construction" because the Court "perverted" the statute. See Richard Epstein, *Forbidden Grounds* (Cambridge: Harvard University Press, 1992), pp. 192, 197.

THE SUPREME COURT DISOBEYS THE LAW

Court able to read the Act?* It says very clearly that a business can be punished only:

"If the court finds that the respondent has *intentionally* engaged in or is *intentionally* engaging in an unlawful employment practice charged in the complaint . . ." [emphasis added]³

Didn't the Court know about those words in the Act and know the legislative history, both of which said just the opposite of what it was holding?

- **The Supreme Court approved the power that the EEOC had usurped to interpret what Congress meant.**

The EEOC had written many, many pages of "Rules" amplifying and explaining to the businesses of America exactly what was *required* of them under this new law. They did so even though Congress had specifically withheld that power from them.** Nevertheless, the Supreme Court said that these rules of the EEOC are entitled to "great deference."⁴

Why did the Court do that? It did so because it knew that it was violating the law and substituting its own view for what Congress had actually said. Therefore, it needed the support of everyone it could find. The rules which the EEOC had promulgated agreed with the court's opinion and it made the court's opinion more "respectable" if the court could show that the "President's people" at the EEOC agreed.

Therefore, all of the rules that the EEOC would make in the future regarding the definition of "discriminate" would be as good as law—*even though Congress had specifically refused to give it that power.*

---

*   Act says at 2000e-5(g): "(1) If the court finds that the respondent has *intentionally* engaged in or is *intentionally* engaging in an unlawful employment practice charged in the complaint, the court may enjoin the respondent from engaging in such unlawful employment practice, and order such affirmative action as may be appropriate, which may include, but is not limited to, reinstatement or hiring of employees, with or without back pay (payable by the employer, employment agency, or labor organization, as the case may be, responsible for the unlawful employment practice), or any other equitable relief as the court deems appropriate." [emphasis added]

**   The Act says at 2000e-12(a): "The [EEOC] shall have authority from to time to issue, amend, or rescind suitable *procedural* regulations to carry out the provisions of this subchapter." [emphasis added]

Any business would have to be very careful about what these bureaucrats instructed them to do in the future. Their rules would carry the same weight as Congressional laws.

- **The Supreme Court approved the use of "class actions", which allow a whole "class" of persons to join together in one suit or a single person to sue for everyone without their permission or even their knowledge.**[5]

The Supreme Court got through this discussion very rapidly, saying, "Congress provided in Title VII of the Civil Rights Act of 1964, for class actions..."

The only problem is that this is not true. This statement is devoid of any citation. The reason the court hurried over this point so quickly without any discussion or citation is that the court was not telling the truth. There is nothing in the Act about class actions. The leading commentator for lawyers says, "Title VII does not expressly provide for the use of a class action...."[6]

What This Betrayal Meant to Businesses

What did this total and illegal* usurpation of power by the Supreme Court mean in a practical sense to the businesses and workers of America?**

With the preliminary points out of the way, the Court went on to say: 1) a high school education could no longer be required by America's businesses,[7] and 2) tests could not be used[8] if the "inferior education" of blacks would cause them to do poorly.

---

* Some lawyers have quarreled with my use of "illegal." However, it is clear that trial judges often make erroneous rulings that are, in effect, illegal. If no one appeals their decision, that ruling will remain even though it was illegal. By the same token, when the Supreme Court makes an illegal decision, it is still illegal even though there is no place to take an appeal from their illegal decision.

* The Supreme Court made another false statement. It said that it was "plain" from "the language of the statute" that the "objective" of Congress was to: "remove barriers that have operated in the past to favor an identifiable group of white employees over other employees." Despite what the court said, what is "plain" from reading the statute is that the Act is color-blind. And there is nothing in the history or the language of the Act about removing "barriers;" it was intended merely to outlaw discrimination.

THE SUPREME COURT DISOBEYS THE LAW

In other words, America was still *not* "color-blind". Employers would now be *required* by the federal government to look at race when they did their hiring. This is exactly the opposite of what Congress and the American public had decided. America had become *more* "racist" as the result of a federal law that encompassed the entire nation.

All businesses were forbidden from 1) requiring a diploma or 2) using a test unless they could prove to the satisfaction of a federal bureaucrat or judge that the same percentage of blacks had a diploma or could pass a test. Or unless a diploma or test was necessary to the life of that company, a very difficult, if not impossible, burden of proof.*

The judges on the Supreme Court made it clear that they, the judges, knew how to run a business. They knew what skills and knowledge are needed by American businesses and they know how to judge an employee's ability. They wrote:

"The facts of this case demonstrate the inadequacy of broad and general testing devices as well as the infirmity of using diplomas or degrees as fixed measures of capability."

Let's stop there. That, of course, is contrary to everything that the psychologists and the experts believe. The businesses of America had been using these tests for almost the entire century, not because they wanted to spend the money but because they were a very useful tool in placing people in jobs in a very fair and impartial manner.

---

* If you ever wonder why companies are forced to "buy-off" almost any plaintiff and settle every case, just consider what the Supreme Court had required. Any business must prepare a statistical analysis before it can use a test. Very few businesses could afford the time to try to understand what is required as outlined in the following explanation:

"Although it is impossible to review even a tiny fraction of the literature here, it is sufficient to say that the professionals in the field all agree that there is a positive correlation between test performance and job success; they debate only its extent. The relative doubters place the correlation coefficient at around 0.3, while those who are more supportive of the practice tend to place it at around 0.5. In addition, extensive work has been done in 'validity generalization' techniques, which allow for an assessment of the validity of various tests without any need to pretest them in some narrow or particular environment. The major study is

FREEDOM WILL CONQUER RACISM (AND SEXISM)

As the leading text for lawyers says,

"[T]he use of aptitude, ability and intelligence tests as aids to employment and promotion decisions was not originally related to their potential for indirect race discrimination. If anything, the opposite was true, in that the "objective" character of such tests presumably had the salutary effect of ruling out the factor of subjective racial bias on the part of supervisors and personnel managers. In any event, well before testing became embroiled in the race discrimination problem, it was a well-established feature of American business life."[9]

But the court knew better than this *entire profession* of industrial psychology. It continued:

"History is filled with examples of men and women who rendered highly effective performance without the conventional badges of accomplishment in terms of certificates, diplomas, or degrees. Diplomas and tests are useful servants, but Congress has mandated the common sense proposition that they are not to become masters of reality."[10]

What arrogance!

Did Congress ever "mandate" a "common sense proposition", as the Court just said, that the use of tests and diplomas are to be curtailed by business? They never said that.

*The U.S. Supreme Court had wilfully disobeyed the law.**

Hunter, Schmidt, and Jackson, *Meta-Analysis*. Crudely stated, the intuition behind their basic strategy is to unpack the aggregate data, which are usually presented in an abbreviated form as 'significant' or 'no significant' correlation (at the 0.05 level), and to look at the confidence intervals...."

This can be found in Epstein, p. 237. *Do you understand what he said?*

* When Thurgood Marshall, the revered black Justice on the Supreme Court, argued for the NAACP before the Supreme Court in 1948, he declared, "Classifications and distinctions based on race or color have no moral or legal validity in our society." He said this in *Sipuel v. Board of Regents of the University of Oklahoma,* 332 U.S. 631 (1948).

Yet, in 1971, when he was a Justice on the Court (the same year as the *Duke Power* case), he was asked by Justice William O. Douglas (who had liberal credentials equal to anyone) why a white applicant to be a lawyer should be treated more harshly than a black applicant. To this question, Justice Marshall answered, "You guys have been practicing discrimination for years. Now it is our turn."

THE SUPREME COURT DISOBEYS THE LAW

Because this was a totally new ruling, the Supreme Court attempted to quiet the fears of America. After all, they were using this law only against a "bad" company that had openly discriminated for many years against blacks (even though everyone agreed that the company was no longer doing so). Surely, this would not happen to "good" companies.*

Not What Congress Said

Despite what the Supreme Court said, the Civil Rights Act was intended to *stop* businesses from giving different treatment to people because of their race. If a business gave a different treatment to a person because of race, then it would be discriminating.

Nothing was ever discussed or mentioned *anywhere* in the very long debate in Congress that our courts would judge a business other than by how the business treated each individual person and each employee, certainly not by how its treatment would affect an entire race or sex. As we have learned, the written memorandum from Senators Clark and Case had said, "There is no requirement in Title VII that an employer maintain a racial balance in his work force.[11]

Justice Douglas reports this in his autobiography, *The Court Years,* at page 149.

This meant, of course, that a non-culpable, young white man was punished for the sins of other white people, sometime in the past, solely because this young man had white skin.

* To give you just a tiny realization of what this meant to our businesses, you should know that the EEOC set out the following guidelines in 1978 as to how a business is supposed to determine whether a test has a "disparate impact" on the races.

"A selection rate for any race, sex, or ethnic group which is less than four-fifths (4/5) or (eighty percent) of the rate for the group with the highest rate will generally be regarded by the Federal enforcement agencies as evidence of adverse impact, while a greater than four-fifths rate will generally not be regarded by Federal enforcement agencies as evidence of adverse impact." *Uniform Guidelines on Employment Selection Procedures* (1978) 29 C.F.R. ss 1607.4D (1989).

This has led to an entire industry of statisticians using complicated formulas that are completely foreign to anyone except statistician. A business which wishes to protect itself must go to the cost of hiring lawyers and statisticians.

FREEDOM WILL CONQUER RACISM (AND SEXISM)

"On the contrary, any deliberate attempt to maintain a racial balance, whatever such a balance may be, would involve a violation of Title VII because maintaining such a balance would require an employer to hire or to refuse to hire on the basis of race. It must be emphasized that discrimination is prohibited as to any individual. While the presence or absence of other members of the same minority group in the work force may be a relevant factor in determining whether in a given case a decision to hire or to refuse to hire was based on race, color, etc., it is only one factor, and the question in each case would be whether that individual was discriminated against."

And yet the Supreme Court said in this case that it would look not only at how the individual is treated, but how the treatment affects a race as a whole.

After this case, the courts of America were now *required* to look at race as a result of the Supreme Court decision which:

1) Allowed a class action.
2) Made irrelevant the "intent" of the company.
3) Looked at the impact that the treatment would have on a particular race.

This meant that a business could no longer treat each employee fairly; it now had to determine the effect its treatment was having on blacks, women, Puerto Ricans, Christians, Jews, etc. *as a group.* And, if it were sued, its decision as to the needs of the business could be second-guessed by any judge in the country; and the judge's decision would be final, not the company's.

The Supreme Court said: "The Act proscribes not only overt discrimination but also practices that are fair in form, but discriminatory in operation. The touchstone is business necessity. If an employment practice which operates to exclude Negroes cannot be shown to be related to job performance, the practice is prohibited."

It said further:

"The Company's lack of discriminatory intent is suggested by special efforts to help the undereducated employees through Company financing of two-thirds the cost of tuition for high school training. But Congress directed the thrust of the Act to the *consequences* of employment practices, not simply the motivation. More than that, Congress has placed on the employer the burden of showing that any given requirement must have a manifest relationship to the employment in question.

THE SUPREME COURT DISOBEYS THE LAW

"The facts of this case demonstrate the inadequacy of broad and general testing devices as well as the infirmity of using diplomas or degrees as fixed measures of capability."[12]

Remember the "Testing" Amendment?

But, said Duke Power to itself, we will certainly win on the testing issue because Senator Tower's amendment made it clear that a company could use any test that was not intended to discriminate.

Do you remember what the official "Captains," Senators Case and Clark wrote to assure the public and the other Senators (and to provide more "legislative history")? They wrote:

"There is no requirement in title VII that employers abandon bona fide qualification tests where, because of differences in background and education, members of some groups are able to perform better on these tests than members of other groups. An employer may set his qualifications as high as he likes, he may test to determine which applicants have these qualifications, and he may hire, assign, and promote on the basis of test performance."[13]

And do you remember the memo prepared by the same Senators: **"Objection:** The bill would make it unlawful for an employer to use qualification tests based upon verbal skills and other factors which may relate to the environmental conditioning of the applicant. In other words, all applicants must be treated as if they came from low-income, deprived communities in order to equate environmental inequalities of the culturally deprived group.

"Answer: The employer may set his qualifications as high as he likes, and may hire, assign, and promote on the basis of test performance."[14]

But it didn't matter what Congress had said. The Supreme Court totally distorted the meaning of Tower's amendment and totally ignored the legislative history of his intent so that it could impose its own will on the American people.

The Supreme Court Had Written A Law of its Own

The Supreme Court had written a whole new law of its own. It had invented a new test so that lawyers and professors could write volumes about it in their erudite way and fly around the country to discuss it in detail at their seminars. This truly does make the lawyers very important to businesses which find it impossible to keep up with all of this.

FREEDOM WILL CONQUER RACISM (AND SEXISM)

The entire debate in Congress and the thrust of the Civil Rights Act had been about the "treatment" that must be given to individual employees. We did not want a business to "treat" someone differently because of his race. But this didn't matter to the Supreme Court.

The Court wrote its own laws. It said that what was important was not only how the company "treated" each individual employee but what "impact" the company's practices had on a particular race as a whole.

Thus, it invented a whole new test for judges and lawyers to write about. It labeled the two types of tests as "disparate treatment" and "disparate impact".

Under "disparate treatment", which is what Congress had intended, a court determines how an individual employee has been treated.

However, under the new test, "disparate impact", a court determines what "impact" the company practices have on *all* of the members of a particular race.

And so the use of "quotas" was given a tacit approval.

6

THE U.S. GOVERNMENT ATTACKS OUR BUSINESSES

Whereas most countries help and protect their businesses, this chapter tells the sad story about how the U.S. government *attacks* our businesses.

The U.S. government began a relentless "attack" on American business in 1974.

There is no other way to describe what happened. The assault was conducted by the EEOC. There was even an "enemies list", i.e., a list of the American companies that would be targeted.

Needed More Power

Before it could really go after our businesses and subjugate them, the EEOC had to get more power. Under the Civil Rights Act, it was told to use "conciliation" and "persuasion." When that failed, it could go to the Attorney General and ask that a lawsuit be started.*

---

* A reference book for lawyers says it this way: "[I]t must be remembered that Congress' original plan in writing Title VII [the section of the Act dealing

FREEDOM WILL CONQUER RACISM (AND SEXISM)

But the EEOC was frustrated. It wanted to sue without going through the U. S. Attorney General. It wanted to be independent. And the "elite" wanted it to have even more power than that; the "elite" wanted it to have the power to issue its "orders" *directly* to a business without even having to go before a judge.

The "elite" made this an issue in Congress in 1972, *right before the presidential election*. President Nixon was a good politician; he straddled the fence. He supported a law giving the EEOC the power to begin its own suits in federal court but a federal judge had to make the "orders." The President's "compromise" won. Now the EEOC no longer needed to ask the Attorney General to sue for it. It could be its own lawyer.[1]

It's interesting to note that all during the debate the *New York Times* was misleading its readers. It kept making statements such as, "But if voluntary conciliation fails, the commission is powerless."[2] It even had a feature story about a black man who could not sue because the EEOC could not bring suit. The story said "[C]onciliation has often failed, and, when it has, the commission had no further weapons in its arsenal."[3] That, of course, was not true. The EEOC always had the power to sue, but first it had to convince the Attorney General that it had a valid case before someone could be hauled off to court. (An individual always had the power to sue if the EEOC did not.)*

---

with employment] was that instances of alleged discrimination could best be handled through informal methods of persuasion, conciliation, and settlement. In order to effectuate this ideal, Congress included in Title VII an administrative scheme whereby charges of discrimination in the workplace were to be referred to state and federal administrative agencies which would then work to effect agreement between the parties. For a variety of reasons ... the emphasis in Title VII cases has apparently shifted from the scheme envisioned by Congress to formal court actions." Larson, ss 48.00

    * Another important development took place in 1972. The Senate tried to make the Act easier for plaintiffs to sue by taking out the word "intentionally." If this happened, a plaintiff would not have to show that a business had *intended* to discriminate.

But the House would not go along with the Senate, and "intentionally" was left in. Therefore, if any liberal tries to say that the Congress approved the actions

THE U.S. GOVERNMENT ATTACKS OUR BUSINESSES

The Voters Are Deceived

A few voters were beginning to sit up and take notice about this time. But they were quickly put back to sleep.

In the 1972 presidential campaign, even liberal George McGovern repudiated "quotas." And, of course, Nixon did also.[4]

But it didn't matter what the candidates *said*. What they *did* was just the opposite. Nixon had been elected by the "silent majority" who were already tired of the liberal ideas of the 1960's. But Nixon was talking on both sides of the issue. He had already encouraged quotas with the federal contractors.

After the election was over and after the Supreme Court had given the EEOC a green light, the EEOC began to use its new power to sue. It was allowed by Nixon to begin its grand march against American business.

No person likes it when the IRS is ready to audit them at any moment, with or without reason. The inspectors from the EEOC are no different. Of course, there are good people in all of those agencies, but we all know that power corrupts anyone. Give power to any people and they tend to become arrogant. We've all seen it happen.

But this is even worse.

These inspectors from the EEOC are zealots.* They are not just the ordinary bureaucrat or any person off the street. They sincerely

---

of the Supreme Court because it did not reverse the *Griggs* case in 1972, a conservative can just as easily point to the 1972 vote to show that Congress was not approving. It refused to remove the word "intentionally," and it refused to repeal Sen. Tower's amendment on testing.

* Who were the members of the EEOC in 1974, to whom we had given this awesome amount of power?

—John H. Powell, Jr., Chairman. A black, 43-year-old lawyer, he had graduated from Howard University, Harvard Law School, and the Graduate School of Law at NYU. He had worked in various positions in the government, four years in a law firm in Mineola, New York, and four years with corporations.

—Ethel Bent Walsh, Vice Chairman. A 51-year-old graduate of Katherine Gibbs secretarial school and a Republican, she came to Washington with Nixon and worked in the Small Business Administration. According to the EEOC, "[She] rose from typing clerk in a small firm to vice president for operations of ... the

FREEDOM WILL CONQUER RACISM (AND SEXISM)

believe they have a mission to correct our society and to get the "racists" and "sexists."

The "Enemies List"

After the EEOC was given the power to sue, it made an "enemies list," i.e., a list of the big companies that it would attack. The top three were:

General Motors
General Electric
International Paper

The others were:
American Cast Iron Pipe
Lockheed Aircraft
North American Rockwell
McDonnell Douglas
Coca-Cola
Firestone Tire and Rubber
Sears, Roebuck
Libbey-Owens-Ford
Hughes Aircraft

---

largest aerosol contract packing corporation in the world....[She] learned first-hand about discrimination based on age when she was looking for a position. She noted that there are a lot of people looking for employment today which crosses racial, professional and cultural lines. The situation becomes increasingly difficult when age is added as a factor and really difficult when sex and age both are a factor. Although she doesn't know what she is going to do to help remedy the situation, she says there is a need to raise the recognition of these problems."

—Colston A. Lewis. A black lawyer from Richmond, he had graduated from Virginia Union University and Howard University Law School. A Republican, he had worked on many civil rights issues in his native state.

—Raymond Telles. An Hispanic, he had served as mayor of his native El Paso and Ambassador to Costa Rica. He had been Senior Vice President at First Financial Enterprises in El Paso.

—Luther Holcomb. A 63-year-old Baptist minister from Dallas, he had served on many local, state and national boards including the National Conference of

THE U.S. GOVERNMENT ATTACKS OUR BUSINESSES

Lone Star Steel
United Air Lines
Ingalls Shipbuilding
FMC Corp.
Ford Motor
Bethlehem Steel
Sperry Rand

The next level was:
American Tobacco
International Harvester
Western Air Lines
Kaiser Aluminum
Dan River
Rexall Drug
Santa Fe Railroad
General Electric (this company was listed twice by the EEOC)
Westinghouse
St. Regis Paper
Southern Railway
Liggett & Myers
Avondale Shipyards
Yellow Freight System[5]

Christians and at Jews, the Legal Aid Society and the Child Guidance Clinic. He had been an original member of the EEOC.

According to *Dun's* magazine, Colston Lewis was "a minority of one" on the Commission. "[Chairman] Powell disagrees with [Lewis]. The Chairman believes that if minority people are given a crack at the opportunities, they will soon measure up. 'We must eliminate the barriers,' he argues, 'which impede the ability of minorities to aspire to and achieve their economic objectives. Once these barriers are eliminated, minorities will soon be competing on an equal footing.'

"Besides Powell and Lewis, the other EEOC Commissioners are Luther Holcomb, a folksy Baptist minister from Dallas, Texas; Raymond Telles, a former mayor of El Paso, Texas; and Ethel Bent Walsh, a businesswoman from New Jersey. Ms. Walsh occasionally joins Colston Lewis in his opposition to the Chairman's policies. But Powell can usually count on the votes of Holcomb and Telles for a majority." See *Duns,* June 1974, p. 84

FREEDOM WILL CONQUER RACISM (AND SEXISM)

The head of the EEOC, John H. Powell, Jr., who assumed the post in January, 1974, did not hide the fact that he was brazen: "Once we get the big boys, the others will soon fall in line."[6]

A chief attorney on the Attorney General's staff wrote in 1976 to a Deputy Attorney General that under the EEOC's new rules it could attack *any* business in the country that it wanted to get:

"[F]ew employers are able to show the validity of *any* of their selection procedures . . . [This gives] great discretion to enforcement personnel [i.e., the EEOC] to determine who should be prosecuted . . ."[7]

The EEOC no longer needed any approval to sue. So it filed suit against most of the largest companies in American industry; in less than two years it filed some 300 suits.[8]

Is it any wonder that many companies decided to give up all testing? Or to move a lot of their manufacturing overseas to foreign countries?

And so the EEOC began its grand march. In order to make it clear to all businessmen that it was serious, the EEOC took on the largest, most visible ones. AT&T fell in 1973 by "agreeing" to pay $83 million in compensatory payments to women and blacks.[9] It even "agreed" to put 750 people in its equal employment opportunity office.

This meant that AT&T now had its own "EEOC" right inside the company, watching every movement and every word that anyone ever uttered. Now you can understand why every big business in America is always in "strong support" of the Civil Rights Act; they are being watched very carefully. They have no choice.

General Electric "agreed" to pay more than $32 million; Chase Manhattan Bank paid $1.8 million. General Motors settled for $42.5 million, even though it had 17% black and 15% female employees.[10]

The head of the EEOC, Mr. Powell, said, "There are going to be quite a few trials during my term of office."[11]

The EEOC attacked the entire steel industry which settled to avoid the endless litigation and bad publicity that would follow, agreeing to pay $31 million in back pay to workers who were said to have suffered discrimination. In addition, it agreed to do the following:

- 50% of the openings in trade and craft jobs would go to minorities and women.

THE U.S. GOVERNMENT ATTACKS OUR BUSINESSES

- 20% of all openings in maintenance jobs would go to women and 15% of all clerical jobs to blacks during the first year.
- 25% of management-training and supervisory jobs would be filled by either women or blacks.[12]

The head of the EEOC said further: "It is *our* judgment whether these companies are in compliance. Companies had better come to the realization that compliance is in their own self-interest. Louis XVI and the Czar of Russia resisted change, and what happened to them is history." [emphasis added]

And so the big corporations decided that they could never win by fighting, only by 1) submission or by 2) leaving the country.

It did not matter whether they intended to discriminate. "We need this power," said the head of the EEOC, "to prod those many companies who honestly do not believe that they discriminate. A lot of this discrimination, I must admit, is not overt on the part of management."[13]

The irony is that most of these companies usually had the best civil rights records of anyone in the country.

One of the five Commissioners on the EEOC disagreed with the chairman, but his was a lonely voice.

"The Commission is harassing Sears and GM," said Commissioner Colston Lewis, a black civil rights lawyer from Richmond, "because this is the way the chairman can get headlines. Besides, Sears has the best damn affirmative action program of any company in the country."

Lewis was concerned about the hiring of unqualified people. He thought it best to get them qualified.

"It is wrong to force companies to hire unqualified applicants just because they are minority people. In the end, such practices will only serve to hurt the minorities. We must eliminate the barriers which impede the ability of minorities to aspire to and achieve their economic objectives. Once these barriers are eliminated, minorities will soon be competing on an equal footing."[14]

The Supreme Court Watched

While all of this was going on, the U. S. Supreme Court, which has the power to review any case that it wishes, *refused* to hear the major ones on this subject for another eight years. America's highest court sat idle, refusing to accept any appeals, watching the chaos as different courts said different things about what the word "discriminate" meant.

FREEDOM WILL CONQUER RACISM (AND SEXISM)

There was, however, one troublesome problem for the people who ran the EEOC. They could promise a business that the U. S. government wouldn't sue if it did what it was told. But the EEOC could not stop the angry white employees who were starting to bring their own suits because of being denied jobs or promotions as a result of the quotas which were being required by both the EEOC and the President's OFCCP.

Finally, in 1979, the Supreme Court agreed to hear a case, 15 years after the passage of the Act.[15] It involved a steel mill in Louisiana which had agreed (after pressure from the President's OFCCP) to put one black for every white into its training program.*

The Court agreed to take the case, probably because it realized that it was becoming necessary to stop the whites from suing or else the large American businesses would always be in the middle and therefore they would stop cooperating with the EEOC. And so the Supreme Court heard *United Steelworkers v. Weber*. It decided in that case that white persons could not complain if a company was using quotas and discriminating against whites. It didn't matter that qualified whites were being turned down in order to hire less qualified blacks. And it didn't matter that we now had quotas.

How did the court get around the obvious intent of Congress? It said that it would not look at the "literal construction" of the law; i.e. what Congress had said. It did so by looking at the "spirit" of the law. Not at the words of the law, but at its "spirit." The court said, quoting a case from 1892: "It is a 'familiar rule that a thing may be within the letter of the statute and yet not within the statute, because not within its spirit nor within the intention of its makers.'"[16]

And it went on to show that the "spirit" of Congress was to improve the plight of blacks in our economy, and if the judges on the Supreme Court decided that something improved the "plight of blacks," it didn't matter what the words in the law said.

Let me state that again because it is important. The opinion said that if the judges decided that the law *should* be read in a certain manner, it didn't matter what the law actually said.

---

* It is interesting to note that this case really involved a labor union which had been discriminating against blacks with the help of the power of the federal government.

And do you remember the amendment that was passed to avoid this exact situation? The amendment says that nobody can "require" an employer to give preferential treatment. When the amendment was introduced on the Senate floor, Sen. Humphrey said: "[We] have carefully stated on numerous occasions that [this bill] does not require an employer to achieve any sort of racial balance in his work force by giving preferential treatment to any individual or group. Since doubts have persisted, [this amendment] is added to state this point expressly. [It] does not represent any change in the substance of the [bill]."[17]

But the Supreme Court twisted the amendment which both 1) in its language and 2) in its legislative history was clear. The Court twisted it to further the Court's own goals. It turned the amendment around and said that the amendment meant that an employer could *"voluntarily"* discriminate against white people.[18] Of course, we know how eloquently Senator Humphrey and others had assured us, but it didn't matter now. Not only did Congress not give anyone the power to discriminate "voluntarily," but the discrimination in this case was not done voluntarily; it was done solely under intense pressure from the OFCCP and the EEOC. The Civil Rights Act of 1964 now meant only what that handful of "elite" in Washington said it meant.*

And thus were quotas (known to the "elite" as "affirmative action") born.

President Reagan Comes Aboard

When President Reagan was elected in 1980, there were high hopes among some people that the "great communicator" would be able to change all of this.

But there were a few things going against him.

First. By 1981 the big companies of America were already used to quotas and really didn't care anymore. They all had big "Affirmative Action" staffs that were watching all of the employees very carefully, and the companies were afraid to stop for fear they

---

* If any reader is interested in a detailed history of the Act replete with unassailable proof that Congress did not intend this result, they can find no better place to look than at the dissent of Justice Rehnquist in *United Steelworkers*.

FREEDOM WILL CONQUER RACISM (AND SEXISM)

would be called "racist" or "sexist". Once any big organization has vice presidents in charge of something, it can't stop it easily. And so the time had passed for the big companies to really care anymore. Their sense of outrage was gone. So the word went out that American business was not enthusiastic about a change. They could see what had happened to the companies which had resisted.

Therefore, big business did not support Reagan in his efforts. As one commentator noted:

"[I]n the struggle that developed in the early months of the Reagan administration between Congressional opponents of quotas and liberals and the civil rights lobby, most businessmen remained on the sidelines. Some of them supported quotas as morally justifiable; others opposed quotas but were reluctant to say so for fear of appearing unsympathetic to civil rights."[19]

They had learned to live with quotas, and to pass on the costs or move out of the country, according to the commentator, who continued:

"Most businessmen, having no inclination to test the agencies' interpretation of antidiscrimination in court nor any desire to appear unsympathetic to civil rights, tried in their pragmatic way to make the best of a bad situation. They were told—and they told themselves—that 'equal employment opportunity' was good business, ignoring the fact that affirmative action was *not* equal opportunity... In this spirit, companies appointed EEO officers, built affirmative action compliance into the corporate structure, and tried to absorb the costs. By the end of the decade, businessmen were still generally critical of affirmative action, but their idea of reforming it was to cut down on the paperwork rather than to get rid of racial quotas."[20]

Second. How could one man, even a President, change a big bureaucracy like the EEOC where there were over 3000 employees and where almost all of them were protected by civil service? The employees of a department such as this are never "neutral;" they are zealots who are fighting for a cause. And how does a President change the direction of an organization when all of the employees in it are saying, "He'll change this over my dead body!"

Third. Most of the working press in America voted against Reagan and were of the opinion that he was wrong and dangerous. It was difficult, if not impossible, for them to write without bias.

THE U.S. GOVERNMENT ATTACKS OUR BUSINESSES

Fourth. The name of "Civil Rights" had a magic to it that made it difficult for anyone to appear to be against it, even such a popular President.

Fifth. An effective campaign was instituted against any change, with the Chairman of the NAACP, William F. Gibson, even going so far as to call President Reagan a "reactionary and racist."[21] Many in America knew that was a disgraceful remark, but no one called him on it.

Last. And most important of all, most people still agreed that blacks needed some type of help, but the rigid, political positions of the "elite" totally eliminated any intelligent discussions on the issues. Therefore, a workable alternative was never reached.

Even though President Reagan and some of his appointees kept trying to make a point to the people of America, they were unsuccessful. They attempted to get America back to a "color blind" society, but, in response, the press kept saying that Reagan was "soft" on civil rights and no newspaper readers or television listeners knew what that meant.*

It was always "Reagan" against the "civil rights movement."

When a proposal was floated in 1985 to have Reagan rescind the President's OFCCP, which requires quotas by businesses which sell to the government, the Associated Press began its story this way:

"Civil rights and labor groups Thursday sharply criticized a Reagan administration draft proposal to abolish requirements that

---

* One year after Reagan took office, one commentator said that it was partly a lack of courage by the administration that was causing his weakness.

"There may have been a time, in Reagan's first days in office, when it would have been feasible and popular to wipe out goals and timetables and revert, with a stroke of the pen, to a color-blind antidiscrimination system. But now in the wake of those various initiatives, retreats, and confusions on the tax-exempt status of discriminatory schools, it is much harder to act. In any case, it seems clear that nobody in the Administration now has the heart to throw on the table any large initiatives in the civil-rights area. Supporters of the present system will find this welcome news, but critics of the system fear that the Administration has blown a historic opportunity to do something about quotas." Daniel Seligman, *Fortune,* April 19, 1982, p. 162.

FREEDOM WILL CONQUER RACISM (AND SEXISM)

businesses with government contracts set numerical goals for hiring women and minorities."[22]

The Associated Press quoted many of the "elite" as to how terrible this proposal would be.

"'It's an unconscionable proposal,' said Ralph Neas, executive director of the Leadership Conference on Civil Rights 'We hope that the more moderate and thoughtful persons in the administration will prevail and that it will not be implemented.'

"Richard T. Seymour of the Lawyers' Committee for Civil Rights Under Law called the draft 'an astonishingly extreme document.'

"In Pittsburgh, the AFL-CIO's executive council, concluding a three-day policy making meeting, said 'such a move would represent a giant step backward in the fight against employment discrimination.'

Were the reporters at the Associated Press really unable to find *any* responsible person who thought it might be a good idea to eliminate racial and sexual quotas? The reporters would have you believe they couldn't and that it was merely that racist President against the world again.

And it hasn't changed any since then.

On June 24, 1996, *Newsweek* had the following:

"Traditionally—at least since Nixon's 'Southern Strategy'—Republicans have been truly despicable on race, and there are more than a few stalwarts who continue to bloviate disingenuously in support of a 'colorblind' society, by which they mean a tacit relapse into segregation. Bob Dole flirted with this last year, proposing legislation that would end racial preferences [i.e., quotas]."[23]

We must wonder about the ignorance of *Newsweek*.

- We readers know that it was Republicans who pushed the Civil Rights Act even before President Kennedy got on board, and this was despite the fact that the Republicans knew it would hurt them in the South which was just beginning to go Republican. And we remember how angry Congressman McCulloch got at Congressman Celler who was breaking his promises in order to placate the Democrats in the South.
- And we know that it was President Nixon who implemented the quotas in the 1970's.
- And we know that the work of the EEOC increased under Reagan.

THE U.S. GOVERNMENT ATTACKS OUR BUSINESSES

- But, most important of all, we know that trying to end quotas is not "despicable disingenuous bloviating"*

---

* The sad part about this comment by Newsweek is that it was written in an article by Joe Klein which criticized Gen. Powell for waffling on quotas. Klein said: "[A]ffirmative action has become the euphemism of choice for not-so-subtle racial quotas, for lowered standards instead of expanded opportunities." How Klein jumped from that to the above "despicable" quote is difficult to understand.

7

THE SUPREME COURT MAKES IT WORSE

On a Wednesday in June, 1988, the U. S. Supreme Court once again changed the basic foundations of American society.

It decided a case involving a small bank in Fort Worth, Texas, with about 80 employees. Like most small businesses, the bank had always, since the day it was founded, decided who would get promoted by listening to the supervisors who were acquainted with the candidates and the nature of the jobs to be filled. That sounds reasonable, doesn't it? That's the way all businesses have always made these decisions.

Well, they've been *ordered* to stop.

The U.S. Supreme Court says that this is a reasonable method *only* if there is a sufficient number of blacks being promoted. If the number of blacks who are promoted isn't high enough, then the court will *presume* that the company is run by racists..

By the time that this case came before the Court, the legal terms "disparate treatment" and "disparate impact" had become common knowledge to everyone in the legal profession (and, regrettably, many people in business also had had to learn about them). Both the

THE SUPREME COURT MAKES IT WORSE

trial court and the Court of Appeals held that this case was obviously one of "disparate treatment," which meant a court would look only at the particular employee who was suing to see if she had been discriminated against because of her race.

But the Supreme Court said that this was wrong. This should be treated as a case of "disparate impact," which meant a judge had to look at this "employment practice" and its effect on the black race.

But, wait a minute! The bank (or their lawyers) knew as a result of *Griggs v. Duke Power* that it couldn't use I.Q. or other tests or diplomas *unless the proper percentage of blacks passed the test*. Now was it being told that it couldn't even observe its employees to see who is the best *unless the proper percentage of blacks were promoted?*

What *could the bank* do to promote its employees?

There would appear to be no method that it could use to promote its employees *except to make sure that the quotas are met.*

What other method is there to decide whom to promote?

As a result, every business in America with more than 15 employees is required to keep a "balanced" workforce.* Every business must have strict quotas as to how many black employees it has and how many whites. And this is true for every position in the company. A "balanced" workforce is also necessary with regard to the number of *women* who are employed in every position.

Up until this opinion, there were a lot of signals being sent to American business that quotas were always a good idea, but it was never made "official."

What do we mean by "quotas?" This means that if 29.3% of the laborers in Atlanta are black, then a company must have close to 29.3% black laborers. If 33.4% of the typists in St. Louis are black, then a business must make sure that about 33.4% of its typing pool is black.

If 38.3% of the lawyers in the New York City area are women, then a law firm must have approximately 38.3% women in its firm.

---

* And even part-time employees "count" in determining whether a company has enough employees to be covered by the Act as the result of a January 14, 1997, decision of the U.S. Supreme Court. *Walters v. Metropolitan Educational Enterprises, Inc.,* 117 S.Ct. 660 (1997).

FREEDOM WILL CONQUER RACISM (AND SEXISM)

Why Haven't You Heard?

Why is it that you have never before heard about this astounding fact? The answer is that the businesses are attacked *one at a time;* and they no longer dare complain or things will really become nasty. And they don't have time for this; they're trying to run a business. So they "settle."

Remember what the head of the EEOC said back in 1972? "Companies had better come to the realization that compliance is in their own self-interest. Louis XVI and the Czar of Russia resisted change, and what happened to them is history." Well, the executives of the big businesses were very fast learners.

And do you remember that the chief in the Civil Rights Division of the U.S. Attorney General warned that the EEOC could attack almost any business in the country that it desired? This means that a politician or lobbyist with good connections could have a competitor "driven crazy" by the EEOC because the EEOC could attack almost any business in the country it wanted to since these quotas were impossible to fulfill.

Do you remember how clear it was when the Civil Rights Act was passed? The very difficult burden of "proving" a case would always be on the person who was suing. And when anyone even suggested that it might not happen this way in actual practice in the real world, he was denounced as a *racist!*

And we must wonder what President Kennedy's reaction would have been when his feelings were: "I do not think we ought to begin the quota system.... We are too mixed, this society of ours, to begin to divide ourselves on the basis of race."[1]

All of this has happened because nine people on the Supreme Court are allowed to define the word, "discriminate."

How odd it is that the *Fort Worth* decision went virtually unnoticed by the press. *The New York Times* had a page one, banner headline for another decision which was written the same day. But it buried this important decision in an article on page A19.[2]

Only a Small Bank

The case involved a small bank in Texas. Its name was *Watson v. Fort Worth Bank and Trust.*[3]

THE SUPREME COURT MAKES IT WORSE

The Fort Worth Bank had about 80 employees. Clara Watson was a black who started working for it in 1973 as a clerk. In 1976, she was promoted to a teller. In 1980 she tried to become a supervisor in the main lobby but a white male got the job. She then sought to become a supervisor at the drive-in bank, but this position went to a white female.

While Watson was on sick leave, she applied for two more promotions. She never returned to work and resigned in August, 1981.*

Therefore, this woman had received one promotion and was denied two more while she was working there and denied two more after she went on sick leave. And then she sued.

Should Businesses Worry?

But must the average business worry about this case?

It's pretty hard to imagine a more average employer than the Fort Worth Bank. This wasn't a "bad" company. Even the Supreme Court noted with satisfaction that "the percentage of blacks in the Bank's work force approximated the percentage of blacks in the metropolitan area where the Bank is located."[4]

Both the bank and the Reagan administration had argued before the justices of the Court that such a decision would lead to quotas. According to the *New York Times,* they argued, "[A] ruling in favor of the plaintiff would force thousands of employers to adopt quota systems in order to avoid litigation."[5] But the Court says we shouldn't

---

*   The Supreme Court never revealed in its decision that Watson was applying for a promotion while she was on sick leave and not available for work. Although this fact is not *theoretically* important to the court's decision, it would be important to any employer that Watson was trying to obtain a promotion while she was not at work and her attitude might be shown by the fact that she never did return to work. These facts certainly make her position less tenable and raise speculation as to whether any company would promote her under those circumstances. Apparently the Supreme Court also had doubts and this is the reason why it did not reveal these facts. Obviously, the Supreme Court was not deciding the particular case of Clara Watson and the bank as it is supposed to. It was, instead, legislating a broad policy question, which is the role of Congress. The complete facts are found in the Court of Appeals decision, *Watson v. Fort Worth Bank & Trust,* 798 F.2d 791, 793.

FREEDOM WILL CONQUER RACISM (AND SEXISM)

worry. A company is free to go to court and present evidence that it was not discriminating.[6]

We've heard that before, haven't we? Doesn't it sound familiar? Of course it does.

The Court has expanded the ruling of *Griggs v. Duke Power* and said that even if you don't use tests, you are still going to have to show that the particular method that you use to hire or promote people is "necessary"—*unless* of course, you just happen to have the proper "balance" in your work force of white and black, of male and female, of Jew and Christian, of Asian and Puerto Rican, and so on.

Which means that every employer must now use "quotas" or else spend his or her day in court.

Now ask yourself: If a business person knows that he or she can be taken to court by the full power of the United States government with a case already presumed against it unless it has the proper number of blacks or women, what do you think it is going to do?

Not only does an unscrupulous woman or minority person have the right to extort money because he or she has the right to sue, now it is much, much easier. They can just point to the "numbers" to "prove" that a business is "racist" or "sexist" no matter what method a company uses to do its hiring. The only intelligent thing a businessperson can do is to start using quotas.

In the *New York Times* article about this case, they said the court's decision was "a bitter defeat for the Reagan Administration." Did you note the thrust of that quote? Not a defeat for America, but "for the Reagan Administration."[7]

All of this has happened because nine people in Washington are allowed to define the word, "discriminate."

Court Says, "Don't Worry"

It may be comforting to know that Justice Sandra Day O'Connor says in the opinion that we mustn't worry about this decision. It won't create a burden for business because the "burden of proof" for the person who is suing is very high in a case like this.

Yes, says O'Connor, a business will have to spend hundreds of thousands of dollars on psychologists, statisticians and lawyers because it terminated an incompetent employee ... but not to worry because it *may* be able to eventually convince a bureaucrat, judge or jury that it was not "discriminating."

THE SUPREME COURT MAKES IT WORSE

It is obvious that judges and lawyers believe that the center of the world is in their courthouses. Any work that happens to take place in the rest of the world is not as important as what happens in a courthouse.*

A False Hope

Employment lawyers are excited by any small crumb of hope and many were cheered by the case of *Wards Cove Packing Co.*[8] in 1990. It didn't do much except to say that instead of requiring a business to show a *"business necessity"* in order to use a test or have the supervisors pick the best person for promotion, the business would only have to show that the practice serves in a significant way the employer's legitimate goals; i.e. that it actually furthers its interest.

But only a lawyer could get excited over such a crumb and even that was swept away in 1991 by the combination of a Democratic Congress, a weak Republican president and a business community that had indeed "seen the light" and had no desire to end up like the Czar of Russia, as the head of the EEOC had threatened.

Have We Ratified It?

Many of the "elite" will attempt to say, as I have pointed out along the way, that the people have ratified all of what has happened in Congress and the courts since 1964. They will say this is evident because of some of the actions by both Congress and the courts. But, as we have seen, there is also a lot of action that also shows to the contrary. And even more important, we know that the press has never reported these actions to us accurately. We have never been aware of what has been happening in each courtroom or even in Congress. That has been demonstrated many times in this book.

Does This Apply to Judges?

When the civil rights activist, Ruth Bader Ginsburg, was nominated to the Supreme Court in 1993, her excellent record as a civil

---

* Justice O'Connor's words were: "In sum, the high standards of proof in disparate impact cases are sufficient in our view to avoid giving employers incentives to modify any normal and legitimate practices by introducing quotas or preferential treatment." *Watson v. Fort Worth Bank & Trust,* 487 U.S. 977, 999.

rights activist was praised by all. She was nationally known for her work in favor of minorities and women.

But Sen. Hatch discovered that although Ginsburg had been a judge in the largely black city of Washington, D.C. for 13 years and had hired 57 law clerks, secretaries and interns, not one of them was black.

Sen. Hatch talked about that and the following colloquy took place:

Hatch: "Naturally, I am concerned about preferences and I know you are, and I know that you are a very good person. But I just want to point that out, because that happens every day all over this country, where there is no evidence of intent and, in fact, was no desire on the part of the employer to exclude anybody."

Ginsburg: "I appreciate that, Senator Hatch, but I do want to say that I have tried to ... ."

Hatch: "I know you have."

Ginsburg: "And I am going to try harder, and if you confirm me for this job, my attractiveness to black candidates is going to improve." [Laughter]

Hatch: "That is wonderful. . . . I would like the Justices to think about the real world, real people out there who really aren't intending to discriminate. And if you just use the statistical disparity to make final determinations, you can create an awful lot of bad law and an awful lot of expense to the small business community that may very well not be willing to discriminate."

And it is wonderful to know that a member of the "elite" can laugh off the fact that she hired no blacks despite the fact that her office was surrounded by them. She can do that because everyone knows that she would never discriminate.

But, now about the rest of you . . .

8

WERE THE "ELITE" SURPRISED BY THE SUPREME COURT?

Ordinary citizens are astonished to discover we do not have a color-blind society and . . . *our leaders do not want us to have one.*

However, the "elite" were not surprised by the Supreme Court. The sophisticated observers in 1964 knew that we were heading toward a quota system.

The leaders of the civil rights movement muted their ideas during the congressional debate on the Civil Rights Act.

The U.S. Supreme Court had given us a very large hint in 1954. It did so in its decisions under the Constitution[1] about segregation in the public schools.

Here's a quick look at two important cases from the Supreme Court.

1896 - Plessy v. Ferguson. In this case, a state was allowed to require that railroads have separate seating for black people and separate seating for white people. This did not violate the Constitution, according to the Court. If a white person wished to sit on the train with his black friend, the state could make it *illegal* for him to do so.

FREEDOM WILL CONQUER RACISM (AND SEXISM)

In other words, a state could *require* segregation. It could forbid integration by anyone. The citizens had no right to choose what they wanted to do. There was no guarantee of freedom. The state could tell them what to do.

1954 – *Brown v. Board of Education.* The Court skipped right over "freedom" and went to the opposite extreme. Integration was not only allowed; it was now *required,* under the Constitution. There was still no choice. There was no *freedom*. If a Chinese person in Boston, for example, wished to live with other Chinese people in Chinatown he was essentially violating the law (at least in spirit and often in fact) by living with other Chinese. The Italians were violating the law by living in the North End, the Irish in South Boston and the Jews in Brookline. This became apparent when the federal courts began to require that the children of these people be bussed around the city to achieve integration. The citizen no longer had a choice. There were many citizens who wished to integrate with other races; there were others who did not. But the choice was removed. Whereas the Supreme Court had said in 1896 that it was okay to prohibit the mingling of the races; now it had suddenly changed. Everyone *must* integrate.

As far as the Constitution was concerned, we had skipped right over a color-blind society where a citizen could do what he or she chose to do.

As one liberal commentator gleefully said of the Court's decision, "When the Supreme Court ordered desegregation, it...also exposed the more savory doctrine of 'color blindness' to reexamination" and exposed its weaknesses.[2]

The new doctrine of forcible integration was even more evident in the Supreme Court's second *Brown* decision in 1955. It held that black students who suffered from segregation had no individual rights to desegregated education apart from the rights of the rest of their race.[3] A black student could be delayed in pushing for his rights if progress was being made in the legal status of blacks *as a group.*

This decision had bad results. "This reluctance [by the Supreme Court] to declare and enforce a strict color-blind constitutional rule not only delayed the desegregation of southern schools for over a decade, but helped make possible the application of color-conscious remedies in education, voting and employment after 1965."[4]

Who Saw the Possibilities for Quotas?

In those cases about the Constitution, the U.S. Supreme Court had given an opening for quotas. Who would be the first to seize it? Let's find out.

The first state to enact a law that forbid discrimination in employment had been New York in 1945. By 1963, twenty-five other states had also enacted such laws. But New York remained the leader. Although its policies changed as a Republican and Democrat replaced each other as Governor, the Commission's policies predominately remained ones of conciliation and persuasion.

As the federal government sought to enact a similar bill in the 1940s and 1950s, the state laws were cited as a model until 1953. The experience from the states showed that conciliation was the most effective method and that enforcement orders against recalcitrant offenders were seldom necessary.

This fact was noticed by the leader of the Republicans in the U.S. Senate, Robert A. Taft, who supported a federal law that was modeled after the state laws. But he was strongly against a compulsory one. He said:

"As I see it, the compulsory act, if duplicated in every state as its proponents plan, will finally force every employer to choose his employees approximately in proportion to the division of races and religions in his district, because that will be his best defense against harassing suits." In the 1940's and 1950's Taft endorsed a gradual, voluntary educational approach without compulsory enforcement.

However, in the early 1960's when Congress again looked at the subject, it was being cast in a different light.

The civil rights groups were now saying that the problem of discrimination in employment was more complicated, deeply rooted and structural. The major challenge was no longer in hiring but in training, upgrading and promotion in the skilled, professional and managerial areas.

Although the civil rights groups had always insisted on a color-blind society in which employers were prohibited from classifying their workers by race, they were now beginning to say it was necessary to be color-conscious.

FREEDOM WILL CONQUER RACISM (AND SEXISM)

A New Way of Thinking

After the Supreme Court's decision in *Brown* in 1954 there was a new wave of thinking. The boycott of busses by Martin Luther King in Montgomery in 1955-1956 also raised the expectations of the black people. The most prominent leader of the new intellectual thought was Whitney Young of the Urban League, who said in 1963 that "if the United States drops legal, practical and subtle racial barriers in employment... the American Negro still will not achieve full equality in our lifetime."[5]

In 1955 the new Democratic Governor in New York, Averell Harriman, appointed the liberal Charles Abrams to head its Fair Employment Practice Commission. This was the man who had said that the *Brown* decision of the U.S. Supreme Court had put the spotlight on the principle of color-blindness and exposed its weaknesses. Because he believed that the blacks were being held back by their concentration in urban ghettoes, he would keep the number of blacks in public housing below the point where "white flight" would ensue. When he was accused of endorsing the violation of civil rights for purposes of integration, he warned against an overweening regard for individual rights and color-blindness. He denounced "an atmosphere in which public officials loosely hurl words around like 'quota system' the minute anyone tries to desegregate." According to him, quotas were "wicked catch-words," used by foes of desegregation.

This type of rhetoric led one commentator to say, "Organizations committed to fighting for minorities and/or civil rights in general, exhibit a carefully thought-out sort of schizophrenia: it's okay to use a quota—in fact, it's necessary—but you should never talk about it."[6]

The intellectuals began to say that to freeze the Constitution in the rules of color-blindness and individual rights would be the triumph of formalistic, mechanical jurisprudence. Quotas could be used as a temporary expedient, recognizing, they claimed, that the choice was between perpetual segregation or integration by social control.

Meanwhile, the President's Committees that worked with government contractors (under Presidents Truman, Eisenhower and Kennedy), were also having a difficult time in trying to deal with this perplexing problem. Although all these Committees gave lip-service to a color-blind policy, they all tried various schemes of trying to help the black worker. In 1962, Vice President Lyndon

WERE THE "ELITE" SURPRISED BY THE SUPREME COURT

Johnson was in charge of the Committee. He brought in a consultant who stated that the lack of *qualified* black workers should no longer excuse an employer for having a lack of such employees. It was the employer's job to seek them out and then to train them.

So the deck was stacked when the Civil Rights Act was passed in 1964. The "elite" knew exactly what was coming. But they either kept quiet while the Act was being debated, or they deliberately misled the public. The vast majority of Americans had no idea what was going to happen next.

Section III

THE CIVIL RIGHTS ACT HASN'T HELPED BLACKS ... IT'S HURT

"So what!?"

That's what "elite" readers will be yelling in passionate protest. They'll continue:

"It was worth any price, even giving up some freedom, to make the progress that we've seen since 1964."

But the Civil Rights Act has *not* given us progress.

It's hurt the people we were trying to help.

Blacks did remarkably well after they gained their freedom in 1865. They could compete, just like any other group, despite the great obstacles they faced. It was not until the intrusion of politicians and government that the blacks stopped their upwardly mobile movement. The first intrusion by the government occurred at the end of the 1800's when the "Jim Crow" laws were passed by the southern states (with the approval of the federal government). The second intrusion occurred in 1964 when the federal government passed the Civil Rights Act.

Both intrusions occurred because many politicians were trying to stay in power by winning votes; in the 1800's they were trying to gain the vote of whites and in 1964 they were trying to win the votes of blacks and the liberal "elite."

9

"FREEDOM" WAS THE ANSWER

There was considerable chaos in the first days of freedom after the Civil War.

Some Congressmen were saying that all of the newly freed slaves should each be given 40 acres from the plantations of their former owners. Therefore, many blacks were searching to discover how they could obtain this land.

To others, emancipation meant not only freedom from slavery but also freedom from work.[1]

This self-corrected very quickly for the most part. In the crop season of 1865, the majority had returned to work on their old plantations. However, they were not motivated, and therefore not the best of workers. The acreage that was planted in 1866 was less than half of the prewar period; and even on those fields which were cultivated, little more than half a crop was produced.

Gradually it occurred to most people that the only way that any progress was to be made was by having the black people in charge of their own lives. (This was the same discovery that had been made by the Pilgrims at Plymouth very early on when poor harvests forced them to give up their communal gardens and give each family its own plot.)

FREEDOM WILL CONQUER RACISM (AND SEXISM)

This proved to be an almost magic answer as the blacks started to make immediate progress. Their main endeavor continued to be agriculture as it was over the entire country, both whites and blacks.

The census of 1880 showed that after 15 years of freedom, the standard of living for blacks was well above subsistence in most cases.[2] By 1910, almost 20% owned their own farms with another 5% owning a part of their land.[3]

The average black family around 1900 did not confine its expenditures to the necessities of food, clothing and shelter but allocated a significant fraction of its income to churches, lodges, consumer durables, travel, amusement and savings. The first half century of black freedom witnessed major improvements in the level of living.[4]

Not Because of Altruism

It was not because of altruism on the part of whites (or other blacks*) that these gains were seen. It was because of freedom. The blacks made it clear that they would not be coerced, and therefore the planters were forced to be fair.

After disastrous crops in 1865 and 1866, the biggest fear of any planter was that he would not have any labor. As one of them wrote in 1877, "[E]very one seemed to fear that everybody else would get ahead of him and that he would have no labor at all. Hence a universal rush at the Negro – each outbidding the other, the Negro in the meantime feeling like a maiden with a dozen suitors at her feet – entire master of the situation."[5]

As another wrote in 1871, "At fair prices and with good management there is money in raising cotton. So he [the planter] speaks to one freedman after another, mounts his horse and rides hither and thither, sends an agent back and forth day after day, announces his willingness to make liberal contracts, does make large offers, bribes his own hands to hire others for him, goes to the towns and villages and addresses the many colored loiterers on the streets, stops at railway stations..."[6]

---

*   Let's not forget that 3,777 of the slave owners were black. In Louisiana, the Ricaud family owned 152 slaves. The DuBuclet family had 94. The Metoyer family, beginning with its matriarch, the ex-slave Marie Therez, acquired 278 slaves and almost 12,000 acres by 1830. *Business History Review,* Autumn 1986, p. 355; John Sibley Butler, *Entrepreneurship and Self-Help Among Black Americans* (Albany: State University of New York Press, 1991), p. 171.

"FREEDOM" WAS THE ANSWER

There were many observers at the time who stated that the intense competition for labor did more to enforce real freedom for the blacks than the U.S. military forces.[7]

The same rules applied to a planter who was trying to get tenants. If he did not deal fairly, he found it extremely difficult to get a tenant.

This did not mean that all planters were fair. Of course, there were some who cheated and lied. There were also tenants and laborers who cheated and lied. But the freedom was working.

The freedom that was most important to the blacks was the right of physical movement. They demonstrated conclusively that they could not be held in place against their will. They went from plantation to plantation, from countryside to city and from east to west. Although the whites often used government in an attempt to stop this movement (with laws such as those against vagrancy or against the enticement of employees under contract, etc.), they were largely unsuccessful.[8]

But perhaps the greatest success was the growth in literacy.

In 1865 between 5-10% of the blacks had any knowledge of the written word; but by 1910, 70% told the census takers that they could read. Even if this is discounted to 50%, this caused one commentator to declare, "For a large population to transform itself from virtually unlettered to more than half literate in 50 years ranks as an accomplishment seldom witnessed in human history."[9]

Many others have also said that the ex-slaves showed a tremendous desire for knowledge. The blacks soon demonstrated that they had the ability to learn as quickly as the whites. And they showed this ability in colleges and universities also. However, like all groups, some of them allowed only a little education to make them proud and arrogant and to exploit the uneducated members of their race.

Government Interferes

As long as there was freedom, the blacks made good progress. But this lasted only while there was an agricultural economy. As long as the vast majority of the people in the country were working on farms, the freedom of the marketplace was working well.*

---

* Except under Franklin Roosevelt's farm programs in the 1930s when the land owners were paid to take their land out of production. This, of course, hurt the black laborers and tenant farmers who were no longer needed to farm the land.

FREEDOM WILL CONQUER RACISM (AND SEXISM)

But when the industrial age started to intrude, this began to change.

The change began, as we learned in the previous section, when the U.S. Supreme Court approved the Jim Crow laws in the late 1800's. They allowed the states to pass laws which discriminated against the blacks. The interesting question is, "Why did the South *have* to pass the Jim Crow laws in order to get its citizens to discriminate against blacks? Why didn't the white citizens just discriminate on their own?"

This is an interesting question.

The answer is that it was not uncommon for public transportation, for example, to be racially *un*segregated in Southern cities after the Civil War, including Montgomery, Alabama. It was not until the turn of the century that the Jim Crow laws which required segregation were passed. And even then they were not followed.

Even after the laws were passed, the streetcar company in Mobile initially refused to comply, and in Montgomery blacks simply continued to sit wherever. In Jacksonville, the streetcar company delayed enforcing the segregated seating law of 1901 until 1905. Georgia's state law of 1891 segregating the races was ignored by the streetcar companies in Augusta until 1898, in Savannah until 1899, and in the latter city was not fully enforced until 1906. In Mobile, the streetcar company publicly refused to enforce the Jim Crow laws of 1902, until its streetcar conductors began to be arrested and fined for non-compliance with the law. In Tennessee, the streetcar company opposed the state legislation imposing Jim Crow seating in 1903, delayed enforcement after the law was passed, and eventually was able to get the state courts to declare it unconstitutional.[10]

These railway companies were privately owned. The mere fact that many blacks as individuals would find Jim Crow streetcars distasteful could reduce the frequency with which they rode, particularly when their white customers obviously did not feel strongly enough about it to cause racial segregation to occur through market pressures, the way that they had demanded that the company segregate on these same railways for smokers and non-smokers.

What is important is that *laws* were necessary to get racial prejudice translated effectively into pervasive discrimination, because the forces of the marketplace operated in the opposite direction.

"FREEDOM" WAS THE ANSWER

It should also be noted that it was not *just* "forces of the marketplace" that caused the whites and blacks to ride side-by-side in the 1890s, but that many white people did not desire to segregate their black neighbors.

Labor Unions Interfered

Although the blacks were excellent workers in the building trades (even during slavery), they faced tremendous opposition from the government with the growth of the industrial age and the corresponding growth of cities.

They began to see discrimination against them in the factories and in the cities begin to grow at the end of the 1800s. Some say that it was because of the great influx of ethnic groups from Europe. But, whatever the reason, the prejudice against them spread even into the South. Even in Durham, North Carolina, which is heralded as a community where blacks were able to prosper, the whites formed labor unions and excluded the blacks, regardless of their skills and abilities. For example, in 1903, there were 110 black masons as compared to 15 whites; but by 1929, there were only 85 blacks and 150 whites.[11]

Although the two black leaders, Booker T. Washington and W.E.B. DuBois, agreed on little else, they both disliked the unions. DuBois even called them the greatest enemy of the black working man.[12]

The unions were successful because they gained the strength of the government behind their monopoly power. Although the employers would like to hire the black men, they did not have the power to go against the government. This contrasts sharply with the agricultural labor markets.

A list compiled in 1902 placed some of the more important craft unions in order of increasing hostility toward blacks:
- Miners – Welcome blacks in nearly all cases.
- Longshoremen – Welcome blacks in nearly all cases.
- Cigar-makers – Admit practically all applicants.
- Barbers – Admit many, but restrain Negroes when possible.
- Seamen – Admit many, but prefer whites.
- Firemen – Admit many, but prefer whites.
- Tobacco Workers – Admit many, but prefer whites.

FREEDOM WILL CONQUER RACISM (AND SEXISM)

- Carriage and Wagon Workers – Admit some, but do not seek Negroes.
- Brick-makers – Admit some, but do not seek Negroes.
- Coopers – Admit some, but do not seek Negroes.
- Broom-makers – Admit some, but do not seek Negroes.
- Plasterers – Admit Freely in South and a few in North.
- Carpenters – Admit many in South, almost none in North.
- Masons – Admit a few in South, almost none in North.
- Painters – Admit a few in South, almost none in North.[13]

Discrimination Was New

Up until this period, most discrimination was minimal. For example, in the agricultural labor markets, the weight of the evidence was that there was a virtual absence of racial wage differences in the rural South at the turn of the century.[14]

Even among skilled laborers, it was reported that in Memphis, black plasterers and brickmasons belonged to the same union and received the same pay as did white men. Blacksmiths in various Texas towns were described as receiving "wages according to their skill. White men having the same degree of skill would receive no more." Houston had at least two white contractors who paid carpenters "according to skill, white and black alike." One investigator reported that Atlanta's black artisans received "the prevailing scale of wages," but others adduced evidence of racial differences in that city. From Jacksonville came the report that "usually . . . there is no discrimination in wages [for artisans], but this is not always true." Brickmasons and stone cutters in eastern Georgia received "the same wages of whites in the same trade." In New Orleans, "there is no apparent discrimination in wages in this city and the trade unions are open to Negroes in most cases." In the mines of West Virginia, blacks got the "same as white men for like work." Reports from various Mississippi towns, from Greensboro and Hillsboro, North Carolina, and from Murfreesboro, Tennessee, indicated no racial discrimination of wages paid to artisans.[15]

This was true despite the fact that even DuBois said that the average black laborer was less productive than the average white, stating, "[S]ome of these [black craftsmen] are progressive, efficient workmen. More are careless, slovenly and ill-trained."[16]

"FREEDOM" WAS THE ANSWER

There is little doubt that black labor was relatively unproductive on the average; individual blacks were sometimes judged by the accomplishments of the mass; and pure racial discrimination did sometimes occur.

The problems were stated very starkly by DuBois:

"The new industries attracted the Irish, Germans, and other immigrants; Americans too, were fleeing to the city and soon to natural race antipathies were added a determined effort to displace Negro labor—an effort which had the aroused prejudice of many of the better classes; and the poor quality of the new black immigrants to give it aid and comfort. To all this was soon added a problem of crime and poverty. Numerous complaints of petty thefts, housebreaking, and assaults on peaceful citizens were traced to certain classes of Negroes. In vain did the better class, protest by public meetings their condemnation of such crimes. The tide had set against the Negro strongly . . . . A mass of poverty-stricken, ignorant fugitives and ill-trained freedmen had rushed to the city, swarmed in the vile slums which the rapidly growing city furnished, and met in social and economic competition equally ignorant but more vigorous foreigners. These foreigners outbid them at work, beat them on the streets, and were able to do this by the prejudice which Negro crime and antislavery sentiments had aroused in the city."[17]

The number of people who remained on the farms continued to decrease for both blacks and whites in approximately the same numbers.

1890 - 66% still on the farm
1920 - 50%
1940 - 33%
1950 - 20%

And so the fortunes of the blacks were not as good as they had been as the country was transformed from an agricultural economy.

Blacks Were Always Entrepreneurs

Although most modern scholars have dismissed with disdain any claim that blacks were entrepreneurial, there is surprising evidence being discovered to the contrary. Blacks *were* entrepreneurial. This was true even before the Civil War.[18]

FREEDOM WILL CONQUER RACISM (AND SEXISM)

Even blacks still in slavery were allowed to be in business, and the more successful ones purchased their own liberty.

"[B]lacks developed enterprises in virtually every area important to the pre-Civil war business community, including merchandising, manufacturing, real estate speculation and development, the construction trades, transportation, and the extractive industries. In the development of those enterprises, which paralleled mainstream American business activity, the leading black antebellum entrepreneurs accumulated property in excess of $100,000."

The most successful was William Leidesdorff who lived in San Francisco, where he owned a hotel, lumberyard, shipyard, and an export-import business. When he died in 1848 he was one of the richest men in American with an estate of $1.5 million.[19] Stephen Smith of Philadelphia accumulated $500,000 in lumber and real estate. We know of at least 21 blacks who were worth at least $100,000 (the equivalent of $2 million today).[20]

Although the majority were in small shops or were artisans before the war, "[T]hey were simultaneously involved in almost every major industry."[21]

After the war, many of them started businesses, some of which were quite large. Some of the most successful were in insurance and banking, where large, successful companies flourished.* Many of these men were inventors, with the most famous being Elijah McCoy and Granville T. Woods. McCoy invented a device which allowed steam locomotives and other heavy machinery to be lubricated without being shut down. The expression "the real McCoy" came from the demand that his invention be used on the engines. He had 15 other patents during his lifetime. Granville T. Woods was called the "greatest electrician in the world," and the "Black Edison" after he won two law suits which Edison brought against him. The *American Catholic Tribune* said at the time that he would be remembered as "one of the greatest inventors of his time." There were at least 150 other black inventors that we know about.

---

* It is interesting to note that of 27 black-run insurance companies, 23 hired college graduates with a business degree. Of course, this would not be allowed under the Civil Rights Act.

"FREEDOM" WAS THE ANSWER

The reason that this history is so important is that it "means rediscovering the positive role models which are buried so deeply in Afro-American culture."

"[T]heir values and deeds...should serve as the blueprint for Afro-Americans today who find themselves locked into poverty and despair in the core central cities."[22]

10

THE CIVIL RIGHTS ACT HASN'T HELPED

Great improvement took place from 1940-1980 in the economic conditions of blacks...but *the improvement was just as strong before the Civil Rights Act as it was after it.*

The Civil Rights Act did not help.
- Black poverty was lowered dramatically from 1940-1980, but 80% of the improvement took place *before* 1965.
- The wage gap between blacks and whites was also lessened, but the change was as rapid from 1940-1960 as it was from 1960-1980.[1]

It is true that there was an improvement in the economic condition of blacks *immediately* after 1965 when the Act went into effect, but that was largely because the Jim Crow laws had finally been taken off the books. That intrusion by state governments had finally been eliminated, but then the new intrusion by the federal government began to have its effect and soon the improvements to the black economy began to falter.

THE CIVIL RIGHTS ACT HASN'T HELPED

The Terrible Message

A terrible message has been sent by the Civil Rights Act to the black community. It is the same message that was sent early in 1865 when many of the former slaves believed that they no longer had to work because "the government" was going to care for them.

That message was short-lived in 1865 but the message has a much longer life in this century.

The bad message is that the black people cannot take care of themselves. It is a false message because blacks have shown over and over that they are strong and capable of taking care of themselves. But many have been deluded into believing this terrible message. And many politicians and activists have made a very comfortable living while preaching it.

Middle Class is Doing Well

What has happened in recent years is that the black community has split itself into two groups. The larger group is the old business class and entrepreneurs who have always done well, plus the new middle and upper classes, which are both growing rapidly. The other is a small, but hard, underclass which is doing very poorly.

Let's look at the people who are doing well, and then we will express our concerns about the others.

In 1940, one third of blacks were still on the farm and like most farmers, black and white, their wages showed it.[2] Over 70% of blacks lived below the poverty line. Their earnings were little more than 40% of the income of white people. But they were soon forced to leave the farms because they were being replaced by the mechanical cotton picker. In 1950, very little of the cotton was picked by machine, but by 1962 over 70% was.

As the blacks moved off the farm and into the urban north, their education began to improve and their income as a group started to rise.

By 1980, black males below the poverty line had dropped from 73% down to 20%.[3] This was still too high a figure but it showed quite a change from the 73% in 1940.

It was not only that the black people had moved from the farms of the South to the urban North and had improved their education, it was also that the nation as a whole had had a rapid economic growth that had improved the quality of life for everyone.

FREEDOM WILL CONQUER RACISM (AND SEXISM)

It is the black with the training and education who is getting ahead in America, according to all of the studies. The biggest reason for optimism is the growing size of the black middle class and the black upper class.

Black college graduates are moving from government jobs into the private sector where top financial rewards are possible. And there is substantial evidence that these new professionals will maintain their wages throughout their entire careers.[4]

A new black leadership is arising which comprises 20% of all black men.[5] This new group will be able to pass this heritage on to their children.

There was a growing middle class among blacks in the 1980's. In fact, in 1980 more than 68% of black men were members of the middle class and an additional 12% were above that level.[6] This has improved dramatically since 1940 when only 22% were in the middle class.[7]

The black middle class far outnumbers the black poor.[8]

The Magic Answer

If the Civil Rights Act has not been the answer to helping blacks achieve their success, then what is? Here is the magic answer, according to a Rand Corporation study for the Department of Labor study.

"[T]he safest and surest route to permanent black economic mobility rests in additional education in a good school."[9]

The most important thing, according to the study, is "what takes place in urban black schools of the North."[10]

When Business Leaves, Blacks Will Suffer

Another important reason for the improvement from 1940-1980 was that the entire country was growing and expanding. The one time that this did not occur was during the recession of the 1970's which hurt blacks very badly. The Rand study said:

"The virtual absence of real income growth during the 1970s carried a terrible price in limiting reductions in the ranks of the black poor."[11]

How bad was it? It was "cruel," says the study.

"The disappointing American economic performance during the 1970s had many sorry consequences; one of the cruelest was that the

THE CIVIL RIGHTS ACT HASN'T HELPED

ranks of black poor was 25 percent larger than it would have been had economic growth continued unabated at the pace of the 1960's."[12]

The message is clear.

The surest way to insure that blacks increase their income is not by a Civil Rights Act but by making certain that the business of the country is doing well . . . not by chasing it away to other countries.

When business leaves America because it is tired of the pain brought by the Civil Rights Act and weary of lawyers and judges, who will suffer?

We're already seeing this happen and the answer is, everyone will suffer. Many of our jobs have already gone overseas. But the ones who will suffer the most are the newcomers, the ones at the bottom who are struggling to get aboard. And a large number of those people are black.

It is the basic industries that are going overseas. The high-tech industries are doing well because apparently even a federal judge can understand that a person has to prove he or she is highly intelligent in order to have a job in high tech. It is the basic industries that have suffered and will continue to do so.

Why Are They Not Getting the Education?

We understand why the Rand Report says that education is so important, but why are so many blacks not getting the training and education? The answer may be that our country used to be considered literate. This is not true today. We all know that many of our inner-city children are illiterate.

If many of our black youth can't read, what are they going to do out in the business world that is full of computers and high technology?

What do our businesses say? Are they having trouble finding good employees? They all report that their new employees, both black and white, lack basic skills in math, writing, problem solving, and communication.

If these youngsters can't read or write, is it any wonder that they have difficulty in finding jobs? Will a Civil Rights Act find jobs for them?

What a terrible message the U.S. Supreme Court sent in *Griggs v. Duke Power*! Do you remember what it told the young blacks of America? It said:

FREEDOM WILL CONQUER RACISM (AND SEXISM)

"History is filled with examples of men and women who rendered highly effective performance without the conventional badges of accomplishment in terms of certificates, diplomas, or degrees."

But you can be sure that the sons and daughters of the Supreme Court Justices will have all of the "certificates," "diplomas" and "degrees" that money can buy.

When we send a message to the young blacks that they don't have to strain, sweat and study to get ahead like the sons and daughters of judges, what does that do to their initiative and enterprise?

Will spending more money automatically solve this problem? We hear a lot of talk, particularly at election time, that we have to spend a lot more money. Have we spent the money to solve this problem? The federal government never did anything at all to train people for jobs until the 1960's. But starting in 1960, it spent $500 million over the next four years (in 1980 dollars).[13] When the Great Society came along we really started to spend. From 1965 to 1980, we spent $85.5 billion on job training,[14] the same as we spent on space exploration from 1958 through the first moon landing—an effort usually held up as the classic example of what the nation can accomplish if only it commits the necessary resources.

More and more money can't be the answer.

The Tragedy of Ebonics

The tragedy of poor blacks and their failure in education is illustrated by the recent interest in Ebonics, which is an excuse for not knowing English, and not having a good English vocabulary.

One of the great tragedies of life is a person with *high* aptitudes and *low* vocabulary.

One of the greatest gifts you can give a child today is a very high vocabulary so he or she can express him or herself clearly.

So what are we telling black youth?

We're telling them, "It's okay to talk any way you want. You let them guess what you mean."

It's been known for years that a large and rich vocabulary is vital to the success of any person. This has been clearly documented by the Human Engineering Laboratory in its compilations after the testing of hundreds of thousands of people since its establishment in 1920. They say:

THE CIVIL RIGHTS ACT HASN'T HELPED

"Worldly success, money earnings, management titles, all check with scores in vocabulary. Major executives, presidents, and vice presidents, average at the top, above doctors, lawyers, and college professors."[15]

Its testing of thousands of people showed this truth back in 1937:

"[T]he height to which a man has risen in any profession or occupation yet studied can be predicted more accurately from the size of his vocabulary than from any other single mental trait measurable to date."[16]

In the many companies that were studied by the Laboratory, the one key to success was vocabulary.

"In companies the Laboratory has studied, it has found vocabulary of the greatest importance in distinguishing executive rank. In typical industrial firms, for example, those in charge of others, from the leading hand to the president, have much the same inherent traits. They differ principally in vocabulary. Each executive scores higher in the vocabulary work sample than the average of the group he supervises; he is often the highest-scoring individual of the group. Vocabulary, more than any other single characteristic which the Laboratory can measure, determines the executive rank which a man or woman* reaches."[17]

It gave an example as to why a person with a low vocabulary might become rebellious and violent if he or she is also high in inductive reasoning.

"[I]nductive reasoning finds application in sanctioned diplomacy, formalized jurisprudence, and editorial writing, so without vocabulary the same aptitude gropes rebelliously for new forms of government, ideal justice for all, drastic social reforms; but lacking words can express these visionary aspirations only in violent acts, demonstrations, revolutions, and the destruction of the inadequate present....With a vocabulary below the fifth percentile, few born gifts are effective in any modern civilized community."[18]

The people at the Human Engineering Laboratory even hypothesize that when we think, we use our vocabulary to help us. Therefore, even the thinking process requires a high vocabulary.

---

* Please note that even in 1937, they were talking about women executives.

FREEDOM WILL CONQUER RACISM (AND SEXISM)

A random study was done a few years ago of 18 black, non-middle-class children in Washington, D.C. *It showed that these children had the same aptitudes as the overwhelmingly white, middle class people that the Laboratory usually tested*. But the vocabularies of the black children were very low. The good news was that vocabulary is not an aptitude which is genetic and cannot be changed; it *can* be changed because it is merely a measurement of learning. The bad news is that no one is doing anything about it. They gave three examples:

- Fifteen year old boy. High inductive reasoning, high foresight, task personality. "This combination strongly suggests law as an optimum profession. Law, however, requires a large and exact English vocabulary. Without it, he, who scored at the fifth percentile will never become a lawyer."
- Seventeen year old girl. High ideaphoria, high graphoria, extremely people oriented. "Teachers score this way. She could potentially be a fine teacher if she dramatically improves her vocabulary."
- Fourteen year old boy. High structural visualization, high finger dexterity, high inductive reasoning. "A natural pattern for scientific research or medicine. How many scientists have a five percentile vocabulary?"

The Laboratory expressed its frustrations this way.

"Put yourself in the position of a man or woman who is capable but who lacks expression for that capability [because of a low vocabulary]. Imagine the profound frustration and raging bitterness such an intolerable situation can provoke. If a person senses that his talent, his very reason for existence, is being squandered, denied acceptable fulfillment, is it any wonder that he turns to illegal or violent modes of expression for his thwarted aspirations?"[19]

Professor Thomas Sowell of the Hoover Institution at Stanford University, a black man, may have an answer as to why the interest in ebonics.

He says that around the world the common thread of group activists who wish to retain their political power is "separatism."

"Accordingly, group activists often seek separate languages, separate institutions, and even separate territories. Even where most of the group already speaks the language of the surrounding society, as among the Maoris of New Zealand, group activists seek to artificially reconstitute a separate language community."[20]

THE CIVIL RIGHTS ACT HASN'T HELPED

The Black Family Has Been Damaged by Welfare

The greatest disaster to the black community is what has happened to the black family. The policies of the government have destroyed much of it.

We see the problem that exists in the black underclass here. About 75% of black families were below the poverty level in 1940.[21] That figure continued to drop until 1970 when it became stuck at 30%.[22] From 1970 to 1980, it remained at 30%.[23] Does this show that racism is back? Hardly. For the black family which was intact with a father and mother, only 15% were still below the poverty line in 1980.[24] (These figures would go even lower if you included food stamps, public housing, etc.)

The problem is that the number of black families which are headed by a single woman jumped from 17.9% in 1940 to over 40% in 1980.[25] (This figure for white people went from 10.1% to 11.7%.[26]) Why have the number of families with just a woman jumped so high?

Because we set up a system in our major states whereby it was more intelligent for a poor person *not* to get married and *not* to take responsibility.

In a typical state in 1970, a single woman on welfare could live with a man and receive $134 a week.[27] This would go directly to her and not be interfered with or controlled by her man. If he got a minimum wage job, her welfare and his job would go up to $270 a week.[28] However, if they were foolish enough to get married, she would lose her benefits, and they would have to live on his small salary of only $136.[29] But there was another twist to the story. He could, and often did, leave his job and receive unemployment compensation,* which would give them, without any work at all, a total of $202 a week, which was more than a minimum wage job would pay.[30]

Anyone in this situation in 1970 would naturally go for the welfare check, and they did. We were teaching our youth to take no responsibility for themselves, to look only at the short term and not worry about the future because the government will provide.

---

* Although it may sound contradictory to quit a job and receive unemployment compensation, it is not difficult to do if you are skillful about it.

FREEDOM WILL CONQUER RACISM (AND SEXISM)

As a result, many girls, including black girls, have seen welfare as an acceptable life style. Our black teenagers between the ages of 15 and 19 have the most babies of that age group in the entire industrialized world.[31] This rate is twice as high as for any other group of women in the West.[32]

It has been shown that a 10% rise in welfare benefits will cause a 12% jump in illegitimate births among low income women.[33]

In 29 states, welfare will pay more to a mother with two children than the average starting wage for a secretary. The hourly wage equivalent of welfare for a mother with two children in Hawaii is $17.50, in Alaska, $15.48 and in Massachusetts, $14.66.[34]

As a result of all of this, the number of young black men who are not bothering to seek jobs should increase. Has it? The answer is, "Yes," a large number of young black men do not stay in the labor force for any long period of time. They get a job and then leave for a time. At the period of their lives when they should be building a good work record and gaining valuable experience, they are damaging themselves greatly.

What did the federal government spend to fight poverty in 1980 as compared to 1968? After we adjust for inflation, the federal government was spending four times as much per year to fight poverty as it did in 1968.[35] In 1968, 13% of all Americans were poor; in 1980, 13% were still poor.[36]

It would take only $11.4 billion a year to lift everyone above the poverty level, but we spent more than $30 billion a year on welfare.[37]

Welfare Has Destroyed Much of Black Society

The increase in the number of single mothers has helped to destroy the infrastructure of black communities.

A recent study shows that when black households that are headed by a female are on the increase, this is accompanied by increases in the rates of black robbery and murder. "[W]hen single-parent households are the norm, this weakens the formal and informal capacity of communities to exert social control over their members."[38] George Gilder has an opinion as to why this has happened.[39]

"All societies have always been beset by 'invasions of barbarians'—i.e., teenage boys. Unless they are tamed by marriage and the provider role, men become enemies of civilization, and revert to their primordial role as predators."

THE CIVIL RIGHTS ACT HASN'T HELPED

He believes this is what is happening in our cities today.

The minimum wage has made it difficult for young black men to gain the experience they need to get ahead.

In addition, welfare is making the problem much worse.

"In a reversal of the usual pattern in civilized societies, the women have the income and the ties to government authority and support. The men are economically and socially subordinate. Favored by the feminists dominant at all levels of government, this balance of power virtually prohibits marriage, which is everywhere based on the provider role of men counterbalancing the sexual and domestic superiority of women."

He points out that by the 1980s, black women were earning 106 percent of the incomes of white women of similar age and credentials. This prevailed even at the highest levels of the economy where black women college graduates with five years on the job out earned both comparable white women and black men in 1991. And in the underclass, a typical welfare package yielded a monthly disposable income of $995 compared to employment income of $775 after expenses for a typical single mother.

This has had a decisive effect on family formation because the value of female incomes far exceeded the short-term value of marriage, and far out-paced the earning power of marriageable young men.

"Nevertheless, the men retain greater strength, aggressiveness, and sexual compulsions. By threats, violence, and remorseless pressure, these males extort beds, board, money, and other comforts from the welfare mothers. As night falls on an urban culture without marriages, the ghetto games of musical beds account for a large share of inner city violence. All programs addressed to relieve the condition or upgrade the employability of welfare mothers will only ensconce more fully these welfare 'queens' on their leisured thrones and render the men still more optional, desperate, feral, and single."

The answer, according to Gilder, is not to "put these women to work."

"They are on welfare in the first place because they would or could not get jobs that remotely compete with welfare benefits. On the whole, white or black, these women are slovenly, incompetent, and sexually promiscuous. To bring them into the workforce would require heroic efforts...[Also] the very idea that women with small children should work outside the home is perverse. The welfare state has already deprived these children of fathers. The workfare state proposes to take away the mothers as well."

The only welfare reform (apart from denying apartments to teenage single mothers) that makes sense, according to Gilder, is a private economy that grows faster than the public dole.

We must bring our manufacturing businesses back home, instead of chasing them away with the Civil Rights Act and so many other regulations. We must eliminate the minimum wage so that young men can learn a trade.

We must also give our young men a chance to work again and to feel pride in that work.

Can Government Help?

Many black people have believed the story that they can't succeed unless the government helps them.

No other group of people has ever believed that. No group of people has ever become successful in this country by appealing to the government for special help. The Jews didn't, nor did the Japanese, the Cubans or any other group.

Back in the 1950's and early 1960's, it was universally acknowledged that the starting gate should be equal for everyone.

But after Lyndon Johnson became President, the politicians and the black civil rights leaders began to move the starting gate. They began to treat the blacks differently from other groups.

These people are discriminating against blacks and treating them differently by telling them that they can't make it unless the politicians help them.

Is America Racist?

A big question that every black must answer is: Is America so racist that I can not make it by myself? According to the polls, most black Americans believe that they can make it.

And the statistics bear that out.

When we look at black people who come here from the West Indies, it is interesting to note that they do very well in the United States. Their income, even as newcomers, is 94% of the national average, and their children make more than the national average.[40] (One must wonder whether their income is higher because they have an excellent grasp of the English language and a high vocabulary.)

THE CIVIL RIGHTS ACT HASN'T HELPED

The fact that they have black skin does not seem to impede their advance.

A study of blacks and whites with the same reading habits shows that they earn the same incomes, regardless of race.[41]

And, of course, there are the Asians. The accepted theory is that they are discriminated against, and they are included as a protected group in the Civil Rights laws. But the Chinese make 112% of the national average and the Japanese make 132% of the national average.[42]

And what do the Anglo-Saxons make? Only 105% of the national average.[43]

Everyone would agree that there still is racism in the United States among a small minority of all groups, including both white and black; but there is no question that citizens of the U. S. can—and do—still rise above that.

There will always be racism by some. We have done an excellent job in the United States of eliminating racism as compared to other countries. In Africa, the blacks often discriminate against other races and even against other blacks: the Ebos of Biafra versus the Hausa of Nigeria, Watusi versus Bantu, the Kikuyu and Luo in Kenya, and the periodic massacres of the Batutsi and the Bahutu in Rwanda and Burundi.

As a black columnist for the *Washington Post*, William Raspberry, says, there are two interesting things about the Asian-Americans who are making it in our society. They see America as a land of unsurpassed opportunity and as a place for hard work. He says:

"[We blacks] have tended to view everything through the prism of the civil-rights assumption that the absence of the good things of life is proof of discrimination. Sometimes this assumption is correct. The denial of access to certain schools and jobs in the 1960s was blatant.

"But for today's black underclass, school failure, joblessness, adolescent pregnancy, juvenile crime and drug abuse are due far less to discrimination than to inadequate exertion.

"What we need to do is to find ways to make our youngsters understand the critical importance of individual exertion by showing them examples of people for whom exertion has paid off and by making certain that their own exertion is rewarded, beginning in the very earliest years. The way to inculcate middle-class attitudes in the underclass is to teach their children what the middle class takes for granted: that their fate is in their own hands."[44]

FREEDOM WILL CONQUER RACISM (AND SEXISM)

We often hear it said that blacks should be treated specially because, "They didn't ask to come here." But who did ask to come here? Nobody, white or black, who was born in this country "asked to come here." We're all so fortunate that we were born here, and not one of us wants to leave.

If America is so racist, why would everyone still keep trying to come here? No one is lining up at the shore trying to get *out;* but there are an awful lot of people who would like to get *in*.

It's time we stopped listening to those who say that blacks can't make it like other groups have and start listening to people like Professor Walter Williams, head of The Economics Department at George Mason University, who likes the following quote from a black congressman back in the 1800's, Robert Smalls,

"My race needs no special defense, for the past history of them in this country proves them to be the equal of any people anywhere. All they need is an equal chance in the battle of life."[45]

Now, if only we could get the "elite" to believe that.

11

MOST BLACKS AGREE

The vast majority of blacks agree with the preceding chapter.

Numerous polls show that most black people want only a fair chance. One of the most interesting polls asked:
- Can blacks get ahead if they work hard enough?—Four out of five blacks said, "Yes."
- Are most blacks making progress?—Two out of three said, "Yes."
- Should blacks get preferential treatment or should their ability be the main consideration?—Only one in four wanted preferential treatment. Most wanted to be judged on their ability.[1]

Is that astounding?

The vast majority of blacks have the pride to want to get ahead on their own merit and ability. They don't want the special treatment that has been given them.

I don't believe it is astounding. If you look at the polls and other information, I believe that somewhere between 10-20% of both white and black people are the troublemakers. Most people merely want to go about their lives. But in the white South back in the old days and in the black community today, it is that 10-20% that is

FREEDOM WILL CONQUER RACISM (AND SEXISM)

causing all of the noise, the agitation and the problems. And the good people are afraid to raise their voices.

Why The Difference?

If blacks don't want any special treatment, why does everyone think they do? Why are the political leaders and the judges of this country so anxious to "help?"

Here is one clue.

The pollsters asked the same questions to the leaders of civil rights organizations.[2] Their answers were surprisingly different.

Only two out of five of the leaders thought that most blacks were making progress. And four out of five thought that blacks should get preferential treatment.[3]

Why is there this tremendous split between the "leaders" of the black community and the common person?

One answer was revealed in the same poll. Almost half of the people said that black leaders on TV and in newspapers do not speak for them. They say that these "leaders" speak for only a minority of black people.

This is startling. How can this be true?

- Are we implementing a nationwide policy on the basis of a leadership that is no longer in touch with its people?
- Or is the liberal press talking to only the blacks who will give them the answer they want?

One answer to those questions might be to look at the civil rights organizations themselves.

Birth of the NAACP

There was a historic struggle in the early 1900s between two black men. The black community eventually followed the "elite" liberal, who helped to found the NAACP, because he lived longer and he had the liberal, intellectual community behind him.[4]

This was the classic conflict between the belief that blacks must use their own abilities to succeed and the belief that the government would solve their problems for them.

The first man was born a slave and worked in a salt mine after freedom at the age of 9. The other was born in Massachusetts after the Civil War had ended and knew about the life of the poor only by hearsay and observation.

The first man was Booker T. Washington who was born a slave in 1856, worked in the salt mines in West Virginia as a child and walked 500 miles in rags to the Hampton Institute where he worked as a janitor to get an education. He became the first head of the famous Tuskegee Institute for blacks in Alabama where he made certain that every student was also taught a trade and how to perform physical labor. When the first students arrived in 1881, there were no buildings and they had to meet in a church. Washington lined up the students and criticized their dirty shoes and holes in their clothes. He then had them clear the undergrowth so that the land could be cultivated for food. When some protested that they had come for an education in order to avoid "slave work," Washington swung his ax vigorously and said, "There is as much dignity in tilling a field as in writing a poem...It is as important to know how to set a table and keep house as it is to read Latin." Washington was a dedicated Christian.

W.E.B. DuBois, by contract, was born in Great Barrington, Massachusetts in 1868 and studied Greek and German at Fisk College in Tennessee. He received fellowships to study philosophy at Harvard (where he became the first black to earn a Ph.D. at that institution) and the University of Berlin. He loved Paris and the art museums of Europe. In 1961, he joined the Communist Party, left the United States and moved to Ghana.

Washington became famous after a speech in 1895 at the International Cotton Exposition in Atlanta, where he said, "Ignorant and inexperienced, it is not strange that in the first years of our new life we began at the top instead of at the bottom; that a seat in Congress or the state legislature was more sought than real estate or industrial skill; that the political convention or stump speaking had more attractions than starting a dairy farm or truck garden ....Our greatest danger is that in the great leap from slavery to freedom we may overlook the fact that the masses of us are to live by the productions of our hands, and fail to keep in mind that we shall prosper in proportion as we learn to draw the line between the superficial and substantial....No race can prosper till it learns that there is as much dignity in tilling a field as in writing a poem. In all things that are purely social, [black and white people] can be separate as the fingers, yet one as the hand in all things essential to mutual progress."[5]

In 1907, he wrote, "The Negro was also fortunate enough to find that, while his abilities in certain directions were opposed by the

FREEDOM WILL CONQUER RACISM (AND SEXISM)

white South, in business he was not only undisturbed but even favored and encouraged. I have been repeatedly informed by Negro merchants in the South that they have as many white patrons as black, the cordial business relations which are almost universal between the races in the South proved...there is little race prejudice in the American dollar."

In contrast, when DuBois returned from Europe at the age of 26, he was committed to the European notions of broadening the governmental sphere. He became famous at age 35 for a book which criticized Washington. In 1909, he was one of the founders of the NAACP, and his attacks on Washington became more heated. But Washington did not respond directly to the personal attacks, although he did make it clear where he stood in two statements made in 1911.

He wrote about a Yale graduate who went wrong: "Once he gets the idea that—because he has crammed his head full with mere book knowledge—the world owes him a living, it is hard for him to change." Washington noted that he had met many young men of that sort who were "not wholly to blame for their condition. I know that, in nine cases out of ten, they have gained the idea at some point in their career that, because they are Negroes, they are entitled to the special sympathy of the world, and they have thus got into the habit of relying on this sympathy rather than on their own efforts to make their way."

He also worried about occupational choices: He was not pleased that "the highest ambition of the average Negro in America was to hold some sort of office, or to have some sort of job that connected him with the Government." He argued that blacks "in the long run earn more money and be of more service to the community in almost any other position than that of an employee or officeholder under the Government." He acknowledged that "the city of Washington still has a peculiar attraction and even fascination for the average Negro," but he strove to fight the emphasis on politics: "I never liked the atmosphere of Washington. I early saw that it was impossible to build up a race of which the leaders were spending most of their time, thought, and energy in trying to get into office, or in trying to stay there after they were in."[6]

It is interesting to note that Washington spent his entire life living with and helping black people, whereas DuBois appeared to crave the company of white people.

NAACP Supported by Whites

The NAACP has seldom had more than 2% of American blacks as members, and its membership has been going down. It claims 350,000 members (many of whom are white) which is about 1% of the somewhere close to 30,000,000 black people.

The NAACP and similar organizations are supported by white people. This has been well documented by the Capital Research Center,[7] which was established in 1984 to study the "public interest" organizations and to discover where they are getting their money. Since then the Center has produced many studies.

The information shows that the NAACP is getting much of its money from the large corporations it is fighting and from the huge foundations, such as the Rockefeller and Ford Foundations. It also shows that the "Federal Inspectors" have illegally coerced the large corporations to give money to the NAACP and other liberal organizations.

Another indication that the NAACP is out of touch was apparent after the elections of 1996. The black leaders of the country had crisscrossed California to warn everyone to vote against the California Civil Rights Initiative that would outlaw racial preferences, but many were startled when almost 1/3 of black Californians voted *for* the Initiative. This was done despite the enormous pressure on black people to vote against it.[8]

NAACP Has Lost Touch

The NAACP became front-page news in the early 1990s when its president was sued by a woman employee and it almost went bankrupt, being nearly $4 million in debt. The growth of dissension within the organization in 1994 became too much for the liberal press to hide and the rising scorn toward the organization by many blacks became front-page news. The following was clear, according to The Capital Research Center:

- The NAACP reflected the interests of the "elite", not the interests of black people. For example, at the insistence of teachers' unions, it opposed educational vouchers and tuition tax credits that would have given poor, black parents the opportunity (now afforded only the rich) to choose their children's schools. At the insistence of feminist groups, it supported programs that led employers to hire white middle-class women instead of black males. At the insistence of labor unions, it opposed training wages for youth who were not able to get jobs at the adult minimum wage.

- It was representing the rich, not the poor blacks. The *New York Times* captured the feel of an NAACP gathering: "1800 prominent, prosperous men and women, most of them black, strode into the Grand Ballroom of the Waldorf-Astoria Hotel in their tuxedos and velvet dresses to wine and dine. [Executive Director Benjamin] Hooks, in black tie, smiled broadly as he surveyed the crowd: 'We've come mighty far, haven't we?'"
- Some NAACP leaders sounded troubling themes. Legrand Clegg, a speaker at the NAACP's 1990 annual convention, spoke of "Jewish racism in Hollywood." Hazel Dukes, New York state president of the NAACP, complained that immigrants were getting jobs that blacks should have: "Why let foreigners, newcomers, have these jobs...." One NAACP booklet argued that "the enemies of the labor movement" and of the NAACP "are one and the same..." Sadly, the "enemies" today may be Hispanics or Koreans.
- The *Los Angeles Times* reported the NAACP "has lost favor among younger, more business-minded black men and women" and "has failed to attract new members....Many young blacks have shied away from the NAACP, complaining its elderly leaders dismissed ideas that they had to breathe new life into the group." There was also internal dissension as board members "[Julian] Bond, an ex-Georgia state senator and longtime NAACP activist, and [Herbert H.] Henderson, a West Virginia lawyer and board member since 1980, lost their posts over support of a failed attempt to impose term limitations on board members."
- Even liberal black columnists pointed out the NAACP's problems. William Raspberry of the *Washington Post* argued that the NAACP "needs to find new direction" if it is to deal with the tendency of urban black youth "to become school dropouts, adolescent parents, drug peddlers or users, or criminals. The leading cause of death of young black men is not the Klan but young black men themselves....And here's the point: Our civil rights generals are still fighting the last war—demanding that government create and fund the programs we need, that the

courts protect our interests and that white America get religion, even while we're losing our own."

- Liberal, black columnist Carl Rowan wrote, "The NAACP today is not the voice of the black poor. The NAACP has become the organization of a thin slice of middle-class black America." Rather than open "this year's convention by [urging] delegates and the thousands of black youngsters present to believe in themselves and trained intelligence," Benjamin Hooks, "pandered to black frustrations and hatred," and "encouraged them to wallow in the absurd notion that [D.C.] Mayor [Marion] Barry is on trial because of the 'convenient and selective prosecution of black leaders.'" But, "if 'racial solidarity' means defending abominable behavior by any and every black elected official, then 'racial solidarity' becomes a curse upon the dreams of every black child in this land. If Hooks doesn't understand this, we know what's wrong with the NAACP."

- The nationally syndicated columnist Clarence Page said the NAACP was stagnant: "[N]ew names drawn undoubtedly from the aging pantheon of '60's civil-rights veterans will replace the old, and business will go on as usual....[I]t is long past time to inject the old geezer with new blood, new ideas, new priorities and new directions..." A News-Gannett News Service poll of 1211 black adults backed Page's skepticism: 94 per cent said the NAACP had lost touch with the everyday problems of blacks. Rose Beavers, 31, a drug counselor, told the *Detroit News*, "I see the pain, I see the need. I don't see the NAACP." One life member of the NAACP said the organization was a social club for 50- and 60-year-olds, and the executive editor of *Black Enterprise* said that younger blacks equate the NAACP with the Oldsmobile: "It's their parents' organization."

At a meeting of the NAACP in February 1997, the new president, Kweisi Mfume, former head of the Congressional Black Caucus, indicated a possible shift by saying that many of the problems facing blacks are beyond the reach of government. "We must find ways to do for self," he said.[9]

He also scolded the Maryland chapter for forcing Justice Clarence Thomas to cancel a speech at a Boys and Girls Club event because of Thomas' concern about safety after the attacks about his presence. This caused *The Washington Times* to write an editorial praising Mfume.[10] While his action may be commendatory, it is sad that we must praise someone merely because they advocated allowing a person the right of free speech.

And at the annual meeting in July 1997 the group debated anew what directions it should be taking.

How Much Do the Corporations Give?

The big corporations continue to give money to this organization that is fighting them. And they are the ones who keep it alive to this day.

The corporations are likely to think of the NAACP as an organization with a strong past, a safe, harmless buy, which would please black employees, customers, and shareholders while doing good in urban communities as well.

For example during 1992, the NAACP was given $75,000 by AT&T, $90,000 by Chrysler, $190,000 by Exxon (to the NAACP and its Legal Defense Fund), $85,000 by General Motors, and so on.[11] Name a major company and it is there with its contribution to an organization which actively promotes all of these policies which are so damaging to industry. It received $1.6 million in gifts from corporations in 1992.

Why are these corporations doing this? Probably many have a sincere desire to help black people, and they believe that these organizations—which are heard so vocally in the newspapers and TV newscasts—really do represent the black people of America.

Another reason might be that all of these companies have felt the sting of the federal government since 1970 in lawsuits or threats if they do not fill their quotas. Perhaps they feel that this is a way to buy "peace." And perhaps they are right.

The "Federal Inspectors" from the President's OFCCP have been known to coerce a business into contributing to the NAACP and similar liberal organizations, according to its former Director Ellen Shong Bergman, who says:

"The OFCCP, on an individual basis—on a district office by district office basis—has at some time in the past pressured contractors to make contributions of one sort or another."[12]

And, she says, an inspector can always find a violation if he or she wishes.

"[The OFCCP] is free to find that a contractor has violated the [law] if it fails to perform the availability analysis in exactly the way the particular compliance officer wishes...." And another high-ranking official said, "The way the regs are, they can always find a *prima facie* case of numerical disparity."[13]

But for whatever reason, whether because of coercion or otherwise, the civil rights organizations are supported in large part by the very corporations that they harass—even though they do not represent the black citizens of today. At a national convention, Benjamin Hooks said:

"I wish to express the gratitude of the entire NAACP family for the generous support the Special Contribution Fund received last year. We surpassed most previous income records in 1990, the most significant of which was in the corporate realm. With the stellar leadership of William Smithburg, CEO of Quaker Oats, we reached the highest corporate income total in our history, some $3.5 million from almost 500 corporations."

There Are Alternatives

For those who wanted to see increased opportunity for all, however, far better options than the NAACP finally have emerged—and at least a few companies recognize this.

When Amoco wanted to support minority organizations, for example, it contributed $15,000 to the NAACP; but it also chose to invest many times that amount—$500,000—in the National Center for Neighborhood Enterprise, whose model of community action emphasizes resident management of housing projects, privately run neighborhood schools, and the centrality of family and church instead of primary reliance on government.

NCNE founder Robert Woodson argues that the NAACP and other old-line groups "continue to repeat the mistakes of the past. They remind me very much of old retired circus horses out there in the pasture. Every time the circus comes by, they just start prancing and dancing to the same old music."

Amoco's investment in the National Center for Neighborhood Enterprise contrasts sharply with the corporate money given to the NAACP and similar groups of the left. As Woodson said (with a bit of hyperbole) on television's *Tony Brown's Journal*, "[I]f the 150 black organizations that meet annually and spend five billion dollars on liquor, food, clothes and hotels around the country complaining about white folks, instead met in groups of ten once every five years they would save huge amounts of money that they could then direct into developing the human capital of the black urban poor."

One might think corporations would follow Amoco's example, but few do; the influence of liberal managers in the big companies seems to be too great.

Foundations Are Even Larger Donors

But there is an even bigger source of contributions. That is the foundations that are run by white "elites." They were established by wealthy people who have usually since died and whose Boards of Directors are usually the leaders of big business. The NAACP got $696,000, for example, from the Carnegie Foundation in 1986-7, $700,000 from the Ford Foundation, and so on. The National Urban League received $5 million from the Ford Foundation.[14]

A part of the NAACP, its Special Contribution Fund, received $5,200,000 in 1985. Of this, 45% came from corporations and 17% from foundations.[15]

The rest of the civil rights organizations are similar: including the National Urban League, NAACP Legal Defense Fund, Lawyers Committee for Civil Rights Under Law, Joint Center for Political Studies, and the Leadership Conference on Civil Rights.

All are in business because of the generosity of the people that they are supposedly fighting tooth and nail. Is it surprising that these organizations are not responsive to the average black person? They don't need to be. They're getting their money from our large corporations.

The black people and their organizations were in agreement up until 1964. There had to be a way to exclude "race" from this country. We needed a color-blind society where everyone would have an equal chance regardless of their skin.

Most people agreed with that—both black and white. And that is why the Civil Rights Act was passed in 1964 with the approval of most of the country.

But since that time, there has been no consensus as to where we are going in civil rights.

The organizations that "speak for black people" are supported, not by black people, but by the "elite."

12

THERE WAS A BETTER WAY IN 1964 – MORE FREEDOM

Was there a better way to solve our racial problems in 1964?

Or perhaps we should ask, "Was there *any* other way?" Of course there was. There were many other alternatives.

But we weren't allowed to talk about them.

Many scholars today agree that it was an *excess* of government that was causing our problems in 1964.

Did we correct the excess? No, we created an even more intrusive bureaucracy.

We acted as though God had decided in 1964 that House Bill No. 7152 was the *only* way to solve our racial problems.

We passed an intrusive law even though we already had too much government and it had caused our problems. Our problems were caused by the laws which had been passed to *force* businesses to discriminate *against* blacks, the so-called "Jim Crow" laws, which had been the product of big government on both the state and federal levels.

Having a different perspective than the "elite" does not make a person a "racist." There can be a difference of opinion.

FREEDOM WILL CONQUER RACISM (AND SEXISM)

Jim Crow Laws Were A National Disgrace

Jim Crow was a national disgrace, according to Prof. Richard A. Epstein of the University of Chicago Law School.

"The evil of Jim Crow and segregation in the South was a national disgrace. The critical decisions of the Supreme Court, which allowed the southern states (and to a lesser extent the northern ones) to impose this regime, were equally disgraceful."[1]

It was the state governments which kept blacks from prospering. This was accomplished by laws on labor, zoning, licensing, and many other areas, primarily the police power.

For example, in South Carolina, all textile mills were required by law to separate the races. In Louisiana, the railways had to have separate areas and facilities for black and white. In Kentucky, a private college was not allowed to integrate its classes. But the biggest problem in the states was that the sheriffs did not protect black citizens or white citizens who wished to deal with blacks.

But the federal government was not much better. For example, it helped the monopolistic labor unions which were a major detriment to the blacks.

"[Even as recently] as the early 1950's more than a score of unions had white-only membership provisions and monopoly bargaining power vis-a-vis black workers and their employers."[2]

The federal labor laws were used by the unions to keep out the blacks.

The Davis-Bacon Act of 1931, for example, required that construction workers should receive "the prevailing wage" on jobs funded by the federal government. "It was passed with the explicit intention of protecting incumbent white construction workers in the North from competition with those from the South, and was largely effective in achieving its goal, especially in the period before the passage of the 1964 Civil Rights Act."[3]

The federal minimum wage laws also hurt.

"It is the very existence of the minimum wage law that increases the incentive of the employer to discriminate against blacks or other workers whose low skill levels leave them at the fringes of the economic market. In seeking workers whose value to the firm is above the minimum wage, the employer is likely to turn to white or other workers with more education or experience. Predictably, the minimum wage laws have a disproportionate effect on black workers, especially those at the margin."[4]

THERE WAS A BETTER WAY IN 1964 - MORE FREEDOM

If we had simply eliminated these government barriers which were blocking the progress of black people, we would have gone a long way in 1964 toward eliminating their problems. And we would not have divided the country into warring camps and driven our businesses overseas.

The elimination of those barriers was what we had planned after the Civil War.

"The enforcement of a system of small state government was entrusted to the federal government. With the passage of the Civil War Amendments [to the Constitution], there should have been in total less government at all levels after the Civil War than before, as no new and separate grants of power were accorded the federal government beyond its power to limit state misbehavior."[5]

But the U.S. Supreme Court failed in this regard.

It allowed Louisiana to require separate but equal railroad cars[6] and Kentucky to outlaw integrated classes in a private college.[7] It failed to protect the rights of black citizens.

And so the state and federal governments were allowed to limit the progress of our black citizens. In 1964 we failed to correct that abuse of power by both our state and federal governments; and we gave the federal government even more power.

Would It Have "Self Corrected"?

So the question must be, if we had removed the governments from the business of oppression of blacks, would the system have corrected itself?

"Yes," is the response of Prof. Epstein.

He points out that our courts in England and America have historically had as their overriding concern the control of physical "force" by one person against another. And the courts believed that any person had the right to refuse to deal with anyone.

"The control of force was their overriding theme. It never occurred to any of them that the private refusal to deal, for whatever reason, was any threat to the social order."[8]

If we had created a free market, we would not have a serious problem with discrimination.

"Free entry and multiple employers provide ample protection for all workers, even those faced with policies of overt and hostile discrimination by some employers. Where markets do not have formal barriers to entry, the victims of discrimination have effective strategies of self-protection and powerful allies whose own self-interest will operate on their behalf."

Epstein says there will always be some discrimination; and not all of it is negative.

"[A]ll groups have some rational incentives to discriminate on the very grounds—race, creed, sex, age, religion—that Title VII prohibits."[9]

He then explains the many reasons that groups such as employees might like to discriminate, or "sort." It could be because the workers all speak one language, or because they want classical music in the workplace rather than rock. Some of the reasons for sorting may be based on ill will, but this is good for the others because the dissidents and troublemakers will be isolated.

"If all persons who have a rabid hatred for members of different racial, ethnic, or other groups are concentrated within a small number of firms, then it makes governance questions easier for the remaining firms, as they do not have to contend constantly with dissidents and troublemakers."[10]

And a free system without government interference will provide better opportunities for all persons.

"If thousands of prospective employers are offering different associational mixes, then the probability that any employee will find the ideal work-setting is far greater than if all firms have to conform to some rigid state-established classification, which is driven not by consideration of the business pressures on the firm but by some independent ethical idea which the state, by majority rule or administrative order, is prepared to impose on those who refuse to accept it."[11]

We failed in 1964 (or today) to realize the cause of our problems.

"I believe that the received wisdom, both in 1964 and today, does not grasp what was wrong with Jim Crow and segregation. The dominant evil in the pre-1964 period was not self-interest or markets, inflexible human nature, or even bigotry. It was excessive state power and the pattern of private violence, intimidation, and lynching, of which there is a painful record but against which there was no effective federal remedy. The explicit discrimination in the South and elsewhere was preserved by the use of coercion, both by state law and by private individuals (such as the Ku Klux Klan) whose activities were left unchecked by state agents."

The failure in the South was a failure of government.

THERE WAS A BETTER WAY IN 1964 - MORE FREEDOM

"The history of failure in the South is not a history of the failure of individual character or individual will. It is not a history of the failure of markets. It does not demonstrate the need for federal intervention to eradicate the 'harm' that private markets caused. To the contrary, the lessons from our history of civil rights all stem from two sources: first, the abnegation of the principles of limited government, that is, government restricted to those areas where it is required, such as taxation and law enforcement; and second, the massive state legislative regulation of private markets that was left unchecked by passive judicial action."

The big government had fallen into the wrong hands.

"Under Jim Crow, big government fell into the hands of the wrong people, who were able to perpetuate their stranglehold over local communities and businesses by means of a pervasive combination of public and private force. Jim Crow is best attacked from the limited-government, libertarian perspective as another illustration of Lord Acton's insight: power corrupts and absolute power corrupts absolutely."[12]

Another scholar agrees that blacks were doing well in the 1800s and it was only after "less talented whites" used the government to pass Jim Crow laws that the upward mobility of blacks came to an end.

"[T]he vibrancy of black entrepreneurship and inventiveness of the 19th century was largely snuffed out in the 20th. Precisely because blacks were such successful competitors, less talented whites contrived to pass laws that constrained their ability to compete. These have come to be called 'Jim Crow' laws. Also, labor unions organized to exclude blacks and prevent skilled black carpenters, masons and machinists from plying their trades.

"It is important to understand it was not the market nor even racism per se that primarily oppressed the black businessman, but mainly government. Without the power of government to enforce and institutionalize racism, the market does not discriminate. Money and profits are the great equalizers. That is why modern-day barriers to entrepreneurship, such as licensing laws and taxes, do far more to hold back black economic advancement than even lingering racism"[13]

Does This Explain the Stagnation in the Wage Gap?

Can Prof. Epstein explain why when we were midway through the 1970s there was suddenly a stagnation in the improvement that we had seen taking place in the wage gap between white and black males?

There is no question that progress abruptly stopped during the mid-1970s. We had seen a healthy improvement and then ... stagnation. Many economists credited the improvement during the 1960s to the Civil Rights Act, but Prof. Epstein says they are wrong.

It was not the Civil Rights Act itself which had a salutary effect, but the fact that finally something had been done to remove the Jim Crow laws. If we had just eliminated those laws and done nothing else, we would have been much better off. Once the full impact of the elimination of the Jim Crow laws had time to take effect, and the full impact of the stringent, harsh penalties of the new Civil Rights Act had time to take effect, the Civil Rights Act began to impair and damage the country. Epstein says:

"The primary feature of the Civil Rights Act was the removal of the formal barriers to entry that had been erected by the Jim Crow legislation. At this point, the historical evidence tells a liberation story, not a government intervention story....The successes of the civil rights movement derived from the shrinkage, not the expansion, of total government power, both state and federal."[14]

Get the Government Off Black Backs

A black professor believes that blacks in the U. S. are damaged by the many government regulations which did not exist when other groups were climbing up the ladder.

He is Professor Walter E. Williams, who was raised in the ghettos of Philadelphia.

He also points to the minimum wage laws (which were started in the 1930's) as a good example. He says they hurt all youths who are low-skilled and marginal because of their age, immaturity and lack of work experience.[15]

Other studies show that a raise in the minimum wage *always* causes a loss of jobs. The only question is how many jobs are lost.

Even the liberal *New York Times* reported that when the minimum wage was raised in 1990 to $3.80 and to $4.25 a year later, the percentage of teenagers who had a job went from 47.1% to 43% and then to 39.8%. And black teenagers fared even worse going from 28.8% to 22.5% and then to 20.4%.

THERE WAS A BETTER WAY IN 1964 - MORE FREEDOM

The unemployment rate for black youths went from 27.8% in 1990 to 33% and then to 44.6% in April 1993.[16]

The *New York Times* cited a company in Louisiana that would hire a dozen or more young people each summer at minimum wage jobs like weeding or expanding the parking lot—tasks that were not really essential to the company but gave the teenagers a taste of what work was like. But when the minimum wage went up in 1990, the company cut back to three or four workers, and in 1996 when another raise was expected, the company dropped the quarter-century tradition.

The liberal *Washington Post* published an article by Robert J. Samuelson in 1988 in which he said, "Current efforts by Democratic leaders in Congress to raise the minimum wage have more to do with embarrassing the Republicans in an election year than helping the poor."[17] Samuelson said of those who receive a minimum wage:

"Most aren't from poor families....Most minimum-wage jobs aren't held by heads of families. About two-thirds are held by young (24 and under) and single workers. About a third are teenagers. The typical minimum-wage worker is a teenager from a non-poor family working as a waiter or waitress. A third of all minimum-wage jobs are in restaurants.

"Most workers don't get stuck in full-time minimum-wage jobs; indeed, two-thirds of minimum-wage jobs are part time."

And the same was true in 1997 when for political reasons, the Democrats pushed for a raise in the minimum wage and the Republicans were afraid to oppose it. And again in 1998 when President Clinton proposed another raise.

Why is it, asks Prof. Williams, that we are proud of our freedom in the U.S. that allows two consenting adults to agree to almost anything they desire *except* the right to sell their labor at a price that is agreeable to them?

Who is the strongest supporter of minimum wage laws in South Africa, asks Professor Williams?[18]

The answer is: the white, racist unions of South Africa.

Why do the racist unions in South Africa want a minimum wage? Because, otherwise the blacks will work for a much lower wage and therefore put some of the white workers out of a job.

Prof. Williams believes that much the same thing is happening here as in South Africa. An inexperienced black worker is prevented from competing with a more experienced one under a minimum wage law because the black is told he must charge the same price for his labor. When black youths cannot set their own wage price themselves so as to gain experience and knowledge, they lose out to others. They also lose to machines which take the place of high priced labor, and they lose many entry-level jobs such as movie ushers which are eliminated.

Can you guess who was one of the strongest forces in the fight to increase the minimum wage in 1996?

The AFL-CIO spent $2 million to influence Congress and then added an additional $100,000 for radio advertising over the Fourth of July alone directed at four senators.[19]

Prof. Williams says that the U. S. Supreme Court should once again be as concerned about the "right to work" as it is with the "right to free speech." And he notes that there are more than 500 occupations which are now regulated by the government.

He quotes from a 100 year-old case where the Court said, "The liberty mentioned in [the Fourteenth Amendment] means ... the right of the citizen to be free in the enjoyment of all of his faculties; to be free to use them in all lawful ways; to live and work where he will; to earn his livelihood by any lawful calling; to pursue any livelihood or avocation, and for that purpose to enter into all contracts which may be proper, necessary and essential to his carrying out to a successful conclusion the purposes above mentioned."[20]

As an example, Professor Williams points to the licensing of beauticians where most blacks pass the practical examination and know their job well, but they fail the written test.

He points to the taxicab industry where the number of taxis is now strictly limited so that a newcomer cannot get a start unless he or she buys a license for $100,000 or up. It wasn't that way until the 1930's.[21]

He points to plumbers who were among the first trades to become licensed, starting in California in 1885. Some early courts did strike these licensing laws down as a violation of the Fourteenth Amendment of the U. S. Constitution. There was no question that these laws were used to remove blacks from the craft. He cites articles and letters which show without doubt that this was the intent. There was an article in one trade journal back in the 1800's, for example, which said,

"There are about ten Negro skate plumbers working around here [Danville, Va.] doing quite a lot of jobbing and repairing, but owing to the fact of not having an examination board [licensing agency] it is impossible to stop them, hence the anxiety of the men here to organize."²²

The blacks *had been* skilled artisans. One man wrote in 1898:

"In the city of Washington, for example, at one period, some of the finest buildings were constructed by colored workmen. Their employment in large numbers continued some time after the war. The British Legation, the Centre Market, the Freeman's Bank, and at least four well-built schoolhouses are monuments to the acceptability of their work under foremen of their own color. Today, apart from hod-carriers, not a colored workman is to be seen on new buildings, and a handful of jobbers and patchers, with possibly two carpenters who can undertake a large job, are all who remain of the body of colored carpenters and builders and stone-cutters who were generally employed a quarter of a century ago."²³

There is no question but that this "licensing" of 500 occupations has had a tremendous effect upon the black population. But we hear nothing about this from the "leaders."

There is also no question but that the unions, and not business, have been a big stumbling block in the Civil Rights advancement today. When you read the Sheet Metal Workers case in the Supreme Court,²⁴ you understand the tremendous frustration that the judges must have felt and why they went so far overboard in interpreting the Civil Rights Act. The union in that case thumbed its nose at many courts and simply refused to allow blacks in as members. Of course, this was not unique to blacks. It is common knowledge that most of these craft unions have historically allowed only their sons or nephews to join, and that blacks are not unique in being excluded.

Professor Williams even goes so far as to say that there is a hidden reason why the unions are always so anxious for the government to help the poor.

"[U]nions have incentives to support subsidy programs for those denied job access. Thus, it is very probable that unions will lead the support for income subsidy programs such as Job Corps, summer work programs, CETA, food stamps, public service employment and welfare. The redistribution of income really constitutes a subsidy from society at large, who pay the taxes, to those who have used the various powers of government to restrict or eliminate job opportunity. Income subsidy programs have disguised the true effects of restriction created by unions and other economic agents by casting a few crumbs to those denied jobs in order to keep them quiet, thereby creating a permanent welfare class."[25]

Professor Williams makes a valid point when he says,

"Those clamoring against quotas assume that the economic game is being played fairly. It is not being played fairly. It is rigged and rigged in a way particularly devastating to blacks because of their history in the United States. So the moral question has to be asked: If we are going to retain various laws and regulations that systematically discriminate against black opportunities, what do we do? If we keep the laws, then hard and fast racial quotas, in some areas, may constitute a 'second-best' solution. The first-best solution, in terms of equity and efficiency, is to eliminate the regulations and eliminate the quotas."[26]

As Professor Williams says, the courts should start looking at a citizen's "right to work."[27]

That is a very profound statement. Why are the courts not finding a "right to work" that the government cannot abridge?

13

WHAT WOULD SOLOMON NORTHRUP DO?

Solomon Northrup was a free, black man who was kidnapped and sold into slavery in 1841. It was twelve years before he was rescued from the remote section of Louisiana where he was being held.

While a slave, he was beaten, whipped, and chased with dogs that would have torn him apart if they had caught him.

Yet he never became a racist.

Because he never succumbed to hate.

This man knew more than anyone who is living in our country today about the inhumanity of man against man. But he also realized that people are basically divided into two groups, those who are kind and honest, both black and white, and those who are cruel and dishonest, both black and white. Neither race has a monopoly on either type of person.

Solomon Northrup would be dismayed if he could see the black family today.

He would be incredulous that blacks are accepting the idea that someone else—whoever it is, whether it be white politicians, black politicians, government workers, businessmen or anyone—is going to give them prosperity and freedom.

FREEDOM WILL CONQUER RACISM (AND SEXISM)

He knew that freedom and success (however you define those terms) for *anyone* can come only through hard work and constant vigilance.

No one else will give it to you, he would say.

Solomon Northrup was born a freeman in upstate New York, living most of his life along the Hudson River, north of Albany. However, he learned firsthand the barbarism of slavery, having been kidnapped in 1841 at the age of 33 years and sold into slavery in a remote region of Louisiana, where he languished for 12 years before being rescued. After his return, he wrote a book about his experience, which became a bestseller in its day with over 30,000 copies being sold.

He was literate and married with three children. He had been a farmer, an independent businessman cutting timber and (with his own team of horses and employees) rafting logs from Lake Champlain to Troy, as well as doing other work. In 1834 he had moved his family to Saratoga Springs, which he says was a "world-renowned watering place." He drove a hack, or carriage, and also became well-known as an excellent fiddler, and therefore was not surprised when two men asked him to go to New York City and play for their circus there. But this proved to be a hoax to lure him further to Washington, D.C. where he was drugged, kidnapped and sold as a slave.

When he awoke from his kidnaping, he was chained to the floor of a slave pen in Washington, D.C. When he proclaimed that he was a free man, not a slave, he was beaten severely.

He tells what happened.

"My feet, as has been stated, were fastened to the floor. Drawing me over the bench, face downwards, Radburn placed his heavy foot upon the fetters, between my wrists, holding them painfully to the floor. With the paddle, Burch commenced beating me. Blow after blow was inflicted on my naked body. When his unrelenting arm grew tired, he stopped and asked if I still insisted I was a free man. I did insist upon it, and then the blows were renewed, faster and more energetically, if possible, than before. When again tired, he would repeat the same question, and receiving the same answer, continued his cruel labor. All this time, the incarnate devil was uttering most fiendish oaths. At length the paddle broke, leaving the useless handle in his hand. Still I would not yield. All his brutal blows could not force from my lips the foul lie that I was a slave. Casting madly on

WHAT WOULD SOLOMON NORTHRUP DO?

the floor the handle of the broken paddle, he seized the rope. This was far more painful than the other. I struggled with all my power, but it was in vain. I prayed for mercy, but my prayer was only answered with imprecations and with stripes. I thought I must die beneath the lashes of the accursed brute. Even now the flesh crawls upon my bones, as I recall the scene. I was all on fire. My sufferings I can compare to nothing else than the burning agonies of hell!"[1]

This account of the torture was told in his book.

He wrote the following about the man for whom he labored for the last ten years of his captivity.

"He could have stood unmoved and seen the tongues of his poor slaves torn out by the roots—he could have seen them burned to ashes over a slow fire, or gnawed to death by dogs, if it only brought him profit. Such a hard, cruel, unjust man is Edwin Epps."[2]

Solomon Northrup was not a man to justify or absolve slavery. He would condemn it with all of his passion and all of his being.

And yet Solomon Northrup did not blame or hate all white people. There were even some slave owners whom he praised, including William Ford, his first owner.

"In many northern minds, perhaps, the idea of a man holding his brother man in servitude, and the traffic in human flesh, may seem altogether incompatible with their conceptions of a moral or religious life. From descriptions of [bad owners], they are led to despise and execrate the whole class of slave holders indiscriminately. But I was some time his slave, and had an opportunity of learning well his character and disposition, and it is but simple justice to him when I say, in my opinion, there never was a more kind, noble, candid, Christian man than William Ford."[3]

And of another slave owner:

"I dwell with delight upon the description of this fair and gentle lady, not only because she inspired me with emotions of gratitude and admiration, but because I would have the reader understand that all slave-owners on Bayou Boeuf are not like Epps, or Tibeats, or Jim Burns. Occasionally can be found, rarely it may be, indeed, a good man like William Ford, or an angel of kindness like young Mistress McCoy."[4]

Lest anyone think that this man who suffered so severely under the lash was addled when he wrote the above, this is what he thought of slavery.

FREEDOM WILL CONQUER RACISM (AND SEXISM)

"The existence of Slavery in its most cruel form among them [the white owners] has a tendency to brutalize the humane and finer feelings of their nature. Daily witnesses of human suffering—listening to the agonizing screeches of the slave—beholding him writhing beneath the merciless lash—bitten and torn by dogs—dying without attention, and buried without shroud or coffin—it cannot other be expected, than that they should become brutified and reckless of human life. It is true there are many kind-hearted and good men in the parish of Avoyelles—such men as William Ford—who can look with pity upon the sufferings of a slave, just as there are, over all the world, sensitive and sympathetic spirits, who cannot look with indifference upon the sufferings of any creature which the Almighty has endowed with life. It is not the fault of the slave holder that he is cruel, so much as it is the fault of the system under which he lives. He cannot withstand the influence of habit and associations that surround him. Taught from earliest childhood, by all that he sees and hears, that the rod is for the slave's back, he will not be apt to change his opinions in maturer years.

"There may be humane masters, as there certainly are inhuman ones—there may be slaves well-clothed, well-fed, and happy as there are surely those half-clad, half-starved and miserable; nevertheless, the institution that tolerates such wrong and inhumanity as I have witnessed, is a cruel, unjust and barbarous one. Men may write fictions portraying lowly life as it is, or as it is not—may expatiate with owlish gravity upon the bliss of ignorance—discourse flippantly from arm chairs of the pleasures of slave life; but let them toil with him in the field—sleep with him in the cabin—feed with him on husks; let them behold him scourged, hunted, trampled on, and they will come back with another story in their mouths. Let them know the *heart* of the poor slave—learn his secret thoughts—thoughts he dare not utter in the hearing of the white man; let them sit by him in the silent watches of the night—converse with him in trustful confidence, of "life, liberty, and the pursuit of happiness" and they will find that ninety-nine out of every hundred are intelligent enough to understand their situation, and to cherish in their bosoms the love of freedom, as passionately as themselves."[5]

The "love of freedom" is what all people cherish, according to Solomon Northrup. His saga and his thoughts about it should be known by all. His book, *Twelve Years A Slave*, is available from

WHAT WOULD SOLOMON NORTHRUP DO?

Louisiana State University Press, Baton Rouge, Louisiana. I recommend it highly.

There Will Always Be Discrimination

Will there continue to be discrimination?

Of course there will. Solomon Northrup knew that. There will always be some discrimination by some white people against blacks. And there will always be some discrimination by some black people against whites.

The title of this book is that freedom will *conquer*, not that it will *eliminate* it. But who wishes to say that black people are not capable of rising above that discrimination, the same as others do?

If someone told me, "You can't make it because you're not smart enough," I would be very angry.

The black economist, Thomas Sowell agrees:

"[B]lack people just don't have it." That's what the arguments for quotas are really saying, according to Sowell, who continues:

"The devastating impact of this message on black people—particularly black young people—will outweigh any few extra jobs that may result from this strategy."[6]

What a terrible message we are sending.*

In a recent column, Sowell cites the black talk show host, Ken Hamblin, and his recent book, *Pick a Better Country*, wherein

---

* A concern about this "terrible message" was stated clearly in 1973 in *Fortune* in a story about the person in charge of General Electric's equal employment opportunity programs, Jim Nixon, a black man.

"It is very difficult for a large corporation to discriminate in favor of any group without, to some extent, stigmatizing all members of the group who work for it. G.E.'s Nixon, who is himself black, says that talk about hiring less-qualified minority-group members makes him uneasy—that 'it puts the "less-qualified" stamp on the minorities you do hire.' In companies where reverse discrimination is the rule, there will be a nagging question about the real capabilities of any black man who gets a good job or promotion. The question will occur to the white applicants who didn't get the job; it will occur to customers who deal with the black man; and of course, it will occur to the black man himself. Perhaps the cruelest aspect of reverse discrimination is that it ultimately denies minority-group members who have made it on their own the satisfaction of knowing that."

FREEDOM WILL CONQUER RACISM (AND SEXISM)

Hamblin challenges anyone to pick a better country than the United States. Sowell says:

"'[Hamblin] is indeed a man from a different era, when poverty was something you escaped and obstacles were things you overcame. Racism was something you looked down on, not something you clung to as an excuse....

"Hamblin regards blacks like himself as the rule and the welfare and criminal classes in the ghettos as the exception, [and] much of his energy goes into opposing those who promote that sick lifestyle and the 'poverty pimps' who make a career out of keeping that system going. He includes not just members of the welfare bureaucracies, but also politicians like Washington, D.C., Mayor Marion Barry and the Congressional Black Caucus.

"Hamblin understands that the careers and the clout of these people with a vested interest in poverty depends on keeping their constituents isolated, paranoid and pumped full of resentments of everyone—black or white—who is beyond their closed-in world of narrow values and narrow visions. That requires, among other things, the demonizing of blacks who have succeeded in the larger society, including Ken Hamblin....'

"Hamblin doesn't let such people intimidate him, however. 'I have them surrounded,' he says."[7]

Another black scholar, Shelby Steele, agrees. He was a child of the civil rights movement, marching in demonstrations through his childhood.

But he knew that the movement had taken a wrong turn.

"If my benefits come to me primarily as a black, and not as an American, then the effect over time is to undermine common society—the common culture and democracy of America. I as a black don't identify with America—America is my enemy. This kind of thinking causes me not to move into the American mainstream. Which correspondingly causes me to fall farther and farther behind.

"Let me put it this way. Black America is a one-party system....organized around the use of our historical victimization as the source of our power. Jesse Jackson's power is the power of victimization. He is an ambulance chaser for victimization."[8]

Whoopi Goldberg says that "the idea that we as black people are not part of this country...is a concept that we have to get over. That's why we can't define ourselves as African-Americans. We're not.

WHAT WOULD SOLOMON NORTHRUP DO?

We're Americans. That's why Rosa Parks was on the bus. That's why Martin Luther King and Medgar Evers were fighting to make sure that everyone remembers we were Americans, not African-Americans, not Asian-Americans. We are Americans."[9]

Uncle Toms Do Exist

We hear a lot of talk today about "Uncle Toms."

They do exist. They are the Jesse Jacksons and others who take the white, liberal money that is funding the NAACP, the Urban League and other such "black" groups.

They are the ones who are benefiting from the present racist policies which, as Prof. Sowell discovered, always benefit the prosperous members of the protected group while the poor members of the group see their conditions deteriorate, no matter in what country across the world these policies are implemented.

The "elite" will fight very hard to keep their power. Any black who opposes them will be labeled an "Uncle Tom."

We can be sure of one thing: Jesse Jackson did not teach ebonics to *his* children. He sent them to the finest white, private schools that money could buy.

Are Blacks Concerned About Slavery Today?

When the farmer friends of Solomon Northrup marched out of Washington, Saratoga and Essex Counties in New York in 1865, they were going a long way from home. They were not rich men, anymore than Solomon was. They were leaving their wives and children and intruding into a land far away.

One hears a lot today about the terrible conditions in Africa. We hear about torture, famine, murder. We even hear about slavery.

This world of Africa is much closer to every black person in America today than Louisiana was to a New York farmer in 1865.

Yet, we don't hear a lot about what the blacks of America are doing to help these poor people.

We hear a lot of criticism about the poor New York farmers who "allowed" slavery to exist in the South. There is not a black person in America today who should not be doing something to help those in slavery in Africa today.

When will the help start to flow?

FREEDOM WILL CONQUER RACISM (AND SEXISM)

One black man, Keith B. Richburg, covered Africa for the Washington Post from 1991 to 1994. He had always assumed that the troubles there were the legacy of colonialism and the Cold War. If the blacks were given a level playing field, they too would take their place on the escalator to prosperity that had lifted so many formerly backward nations. But what he found instead was senseless cruelty and repressive dictators, which have not emerged from the sins of the West but are homegrown. Inhumanity in Africa wears a black face, and the more he saw, the most disillusioned he became. He ended his book this way:

"I will also know that the problems are too intractable, that the outside world can do nothing, until Africa is ready to save itself. I'll also know that none of it affects me, because I feel no attachment to the place or the people.

"And why should I feel anything more? Because my skin is black? Because some ancestor of mine, four centuries ago, was wrenched from this place and sent to America, and because I now look like those others whose ancestors were left behind? Does that make me still a part of this place? Should their suffering now somehow still be mine?

"Maybe I would care more if I had never come here and never seen what Africa is today. But I have been here, and I have seen—and frankly, I want no part of it.

"So am I a coldhearted cynic? An Africa hater? A racist, maybe, or perhaps a lost and lonely self-hating black man who has forgotten his African roots? Maybe I am, all that and more. But by an accident of birth, I am a black man born in America, and everything I am today—my culture and attitudes, my sensibilities, loves, and desires—derives from that one simple and irrefutable truth."[10]

One Way to Help

It's my belief that we should help the youth of the ghettoes establish small businesses in order for them to gain experience. Sadly, we could probably never do it. Just think of the problems.

- Minimum wage law
- Child labor law
- OSHA

And those would be just a beginning. The obstacles that the government would put in our way would be insurmountable. In addition, the "elite" would accuse us of running a "sweatshop" and of "exploiting" the teenagers.

And the other businesses would have a right to complain because we would be paying these youngsters a lower wage than the competing businesses must pay.

In addition to all those problems, a study of Boston shows that *any* small business owner, white or black, is going to have a difficult time getting started with all of the regulations and red tape which the city government will throw in his or her face.[11]

What a shame that the government takes away our freedom to help train these youngsters to compete in our world!

If only the liberal "elite" would just "get out of the way."

Section IV

IT HASN'T HELPED WOMEN

The 1960's began with the following attack. Who wrote it?

- **Women in America have everything a person could want!**

"The suburban housewife [in the 1950's]—she was the dream image of the young American women and the envy, it was said, of women all over the world. The American housewife—freed by science and labor-saving appliances from the drudgery, the dangers of childbirth and the illnesses of her grandmother. She was healthy, beautiful, educated, concerned only about her husband, her children, her home. She had found true feminine fulfillment. As a housewife and mother, she was respected as a full and equal partner to man in his world. She was free to choose automobiles, clothes, appliances, supermarkets; she had everything that women ever dreamed of."[1]

FREEDOM WILL CONQUER RACISM (AND SEXISM)

- **This dream world has been created, even demanded, by the women themselves.**

"In the last analysis, millions of able women in this free land chose, themselves, not to use the door education could have opened for them. The choice—and the responsibility—for the race back home was finally their own."[2] "[T]he chains that bind her in her trap are chains in her own mind and spirit."[3]

- **Our women are miserable.**

"It was a strange stirring, a sense of dissatisfaction, a yearning that women suffered in the middle of the twentieth century in the United States. Each suburban wife struggled with it alone. As she made the beds, shopped for groceries, matched slipcover material, ate peanut butter sandwiches with her children, chauffeured Cub Scout and Brownies, lay beside her husband at night—she was afraid to ask even of herself the silent question—'Is this all?'"[4]

* * * * *

These words were penned not by a man, but by Betty Friedan, the founder of the National Organization for Women, known as NOW. It's easy to understand why these words caused many of the men of America, who were working so hard to provide all of this munificence that the women enjoyed, to ask in frustration,

"What do women want, anyhow?"

Friedan would not say what *she* wanted, but it was clear that she was looking to change our society. There was no question about that. And she would see that it would be changed to fit *her* image of happiness. The extent of the change was uncertain. But it could be drastic and deep. She said:

"[W]hether we will finally have to challenge the institutions, the concepts of marriage and the nuclear family—I don't know, I just don't know."[5]

IT HASN'T HELPED WOMEN

Although Friedan would not say whether she would attack the very basic bulwark of our society, the family, and replace it with something else, the other leaders knew that they would be doing so.

Most historians say the modern Women's Movement started in 1963 with the publication of this book by Friedan called *The Feminine Mystique*.

I read it in 1964, and I agreed with a lot of it.

14

IT WAS TIME FOR A CHANGE

Before we decide whether women need special help, and even special *laws*, to 1) help and 2) protect them, we must agree on one thing.

The world is going through great changes.

This may seem trite and simplistic, but it's necessary to state this clearly because many of the leaders of the "Women's Movement" 1) don't realize it or 2) they don't want *us* to realize it.

So, let's look at those changes for just a minute.

Change Is Happening

Only a few years ago, the women of America were "*protected*." Do they *still* need this "protection"? Or has the world changed? Do they still need the special help of a law or can they make it on their own?

This has *never* been debated. "Sex" was added to the Civil Rights Act as a joke in 1964. It was not taken seriously until a very small group of women began applying great political pressure with the help of the media and with the help of the newly written, Civil Rights Act.

IT WAS TIME FOR A CHANGE

It was only a few years previous, back in the 1950's, that the professors at the top women's colleges, Vassar, Smith and others, were <u>desperate</u> in their attempts to engage intelligent women in any intellectual pursuit. "[T]he girls [in these colleges] seemed suddenly incapable of any ambition, any vision, any passion, except the pursuit of a wedding ring,"[1] reported Betty Friedan.

But only a few years later, some of these same women were blaming everyone *except themselves* for the fact that they were not trained to work outside of the home.

Before we can discuss whether women need to be "protected" and whether they need "special help," or what role the federal government should take in forcing tremendous changes in our society and even censoring our thought, we must see if we can agree on some basic, fundamental truths.

We Must Not Be Upset By Change

The changes in our society have accelerated very rapidly since World War II. Those of us who were around 50 years ago have seen it. What are these tremendous changes that are causing such an upheaval in our society?

Back in the 1930's, some member of every family had to go to the grocery store and to the butcher shop (there were no supermarkets, each was a different store) every single day, because most people had only an ice box, which was marginal in preserving food. The new refrigerators were scarce and not very good and, of course, there was no frozen food at all. Meat and vegetables had to be purchased almost daily.

And there were no clothes dryers. All of the laundry was done in a washing machine with a wringer attached and then the heavy load was carried outside to dry on a clothes line. In the winter, it dried on a line in the basement. This included all the diapers; there was not even a diaper service, much less disposable diapers.

All of the cars had stick shifts on the floor and were difficult to drive. In the winter, the roads were often impassable and everyone who did use them had to get down on his back and put on tire chains. The "clink" of tire chains driving down the street was a familiar sound of winter.

FREEDOM WILL CONQUER RACISM (AND SEXISM)

Many people still had coal furnaces in the basement which needed coal to be shoveled into them every few hours and stoked, and the heavy cans of ashes had to be carried up the cellar stairs and disposed of.

On our farms, things were even more primitive. The wonder of electricity was just coming to the farms and the electric motor was combining with the gas engine to gradually eliminate much of the hand labor that was required.

There was plenty of work to go around for everyone. Women were not unhappy to let a man bear the brunt of the hard physical labor that was necessary, and the women were needed inside the home for all of the work that was required there.

It's still that way in many areas of our life.

When the garbage truck rolls up to your door, how many times do you see a woman get off? When a snowstorm blankets your area and the electric lines go down, how many women volunteer to go out and climb the dangerous, icy poles in the middle of the storm to get your power going again? When your car breaks down on an interstate highway, how many of us look for a woman to stop and fix it?

In our rural areas, this is especially true. In the forests of America, you still don't see many women with chainsaws. And on the farms, you almost always see men out driving those big tractors.

This was the way that almost all of our world used to be back in the 1930's. It was a world of heavy labor and hard work before electricity and gasoline engines took over much of that toil.

Women Were Protected

How did our society cope in the 1930s and 1940s?

We did it by giving women a protected role. Every man was expected to give shelter and protection to a woman so that she could bear and raise the children of the society. She *needed* that protection back then. If a society was able to raise those children, it was considered successful.

There was not much quarrel between the sexes. Everyone was able to see that they were all pulling together. Even one of the most radical feminists of our time, Germaine Greer, agrees with this. She spent some time on a farm in her teens and she had "enormous respect for the farm women, for their vigor and strong sense of integrity, their generosity, for what she had come to regard as an unadorned love of family."² The farm women were, in her view, "authentic."*

Many of us have found that to be true, in contrast to the many people today who have never witnessed that rural life.

This does not mean that we want to, or could, go back to the days when manual labor was important and we needed the help of everyone, man, woman and child, to get the work done. But we must have a better sense of why life was so different in those days.

And we must realize that we are indeed going through enormous changes. If we approach these changes with anger, bitterness, and paranoia, we will have a very difficult time.

These changes affect men as well as women. How do they affect men? Let me give a few examples that I have seen in my lifetime. And let me say that I do not disagree that some of these responsibilities should be borne by men. I am merely reporting them for what they are because this part of our society is not known by many today. We hear the strident claims that, "Women have always been subjugated by men." This was undoubtedly true of some men. But there have always been strong, domineering women as well. Men were *also* under great moral and legal pressure to take proper care of their families, i.e. their wives and children. These are examples from the 1960's.

- A client of mine, when I was practicing law, had to pay his former wife so that she had $153/week for 3 people (herself and two children), while he had only $53/week for 3 people (himself,

---

* Betty Friedan agreed with that and even took it a step further.

"Until, and even into, the last century, strong, capable women were needed to pioneer our new land; with their husbands, they ran the farms and plantations and Western homesteads. These women were respected and self-respecting members of a society whose pioneering purpose centered in the home. Strength and independence, responsibility and self-confidence, self-discipline and courage, freedom and equality were part of the American character for both men and women, in all the first generations. The women who came by steerage from Ireland, Italy, Russia and Poland worked beside their husbands in the sweatshops and the laundries, learned the new language, and saved to send their sons and daughters to college. Women were never quite as "feminine," or held in as much contempt, in America as they were in Europe. American women seemed to European travelers, long before our time, less passive, childlike and feminine than their own wives in

his second wife and child). That happened because at that time, a woman had *no* legal duty to pay *any* support whatsoever for her children. Therefore, my client could not introduce any evidence to the judge that his wife was also working. Whether she was working was totally immaterial as to what the father should pay. Because it was impossible to live on $53/week, he had to work two jobs and take money "under the table." But no one cared about his problems. I brought this case to the attention of the ACLU, but they said they were too busy. A week later, there was an article in the newspaper that the ACLU was representing a girl who wanted to be on the boys tennis team at high school.

- A beautiful young woman about 20-years-old came before a judge to ask for child support from her former husband. He was suffering from the trauma of the divorce and was seeing a psychiatrist. She was not working but was having a good time while her mother was caring for the baby. The judge in no uncertain terms told the young man that he didn't care what his problems were, if he didn't have a job in two weeks he would be in jail. The mother had no legal duty whatsoever.
- 17-year-old boys went to jail for corrupting the morals of a minor, i.e. of a 16-year-old girl.
- Children were *never* allowed to live with their fathers after divorce if the mother objected. The "strongest presumption" in all of the law was that a father would not get custody of his children.
- No woman was given a rifle and told by the government to go shoot other men she had never seen who might even be some of her Italian, German or Japanese relatives.

France or Germany or England. By an accident of history, American women shared in the work of society longer, and grew with the men. Grade- and high-school education for boys and girls alike was almost always the rule; and in the West, where women shared the pioneering work the longest, even the universities were coeducational from the beginning.

"The identity crisis for women did not begin in America until the fire and strength and ability of the pioneer women were no longer needed, no longer used, in the middle-class homes of the Eastern and Midwestern cities, when the pioneering was done and men began to build the new society in industries and professions outside the home." Friedan, p. 323.

IT WAS TIME FOR A CHANGE

- The hot, steamy commuter trains, without air conditioning, looked like cattle cars with the men pouring out of them at 6 o'clock at night only to get back on again at 7:45 the next morning to return to a dirty, hot city, while the women and children remained in the cool suburbs.
- The person who was guilty of a crime and went off to jail would almost always be a man, while his "woman" who had watched and applauded the money he obtained from his crimes would just go find another man. Sometimes both a man and a woman would be convicted of a crime, but we lawyers would successfully argue that the woman couldn't go to jail because she was pregnant or had children at home.
- If a man got a woman pregnant out of wedlock, he would have to pay support, but he had no right to the child. This was not his child in any way, except that he had to support it. (Now that we have legal abortion, a woman can engage in sex with the knowledge that if she becomes pregnant, she can have an abortion if she desires. But a man has no such "solution." He has no choice as to whether or not she has an abortion. If he is wealthy or has a job and she chooses not to abort, he will be paying for at least the next 18 years. There is no "free sex" for men; it's still Russian roulette for any man with a good paying job.)
- The only debtor's prison was that for fathers who did not pay their support. The average American male who had a job was paying or he was going to jail. A large number of the people in our county prisons around the country were fathers who did not make their payments. (Fathers often become totally discouraged after their children are torn from them. If we could correct the terrible bias of the courts in awarding custody of the children *always* to the mother, we could avoid much of the problems with fathers.)
- The attitude of the old days (before 1960) was best exemplified by the sinking of the Titanic in 1912. This is difficult to believe today; it is almost like a comic opera. But these men helped the women and children to the lifeboats while the men went to their death. There were no cries for liberation at that point.

FREEDOM WILL CONQUER RACISM (AND SEXISM)

Some of the above was necessary, but it was not a one-sided world against women, as we constantly hear today.

Harder for Women?

Okay, you'll say, so everyone is going through a great period of change. And no one knows exactly where this is going to end.

But why is it more difficult for women? Why are we seeing so much more concern among women than men?

There are two reasons. Probably the most important is that most women love babies and children, but suddenly they are being told that we have too many babies. Our society has suddenly stopped telling women that they are wonderful to be mothering; and they are now getting a message that they should stop "polluting" the world with so many little children.

This is bound to cause confusion and anger.

Another problem is that many women today have a choice. Men know that their role is to provide shelter and food for their family, but the role of a woman is often less clear. Her duties at home are much less difficult and time consuming than they were for her mother. Should she get a job or have children? Or should she do both? And if she does both, is she going to be able to handle it all? *And no matter what route she takes, someone will criticize her.*

These are very difficult decisions for a woman to make. And we as a society have made them even more difficult. Instead of an intelligent discussion of these questions, we have gotten off into rigid camps with everyone yelling and screaming.

The men of America have accorded the women of America the most freedom of any women in the history of the world. But they have received no thanks. When the women were marching in a demonstration on New York's Fifth Avenue, a female Italian journalist was heard to say, "Such a thing could never take place in Italy. The men would destroy them."

Along with the freedom we enjoy, we must also have less anger and hostility if we are going to successfully cope with the great changes that we see in our society.

15

WHO'S LED THE CHANGE?

The role of women has to change as our world becomes more mechanized.

We all agree to that. But who should lead this change? Who has led it? *Are they the people that you want leading you?*

In 1966, President Johnson was accosted by a group of women who wanted to use the federal government as a tool to change the country to their personal philosophies, which were socialist, feminist and radical. They wanted to use the government to coerce people into accepting their points of view.

They had decided they needed an "NAACP for women," as they called it. Therefore, they created NOW in 1966. They knew that the issue of "race" was what had passed the Civil Rights Act. But they also believed that if they pushed hard enough, and were visible and vocal enough, they could possibly make "sex" just as important and use that as a wedge to create an intrusive, socialistic government.

One of their first acts was to complain that the EEOC was not working hard enough for "women's rights." They believed the

FREEDOM WILL CONQUER RACISM (AND SEXISM)

EEOC was hampered by a reluctance among some of its male members to combat sex discrimination as vigorously as they sought to combat racial discrimination. These women asked for more power for the EEOC.

They started picketing the EEOC in 1966.[1] In December, 1967, the offices in New York, San Francisco, Atlanta, Chicago and others were picketed. "They would make some noise, possibly get arrested, certainly get thrown out, meet the press, and all the while give prominent display to large, home-lettered signs," said a woman reporter in the *New York Times*.[2] Her favorite sign said,

"A Chicken in Every Pot, A Whore in Every Home."

Many of their protests seem obvious now, such as the picketing of the *New York Times* and other newspapers which ran "Help Wanted-Men" columns and "Help Wanted-Women" columns.[3]

But some of it was not so obvious. Should marriage and the family be abolished? Should children be raised in communes? Many of these women were afraid to raise those issues in public which would let everyone know exactly what their goals were. The president of the influential New York chapter of NOW, Ti-Grace Atkinson, told the *New York Times*:

"We're afraid of the truth. To say that you can be both a career woman and a wife and mother, and that the institutions won't change and won't be threatened—that's a cop out.... Any real change in the status of women would be a fundamental assault on marriage and the family. People would be tied together by love, not legal contraptions. Children would be raised communally; it's just not honest to talk about freedom for women unless you get the child-rearing off their backs. We may not be ready for any of this yet, but if we're going to be honest, we've got to talk about it. Face it, raise the questions."[4]

But most of the women in NOW wouldn't discuss where they were heading, according to the *New York Times*:

"Within NOW, there is an altogether understandable reluctance to pursue the matter. Here are the radicals, wanting to be heard. Out there are the mothers' clubbers, waiting to be alienated. The feminists are not anxious to alienate anyone, and even mild threats to the abiding institutions do tend to frighten most women to death."[5]

WHO'S LED THE CHANGE?

Many of the leaders were also driven by a hatred of men.*

It Started With Friedan

Friedan was a well-to-do graduate of an ivy-league college who was writing about her friends and peers. She said that these women had been provided with every material thing a person could possibly want, and yet they were miserable.

But who could not help but be sympathetic with Friedan, who had been a brilliant student at college where she had graduated summa cum laude, the valedictorian of her class, when she plaintively said, "I want something more than my husband and my children and my home."[6]

But the problem was that, as she said very clearly, nobody could do anything about this but the women themselves. No one was holding them slaves in bondage. They were the ones who wanted to be totally feminine; they were the ones who drove their husbands to stay away from the home in order to earn always more and more so that they could afford the best for their children.**

It hadn't been that way previously. As Friedan pointed out, what she saw happening in the 1950's was a change:

"[F]ewer of them were going on from college to become physicists, philosophers, poets, doctors, lawyers, stateswomen, social pioneers,

---

* If you doubt that the "elite" are teaching women to hate men, consider this event at Wellesley College. When my wife was reading the lead article in her Wellesley alumnae magazine in 1995, she knew immediately they were not telling the truth. The headline that got her attention was large. It proclaimed with great authority, "In 1899, the president of Harvard called colleges for women 'superfluities.' My wife went to the Wellesley College library, looked at the 1899 article and found that the headline and story were a complete fabrication. She was so disappointed that she prepared a 16-page piece which clearly pointed out all of the lies in the article. She distributed it to the entire faculty, the administration, the trustees and over 1000 alumnae. But she received no answer from anyone, and the alumnae magazine repeated the same lies in subsequent issues. Even worse, all of the conservative columnists, publications, professors and organizations all yawned and said that Wellesley did this all the time. The only one that showed any interest was the *National Review* which published a short critique on August 28, 1995 at page 12.

FREEDOM WILL CONQUER RACISM (AND SEXISM)

even college professors. Fewer women in recent college graduating classes have gone on to distinguish themselves in a career or profession than those in the classes graduated before World War II, the Great Divide.

"Fewer and fewer college women were preparing for any career or profession requiring more than the most casual commitment. Two out of three girls who entered college were dropping out before they even finished. In the 1950's, those who stayed, even the most able, showed no signs of wanting to be anything more than suburban housewives and mothers."[7]

The professors were becoming desperate in their attempts to get women to improve themselves. "[T]o professors at Vassar and Smith and Barnard, resorting to desperate means to arouse students' interest in *anything* college could teach them, the girls seemed suddenly incapable of any ambition, any vision, any passion, except the pursuit of a wedding ring. In this pursuit they seemed almost desperate, as early as freshman year."[8]

In 1942 when Friedan had graduated, it had been different. Over 2/3 of the graduates from her sister college, Mt. Holyoke, had gone on to get a graduate degree.[9]

As I read *The Feminine Mystique* in 1964, I and many other men agreed with much of it, never realizing that we would soon be blamed for all of the ills of the world and that men in the United

---

The New York Times Magazine of March 15, 1970, at page 129, printed the following by Pamela Kearon, a member of an organization, "The Feminists."

On Man Hating

Man hating has been the cause of a deep rift within Women's Liberation. It is a vital issue because it involves ultimately the way we feel about ourselves, and how far we are willing to go in our own behalf. I've been at meetings where women actually left because they thought that "man haters" were on the loose. All arguments which tend to suppress the recognition of man-hating in our midst are reducible to this: FEAR. Man-hating is considered a subversive and therefore dangerous sentiment. Men, who control the definition, have made of it a disgusting perversion. Many men engage in sexual intercourse, often extensively, even marry, while hating women. These men are called misogynist. Now, there is no shame in being a misogynist. It is a perfectly respectable attitude. Our whole society (including too many of the women in it) hates women. Perhaps we need a Latin or Greek derivative in place of "man-hating" to make the perfect symmetry of the two attitudes more obvious.

WHO'S LED THE CHANGE?

States in the later years of the 20th century would be blamed for all the problems that women had ever suffered or were now suffering *throughout the entire history of the entire world.*

A Few Problems

Although Friedan's book was excellent, there were a few problems. The foremost was that she assumed, as do most people, that what was good for her was also good for everyone else. Just because she was a brilliant student did not mean that *every* woman wanted to be an academic or a CEO.

This was pointed up in the fact that she was apparently a lousy housewife. Her husband later said, "Betty never washed a hundred dishes during twenty years of marriage."[10] An "official" biographer would say, "Phoning people is the extent of Betty's kitchen duty. Anything else has proved disastrous. If Betty went out to do the shopping, she would inevitably return with the major ingredient of the meal—the meat, for instance—missing. If she cleaned the table, she'd push and push with one finger..."[11]

She was considering only the plight of well-to-do, highly intellectual women. She viewed women as a monolith with herself as the model.

However, the major problem was that Betty Friedan very quickly lost control of the movement she had created to a much younger, much more radical group of women. Betty Friedan was a genuine liberal who had worked for a small labor newspaper in New York City and was involved in left wing causes before she married. But even a left wing liberal was far too conservative for those who soon pushed her aside.

There were also many hardworking, moderate women who were dedicated to changing the role of women during this time. Unfortunately, the leadership at this watershed in American life was seized by the more radical feminists. They used these critical years in our history to push their agenda.

** And one could also not help but consider the many men who could also say, "Is this all there is that I must sit for the rest of my life in a closet that they call an 'office'?" Or "Is this all there is that I must stand in this assembly line to attach a nut on a car 100 times an hour for the rest of my life?"

FREEDOM WILL CONQUER RACISM (AND SEXISM)

Who Were the Leaders?

Who were the leaders of the "Women's Movement" which put the tremendous political pressure on Lyndon Johnson to use the Civil Rights Act to further their own, personal goals?

There were four leaders, according to a sympathetic book published in 1988, *The Sisterhood, The True Story of the Women Who Changed the World*. This book picked the following four as the leaders of this movement: Friedan, Gloria Steinem, Germaine Greer, and Kate Millett. Let's look at these four people who have been selected as the intellectual leaders of the movement.*

- All four had unhappy childhoods.
- All four had deep conflicts with their mothers, much of which they blamed upon the fact that their mothers stopped working when the children came.
- Because they came from unhappy families, they found it difficult to conceive that there could be such a thing as a happy family. *Instead of trying to improve our families and make them better, they wanted to change the system .... to fit their own particular needs.*

The most normal childhood had been that of Betty Friedan and she was by far the least radical of the group. She had been raised in Peoria, Illinois, in the well-to-do family of a jeweler. But when the depression hit in the 1930's there was never quite enough money for the high life style of a maid, chauffeur, and the big house. And so her frustrated, attractive mother would yell at her father who would storm out of the room with a red face after banging his fist on the table.[12]

Friedan never got along with her mother, whom she saw as a "phony," even much later in life. She would blame all of this on the fact that her mother had given up her job as a society reporter on the local newspaper in order to become a wife and mother.[13]

---

* If any reader believes that these four women are not representative of the leaders of the movement, let me make it clear that I merely looked at the book which is accepted as being a definitive work. The author chose the women. As the publisher, Simon and Schuster, says: "[T]his is a revealing group portrait of the women whose ideas and actions have so profoundly transformed all of our lives....[T]his is a riveting social history that casts light on an entire era by illuminating the lives of some of its key figures."

WHO'S LED THE CHANGE?

In later years, she would say that her mother "belittled, cut down my father because she had no place to channel her terrific energies."[14] She would say that her mother was like many other women who "didn't have any power outside the family...had to have too much in it."[15]

Friedan considered herself ugly compared to her mother and her sister; she had never been good at sports; and so when she was not admitted to a high school sorority because she was Jewish, she retreated to a world of books, at which she excelled. But Friedan was robust and had a wild temper. After graduating from Smith, she turned down a prestigious fellowship in psychology because a boy with whom she was in love had told her, "Nothing can come of this, between us. I'll never win a fellowship like yours."[16]

However, she didn't marry the young man anyway and as a result started getting asthmatic spasms.[17] She sought therapy to which she would return over the years as the asthma would recur. She did marry, have three children and move to the suburbs before returning to Smith College for her 15th reunion. It was there that she distributed a questionnaire to her classmates which would lead to the book, *The Feminine Mystique*.

The childhood of the other three leaders was much worse.

One of them couldn't believe that a daughter would actually like her mother. "I thought about the children who did ... not only love their mothers, but actually like them, hang out with them....I thought they were faking. I thought it was a thing you did for outsiders. You pretended to be good chums."[18]

That was the poignant feeling of Germaine Greer, who lived in Australia during World War II and saw her beautiful mother, who had been a model before her marriage, flirt with the many American soldiers who passed through. The mother would constantly talk about sex, while her handsome husband was off fighting in Africa and later returned as a broken old man.[19]

The mother would beat Germaine, sometimes with a copper stick. And the young girl would run away from home.[20] Finally, at the age of 25, she would make it, in the form of a scholarship, to England for a doctorate in Shakespeare.[21] She also blamed her mother's problems on marriage and motherhood.

"Mother was a gorgeous model before the war and then a bobby soxer. She really thought she was Zelda Fitzgerald and Daddy was

FREEDOM WILL CONQUER RACISM (AND SEXISM)

Scott Fitzgerald and that they were going to dance on ocean liners and play Randolph Hearst and all that. She didn't have a career, and being a mother meant nothing to her; the family meant nothing. She had nothing to build and nothing to make, no idea of what role a woman might play."

"Then suddenly it was all over. There she was with a squalling brat."[22] And the brat was Germaine.

Gloria Steinem had to take care of her sick mother at age 11 when her father left the home. Her mother had her first nervous breakdown before Gloria was born, and she was now a sick and confused woman. She would spend most of her day in bed, unable to even clean the house. She would thrust her arm through a window to protect them from "the evil" outside.

From age 11 to 16, Gloria was the sole caretaker of this poor woman.[23]

Again, this mother had also been a society reporter. Steinem insists, "My mother was not mentally ill. She was defeated by a biased world....Her fate was not uncommon for women."[24]

Gloria also went to Smith and she also graduated Phi Beta Kappa, ten years after Friedan in 1952.

After spending time in India for a few years after college, she was greeted at the boat by her father who was something of a hustler and the two would travel across the country pretending they were very poor and they had to sell the "expensive" rings right off Gloria's fingers. Which led her "official" biographer to say:

"As this attractive, unconventional pair meandered across the country, the trick took in suckers aplenty."[25]

Kate Millett also had a charming, happy-go-lucky father who left their comfortable St. Paul, Minnesota, home when she was 14 years old. So she became a man for her mother. "Now I realized I was my mother's man, opening car doors, driving for her, taking her arm across the ice."[26]

She too graduated from college, the University of Minnesota, as a Phi Beta Kappa.

Betty Friedan said in her book, "Women of orthodox Catholic or Jewish origin do not easily break through the housewife image; it is enshrined in the canons of their religion, in the assumptions of their own and their husbands' childhoods, and in their church's dogmatic definitions of marriage and motherhood."[27]

WHO'S LED THE CHANGE?

Of the four leaders, two came from a Catholic tradition, Betty came from a strong Jewish family, and Gloria had a Jewish father and a Protestant mother.

One cannot help but feel sorry for these four people and their miserable childhoods but one also cannot help but wonder whether their proposed solutions would decrease the number of unhappy children or increase it.

The Beginning of Hedonism

Friedan was the only one who stayed with a man for any period of time or had children.

A young Germaine Greer decided while she was still in Australia that she would never have to be one man's woman. "I could have lovers in every town."[28] And she did. After getting her doctorate, she was teaching at a small college in the English countryside. She would have affairs with other professors, usually married. And then she would wonder why the wives of those men didn't trust her. "The young academic couples wouldn't touch me with a barge pole. They were much too paranoid and insecure. I didn't know what they were afraid of, or why they were so nasty and unfriendly."[29]

She would later start her own pornographic magazine. She told her all-male board of editors that they all had to pose nude:

"That means you guys have got to show your dicks, you know, impressive or otherwise. Little or big, you've got to stand up and be counted. I don't care if it's stiff or lying down or what it's doing."[30]

For her own picture, she lay naked on her back with her knees over her head.[31]

Of a later lover, the manager of a rock group, she said that he wasn't bright enough to read her books. "But I'm sure he's looked at every page for quite a long time."[32] She continued, "I don't feel like some girls who feel they have to sleep with their intellectual equals. If I did I would be scurrying around in a state of sexual frenzy."[33]

Greer's language was dirtier than that of most men and was probably used intentionally to shock.

Kate Millett suffered great emotional troubles after being "outed" at a large public meeting by her lesbian friends after she had become famous. She made six attempts at suicide, was committed for a time by her family, and has since retreated out of the spotlight.[34]

FREEDOM WILL CONQUER RACISM (AND SEXISM)

The "Mother Superior"

Betty Friedan was the leader of the movement because of her famous book, but it wasn't long before she was called the "Mother Superior" of the movement.[35]

Betty kept trying to change society whereas most of the others seemed intent on destroying it. She also tried to keep it from becoming a lesbian movement; but, in this regard, she stood alone.

NOW was organized by Betty in 1966 and she lasted as president until 1970.

Many of the female radicals of the 1960's switched to feminism after they had been treated badly by the male radicals. For instance, radical leader Stokeley Carmichael had wisecracked, "The position of women in our movement should be prone." So these radical women, outraged by their treatment in organized left-wing causes, moved to the feminist movement.[36]

The leader of the New York chapter of NOW, Ti-Grace Atkinson, said, "The institution of marriage has the same effect as the institution of slavery had."[37] It should be abolished, she said, and children should be raised communally.

After she defended a woman who had shot Andy Warhol, saying that the woman was a heroine to feminists, Ti-Grace was finally removed by NOW in 1968. But she went on talking to college groups and others across the country. "My impression is that the prostitute is the only honest woman left in America, because they charge for their services, rather than submitting to a marriage contract which forces them to work for life without pay."[38]

Additional radical groups would be started by others. One had the following manifesto:

"Women are an oppressed class. Our oppression is total, affecting every facet of our lives. We are exploited as sex objects, breeders, domestic servants and cheap labor. We are considered inferior beings whose only purpose is to enhance men's lives...."[39]

Ti-Grace fell in love with Mafia leader, Joe Colombo, who was gunned down in New York City in 1971. She found the Mafia "morally refreshing." "It's the oldest resistance unit in the world—seven centuries of resistance. The value system of the Italian-American community is Mafiosi, and we have a lot to learn from it." She did not explain how the treatment that this group gave to its women was an advance for women.[40]

WHO'S LED THE CHANGE?

The following speech was given at Catholic University in 1971 as the result of a court order which required the college to allow her to speak to its students:

"I, Ti-Grace Atkinson, in the name of all women, most especially the deceased victims of the accused, charge the Catholic church...with murder in the first degree, premeditated and willful.

"...with conspiracy to imprison and enslave women...into marriage and the family.

"...with forcing many...into prostitution.

"...with inciting rape...by degrading and sadistic propaganda...

"In the name of all women, I charge the Catholic Church with constituting, by its very existence, an obscenity on the face of the earth...

"Motherfuckers!...The struggle between the liberation of women and the Catholic church is a struggle to the death. So be it."[41]

Others in the Movement came from radical, Marxist groups of the 1960's. They were angry because they had been treated so poorly by the males in those Marxist organizations. So these women argued about whether the chief problem was capitalism or whether the oppressor was the males of all societies. A *New York Times* article noted, "After all, they pointed out, male supremacy was still flourishing in the Soviet Union, Cuba and China."[42] What was the ultimate oppressor? Man or Capitalism?

This was the type of radicalism that Betty Friedan was fighting and which made her look like a conservative. But in the long run, it boiled down to a struggle between two women, two distinguished graduates of Smith College, Betty Friedan and Gloria Steinem.

Gloria Steinem

After selling rings to suckers across the country with her father, Gloria settled in New York City where her charm and good looks soon made an impression on everyone. She also wrote a book, but not about feminism. It was called *The Beach Book* and it told how to have a good time. It was pure hedonism:

"For the unmarried, New York was all 'red balloons,' in her view, a *Great Gatsby* fantasy, 'an endless snowbound house party.' It was a 'great reprieve,' a long holiday, a way for 'girls to postpone commitment.'"[43]

FREEDOM WILL CONQUER RACISM (AND SEXISM)

Gloria did indeed postpone commitment—forever. She was never committed to anyone. She talked about one lifestyle but followed another. She said, "A woman needs a man like a fish needs a bicycle."[44] But she used her good looks and charm on men at any point she could.

"Gloria was a phony,"[45] said Helen Gurley Brown, the editor of Cosmopolitan.

"[T]his woman, who advanced in public favor by appealing to powerful men, has moved to the front ranks of women's liberation, appealing now to women who do not like powerful men," wrote one commentator.[46]

And Betty Friedan said that Gloria was "ripping off the movement for private profit."[47] Friedan had a press conference in 1972 after Gloria had written an article for McCalls. Betty was angry:

"The assumption that women have any moral or spiritual superiority as a class or that men share some brute insensitivity as a class is female sexism. If I were a man, I would object strenuously..."

"Does this mean that any woman who admits tenderness or passion for her husband, or any man, has sold out to the enemy?...

"If we make men the enemy they will surely lash back at us. If we demand equal treatment from them and still insist on special privilege, we deserve the backlash....

"Men *can* and *must* be with us if we are to change society."[48]

But Betty Friedan was destined to run second to the glamorous media star Gloria Steinem.

Steinem never had any official position in the Movement but she did make many speeches, largely to colleges. At her alma mater, it was Gloria, not Betty, who was asked to deliver the commencement address.

A friend of Betty said, "It was as if they had asked the prettiest girl instead of the smartest."[49]

Steinem told the college women that male rule was a recent thing. Women had always ruled the world until recent times. The discovery of the male's part of reproduction had led to "the idea of ownership ... of property and of children, the origin of marriage, which was really locking women up long enough to make sure who the father was..."[50]

But such talk didn't stop Steinem from using men herself. Although she earned large amounts of money, she never saved any or planned for her future. There was always a man around to handle those affairs. Said a friend:

"The interesting thing about Gloria is that she can do anything except the things that all the rest of us can do, like figure out how to use the postage machine or understand that you have to pay your taxes by April 15th. She's not good at it. She's always in arrears with the government and in a lot of trouble. She doesn't pay bills and she doesn't understand how to keep subscriptions going. She's not a detail person; she's a big thought person, which is a lovely thing to be able to do.

"There's usually some man around to take care of that stuff."[51]

Gloria had originally become famous by being a bunny for a short time at a Playboy club and then writing about it. In order to promote a book, she posed in a bubble bath for People magazine.[52]

Gloria, who had a picture of the revolutionary, Che Guevara, on her wall, would go on to found the feminist *Ms.* magazine. *Ms.* foundered in 1987 and had to be sold. She also delighted her critics, who said she depended upon men, by living with one of the richest men in New York, Donald Trump. That lasted about three years.

Friedan Loses

But the main reason that Betty Friedan lost control, according to *The Sisterhood*, was because she did not want to let the lesbians confuse the issues.

After Kate Millett revealed that she was a lesbian, the pressure on the Movement became intense. At a march on December 12, 1970, some women began distributing lavender arm bands which signified a support for the lesbian cause.

When they handed one to Friedan, she let it drop to the ground.

The biographer of the movement says, "[T]his was the turning point, the moment when the women's movement took on a life of its own, moved beyond Betty Friedan's 'civil rights' structure, leaving the creator of NOW—respected, admired, feared, and sometimes hated—behind. [The others] would come to feel that Betty's approach had dealt only with 'symptoms,' that only those willing to explore the significance of 'women loving women' would come to grips with the underlying causes of women's oppression." In contrast, Gloria supported the lesbian cause.[53]

FREEDOM WILL CONQUER RACISM (AND SEXISM)

Postponement of Sex

Betty Friedan noted in her book that sex at an early age was found in underdeveloped civilizations; and in America, it was found in the slums. She said:

"[A] certain postponement of sexual activity seemed to accompany the growth in mental activity required and resulted from higher education and the achievement of the professions of highest value to society."[54]

In other words, free and open sex was not something new and modern. It was not a sexual "revolution," but merely a regression back to a less advanced society.

But this wasn't what the leaders of the Women's Movement were saying. They were pointing to the less educated males in our society and saying that every male practices free sex; therefore, females should also.

The figures that Friedan quoted were from the Kinsey report which showed that men who went to college had a totally different outlook on women than did the rest of the men in the population.

"[E]arly sexual preoccupation seemed to indicate a weak core of self which even marriage did not strengthen,"[55] according to Friedan.

"[T]he key problem in promiscuity is usually 'low self-esteem,'"[56] according to Friedan.

But still the Movement pushed a return to free and easy sex.*

What Were the Goals?

What were the goals of these people who are the accepted leaders of the women of America:

- Women will work outside of the home.
- Children will be raised by the state in communes or day care centers.
- Free and easy sex will be the norm.

---

*   We're beginning to see a change away from the "free sex" movement with Dr. Laura Schlessinger the apparent leader. Both on her talk show and in books, she is telling women, 1) don't have sex without marriage and 2) if you have children, stay home and take care of them. This is a large change from what we have been hearing for the past 25 years.

WHO'S LED THE CHANGE?

- Marriage will be weakened or eliminated.
- Abortion will be free and available on demand at any point of pregnancy.

Who is winning?

Are the radical feminists winning the battle?

If your answer is "No," consider this. Our society believes that when a person breaks a "promise," this is very important. For over a thousand years, it's been the basis of our legal system.

The most important contract that two people ever make is when they get married. They have promised to be faithful to each other.

Are the rules about a contract quaint and old-fashioned? Should we change our legal system, particularly the "promises" that are made during marriage?

Consider what happened after the Air Force discharged Lt. Kelly Flinn in 1997. This is what our leading newspapers said in their editorials:

New York Times: "The military has stepped up its prosecution of adultery to a point that offends common sense, good management and current societal mores."[57]

USA Today: "The larger question is whether the Air Force—and military in general can fix the fraternization and adultery rules .... Decades after most of society began adjusting to an equal-opportunity workforce, this is just the latest case that suggests the military is lost in the wild blue yonder."[58]

Do these newspapers want us to change our laws about *all* contracts or just those in marriage?

Is the *New York Times* correct that adultery is not a big deal under our "current societal mores?" Is *USA Today* correct that our society is an "equal-opportunity workforce" where adultery is the norm? If our mores are changing so drastically, should we abandon the concept of a "promise" made during a marriage ceremony; and should we let the "village" and the day care centers raise our children? If the answer to that is "Yes," should we continue to allow this change in our society to happen slowly as the feminists and the *New York Times* would have us do? Or should we announce it in advance so that everyone knows what the new rules are?

The feminists told us in 1968: "Any real change in the status of women would be a fundamental assault on marriage and the family. People would be tied together by love, not legal contraptions.

FREEDOM WILL CONQUER RACISM (AND SEXISM)

Children would be raised communally; it's just not honest to talk about freedom for women unless you get the child-rearing off their backs. We may not be ready for any of this yet, but if we're going to be honest, we've got to talk about it. Face it, raise the questions."[59]

We're still moving in the direction that the radical feminists have established. Is this what we want?

16

DO WOMEN NEED SPECIAL TREATMENT?

Are women "equal" to men? Are they able to compete in the marketplace? Or, must women be treated "specially" and "gently"?

We are getting confusing and conflicting answers.

We hear that women are ready for combat duty in the Army and Navy; tough, ready to fight and die in the mud for their country. And in the next breath, we hear that they are too delicate to know what to do when a co-worker makes a "pass" at them.

Do you remember that Saturday afternoon in 1964 when Congress "debated" for two hours whether to include women in the Civil Rights Act?

During those two hours, the women in Congress complained bitterly about the "protective" laws in the various states that were intended to stop women from being exploited. Although these laws had been requested and demanded by their mothers and grandmothers, these Congresswomen didn't want them.

For example, women in Michigan were not allowed to tend bar. But that didn't protect women; it helped men, said Congresswoman

Griffiths. "Most of the so-called protective legislation has really been to protect men's rights in better paying jobs."[1]

Katherine St. George agreed.

"Protective legislation prevents, as my colleague from the State of Michigan just pointed out, prevents women from going into the higher salary brackets. Yes, it certainly does.

"Women are protected. They cannot run an elevator late at night and that is when the pay is higher.

"They cannot serve in restaurants and cabarets late at night, when the tips are higher, and the load, if you please, is lighter. ...

"We do not want special privileges. We do not need special privilege."[2]

It was clear to those Congresswomen back in 1964 that a woman was able to serve a drunk in a tavern at midnight without anyone to protect her. She could take care of herself!

But only a few years later, we were suddenly being told again that the government *had* to protect them. This time it was the *federal*, not the state government, that did the protecting. We were told that a woman employee wasn't capable of telling a co-worker to stop bothering her; she still needed to be "protected."

Are women able to take care of themselves or not? Do they need special privileges? Do they need chaperones? A visitor from outer space would find it a little difficult to understand exactly what was going on.

Is it any wonder that the large businesses of America are just moving out of the country or paying off the more radical, strident groups, such as NOW, which could cause them trouble?

Why Is America Upset?

You can ask a man named Paul Johnson (and possibly his wife) why America is upset. He went all the way to the U. S. Supreme Court for his "learning experience."

Johnson spent 17 years of his life maintaining and improving highways for a private company before being employed by a county highway department in 1967. After seven years at the county, he tried to become a dispatcher but came in second. In 1979 he finally came in first.[3]

But Paul Johnson didn't get the job.

DO WOMEN NEED SPECIAL TREATMENT?

It went to Diane Joyce. Why? Because she is a woman, and therefore *she needs special treatment.*

Johnson was tied for second on a written exam with a score of 75 while Joyce was next with a 73. After an interview, Johnson was selected. But he never got the job because the county's "Affirmative Action Office" told the county director that the woman must be promoted. The decision was solely based upon sex. Naturally, Johnson was a little upset. So he appealed to a U. S. judge who had a trial and agreed with him. The judge found that Paul was "more qualified for the position of Road Dispatcher than Diane Joyce" and that "[b]ut for [his] sex, male, he would have been promoted to the position of Road Dispatcher" and "[b]ut for Diane Joyce's sex, female, she would not have been appointed to the position...." This violated the Civil Rights Act, the judge said.

But his arguments didn't matter when the case came before the U. S. Supreme Court inasmuch as we already know that the Court's goal is to "balance" the workforce. Its goal is to make the number of women equal to the number of men in every position. And that is required, says the Supreme Court, by the Civil Rights Act of 1964.[4]

Do you remember hearing that when the Civil Rights Act was passed?

A dissenting judge pointed out that large corporations are not unhappy with the result (many of them had even gone so far as to file papers with the court arguing against Johnson). It's much easier for big business to go along with the EEOC and hire less qualified workers than it is to fight. And it wants all of the other businesses in the same boat because this is obviously raising the costs for the large businesses. It also doesn't want any white males causing trouble with them. The judge said:

"[T]he cost [to a large corporation] of hiring less qualified workers is often substantially less—and infinitely more predictable—than the cost of litigating Title VII cases and of seeking to convince federal agencies by nonnumerical means that no discrimination exists."[5]

Let me rephrase that quotation just a little:

"It's easier for big business to pay the extortion than it is to fight for the truth. And if *it's* being extorted, it wants all of the other businesses in the same boat."

Many of the "elite" made much of the fact that Paul Johnson was only a "little more" qualified than Ms. Joyce. They will point out that she also worked very hard to learn this position. But neither of these answers the basic question:

Must women receive special treatment?

Sears Roebuck is Unfairly Attacked

Why have the businesses decided that it is easier to pay the extortion than it is to fight? Let's take a look at what the U.S. government did to Sears Roebuck... solely because of the "woman problem."

You may say you're not interested in the problems of Sears. However, it is part of "our team" that would like to hire 1) you, 2) your spouse, 3) your children and 4) many others. And you can rest assured that any increased costs at Sears must be passed on to you, the consumer.

Sears was very proud of its "affirmative action" program. It had a right to be. It was the first major retail store in the entire country to have such a program. It became a model that was followed by other retailers and even by other industries.*

In 1968 Sears appointed its first "Equal Opportunity Director" and it voluntarily declared itself to be a government contractor which meant that it would *voluntarily* be subject to the review of the President's OFCCP. It believed that this would be a good example for other American businesses.[6] No other national retail merchant followed the lead of Sears, but the OFCCP did inspect Sears over 2,000 times.[7] It was favorably impressed.[8]

But not the EEOC. Remember it began its assault on American business in 1972 after it was given the power to sue any business that it wished. It started suit against the big ones first because then the rest would fall into line. It started its suit against Sears in 1973. But unlike AT&T, General Electric, and the rest, Sears did not cave in. Why should it? It was proud of its record. And besides, it couldn't move any of its retail stores overseas as could the manufacturers. It had to stay here.

---

* One of the members of the EEOC, a black, civil rights lawyer, Colston A. Lewis, said:

"Sears has the best damn affirmative action program of any company in the country," and

"The Commission is harassing Sears and GM because this is the way the chairman can get headlines. This kind of pressure isn't even legal." See *Duns,* June 1974, p. 82

DO WOMEN NEED SPECIAL TREATMENT?

Thirteen years later, after years of legal battle and 10 months of actual trial before a U. S. judge, the company won in 1986. But the EEOC was still not satisfied, and it appealed to the U. S. Court of Appeals in Chicago. So back to court again went Sears, and it won again in 1988. What was the cost to an American business of fighting this battle? What was the cost to the taxpayer of the EEOC lawyers, statisticians and clerks? What was the cost of tying up a U.S. judge for all of those years?[9]

And what was it all about?

The EEOC started with a list of grievances of how Sears discriminated against women, but it eventually withdrew all but one of the grievances.[10]

The suit involved the sales people in the appliance department. Have you ever noticed when you walk through a Sears store that you have to hunt for a clerk to help you? But when you are in the section with refrigerators or washing machines, you suddenly have helpful people at your side. That's because the person selling large appliances is on commission. The more he sells, the more he makes. Let's change that to, the more he *or she* sells, the more he *or she* makes. Because the EEOC was saying that most of those higher paid sales people were men. And that was discrimination. It was a violation of federal law.

Sears answered that it knew very well that these sales people were mostly men. But this was true only because women wouldn't take the job. The company was trying as hard as it could to get more women in the commission area, but they simply weren't interested. They didn't want to go. And Sears even changed its standards to try to attract women.[11]

That's right, Sears even changed its standards so that more women would take this job. (How much have American companies lowered their standards as a result of the Civil Rights Act? There is no survey that I know of, but here is one example.)

How did Sears change its standards? It had always made sure that its salesmen were very "hungry." If they didn't make any sales, they didn't get any money. If they made a lot of sales, they got a lot of money. The men liked this system. It gave them a chance to earn good money—if they were good. Until 1977, these commission salesmen were paid commission between 6%-9% of their sales.

FREEDOM WILL CONQUER RACISM (AND SEXISM)

But the female applicants did not like this kind of selling. Many surveys which were taken by a frustrated Sears showed that the women disliked the "dog-eat-dog" competition that prevents friendships at work.[12] They liked the non-commission selling because it was more enjoyable and friendly. They didn't think the increased money was worth the increased pressure, tension and risk. Also, the women didn't feel comfortable selling machinery. It didn't appeal to them.[13]

So Sears changed its policies to make the women happier.

The company did away with commission salespeople. It gave them a salary plus bonus. However, the sales volume of women proved that they didn't like even this. They sold less as a group than men did.[14] Therefore, the cost to Sears of having a woman sell a refrigerator was more than if a man sold it. *And, of course, that added cost must be paid by consumers.*

Despite all of these facts which showed that the "productivity" in the sales department was slipping because of the hiring of more women, Sears was doing a "good job" of selling women on taking the job. From 1973 to 1979, the number of females hired into commission sales went from 20% to 40%.[15] The number in part-time sales was 52.3%.[16]

Just what did the EEOC want from Sears? *If women don't want to sell refrigerators, should we as a society tell them that they have to?* Some feminists will retort that the reason that women don't wish to compete or sell machinery is because that is the way they have been conditioned since childhood and it *is* the responsibility of Sears and other businesses to help women "recondition" themselves to the feminist point of view.

The government did not produce one woman during the entire 10-month trial that had ever been discriminated against.[17] It used statistics to "prove" its case.[18] And the trial judge said that these statistics were "highly misleading" and "flawed."[19]

If the EEOC went through such an expensive and exhaustive lawsuit against a company which had *volunteered* to have government inspectors come in and inspect its policies, what do you think the executives of other companies must think?

The fear of the "big bully" has American business looking at other things than putting together the best work force possible to compete with Japan and the rest of the world.

DO WOMEN NEED SPECIAL TREATMENT?

It was during this period that Sears slipped badly in its business. Was it because this suit was so distracting and caused bad publicity? One must wonder.

No One Knew What The "Law" Was

Or look what the EEOC did to Libbey-Owens, the glass company.[20] This business had *always* required in its production line that the employees be of a certain height and weight so that they could do the heavy work that was necessary in the factories.

The company was concerned about (1) the safety of the workers and (2) the efficiency of the plant.

But then came the Civil Rights Act and someone decided that this was "discrimination" because women are smaller than men. Do you think that Hubert Humphrey or any other Senator would have dared to say that Libbey-Owens was guilty of violating the law?

Don't forget that many state laws at that time still "protected" women. They couldn't be required to lift more than 25 pounds, work at night, etc. etc. So after the Civil Rights Act was passed, many companies had a state law telling them they could *not* hire a woman for a particular job and now a new federal law which told them they *had* to hire them. Which law were they to follow? It was *years* before the frustrated companies finally learned, after many court suits, what law they were expected to obey.

Do you know what a lawyer for the EEOC told a meeting of businessmen during that period?

"Obey the state law and wait until the court says you're wrong."[21]

Just think about that for a moment. <u>No one</u> knew what the law was. No one.

But *if* a business did break a law, whichever one it was, the business would be punished and labeled as *sexist*.

As for Libbey-Owens, a settlement was finally reached in 1971 between the EEOC and Libbey-Owens that the minimum for women would be 110 pounds and 5'4". Imagine the surprise and disgust at Libbey-Owens when it was sued again a few years later by the same EEOC, this time in Illinois. It was told that its previous settlement only applied to its Ohio plant and it was discriminating against women in violation of federal law in its Illinois plant. How could the Civil Rights Act of 1964 possibly mean one thing for women employees in Ohio and a different thing in Illinois?

FREEDOM WILL CONQUER RACISM (AND SEXISM)

Now, we can sit here and argue for days whether the size and strength of an employee in a factory is 1) necessary for the safety of the other employees and for efficient production or (2) unfair to women. But such an argument is useless because that decision will be decided by a federal judge who's never been in a factory in his or her life.

What is more important is, "Why is this company being <u>punished?</u>" If Congress wants to eliminate height and weight requirements, why doesn't it say so? Why didn't it hold hearings on this question and make a decision, instead of passing a Civil Rights law for women in two hours on a Saturday afternoon without any intelligent discussion whatsoever? Why must Libbey-Owens have to try to guess what the law is? Why must it be punished? It wants to obey the law if for no other reason than it has to.

No town ordinance as vague as the Civil Rights Act of 1964 would ever be allowed to stand by a federal judge.

Do you know what finally happened to Libbey-Owens? It fought this case for 11 years. The government spent over $300,000 of our tax dollars on it. You can imagine what Libbey-Owens spent. Finally the company gave in and settled. Do you know why? Because the judge pressured it to do so.

And do you know what the judge said when Libbey-Owens said it had never intended to discriminate against women, and it had merely tried to protect the safety of its workers and improve its production? The judge said:

"[T]he motivation of the Company in initially formulating and imposing the height and weight requirements is *irrelevant*." [emphasis added]

Irrelevant!?

Is that judge talking about the same Civil Rights Act that we are talking about? And the same Act that Senator Humphrey was talking about back in 1964? We know that the "intent" of the company is crucial; it is written right into the Act.

And what was the penalty that Libbey-Owens had to pay for "breaking the law?" It had to pay about $10 million in fines to the women who were known to have applied for jobs. It had to pay even those who said they *would* have applied *if* they had known they could get a job there.

DO WOMEN NEED SPECIAL TREATMENT?

It had to make 342 jobs available to this group of women as openings arose and these new employees got back-dated seniority.

Does anyone doubt that Libbey-Owens has been punished?

If you ran that company, would you think of moving it overseas?

More Special Treatment

What is happening to our country as a result of the Civil Rights Act of 1964 and similar state laws?

- Next time you go to the beach you can wonder whether a lifeguard should weigh at least 135 pounds. It is no longer legal to have that requirement inasmuch as most women don't weigh that much.[22]
- You might wonder about the women appointed as guards in all-male prisons, which disregards the fact that the men have a right to privacy while nude or in the bathroom and the fact that women guards are in danger of sexual attack by the prisoners. The judges have "balanced" the equities and decided that the rights of women are more important.[23] The state of Arkansas agreed in 1997 to hire 400 more female guards in men's prisons after being sued by the U.S. government. The female guards will do everything except strip searches, including monitoring the showers.[24]
- You might question the judge who ordered a prison to hire a woman cook despite the fears of sexual attack.[25]
- How about the psychiatric orderlies who are required to form a close relationship with the male patients? The EEOC decided that the psychiatrists were wrong and that a woman would be a satisfactory orderly for these male patients.[26]
- How about the Catholic High School which was not allowed to dismiss a woman who had an illegitimate child. It did not matter that this was against the teachings of their religion.[27]
- Or the woman construction worker who won in court because the toilets out in the field were dirty.[28]
- Or the woman executive who wouldn't go on trips with her boss unless she could bring a secretary along with her as a chaperone.[29]
- Or the woman executive whose lover suddenly became her boss as well as that of another woman with whom he was also

having an affair. When he transferred the executive to another job, the jilted woman sued the company.[30]
- Or the court that said where a social worker was required to have a college education, this could no longer be required.[31]

These are not isolated cases. They are typical of *thousands* of cases that I could report to you that are affecting every company in America, individually and alone in a quiet courtroom with no fanfare.

Special Treatment Needed?

The majority of American women do not believe that they should be given any "special treatment."

A Gallup poll reports that only one woman in five wants special treatment in hiring.[32] And another poll taken shortly after the *Johnson* case (which concerned the man who was rejected by a county highway department) shows that women disagree with the U.S. Supreme Court's decision by a 2-1 majority.[33]

So we are back to the central issue that women in America must decide.

We cannot approach the changes in our society with hate, anger and fear. We must be able to talk about them in an intelligent way.

Do women need special treatment or do they merely want to be treated fairly, honestly and with respect? Do the laws which "protect" them start with a sexist premise that they are not as capable as men? Will a woman engineer *ever* be able to obtain any respect when everyone wonders if she is merely another "token" that the company had to put on the payroll?

If the society of which our women are a part begins to falter, will she end up ahead or behind? Should American business be punished or should we work together for change that will improve the lives of everyone?

If we create an atmosphere wherein everyone is afraid to discuss the issues, will we have improved our society and our lives, or will we have damaged them?

Can there be one organization that speaks for the needs of *all* of the women?

Those are just a few of the many questions that the women of America must ask themselves.

17

IT'S A CONFLICT AMONG WOMEN — NOT MEN

The "Women's Movement" is usually thought to be the result of a conflict between the men and women of America. But that is not true.

It is a conflict *among women.*

The world is not divided between men and women. How is it divided?

- It's divided between those <u>people</u>, men and women, who wish to have the family as the basic unit of our society and those *people*, men and women, who wish to change that tradition.
- It's divided between those <u>people</u> who believe we must keep our moral structure or our society will decay and those <u>people</u> who believe, incorrectly, that free and easy sex has always been available to males and therefore should also be available to females.
- It is divided between those <u>people</u> who believe that everyone should have the choice of either staying at home and/or having a job to help support their family or having a serious career and those <u>people</u> who believe that *everyone* should be forced to

FREEDOM WILL CONQUER RACISM (AND SEXISM)

work outside of the home, with the children being supported by "the village," which will be the federal government.

It is a conflict between 1) radical, elitist feminists, which includes a large number of lesbians (it is not homophobic to point out the obvious fact that many lesbians feel they do not share in any of the advantages of the traditional family and would therefore like to change to a new system), and 2) the rest of the women who wish to make their own choice.

We readers saw that the four women who were picked as the "leaders" of feminism are not the usual women that you know.

But not many American women realize this. This is a conflict between the radical, elitist feminists of NOW and the other women of America.

Most married women are working just to pay the very high taxes which have resulted from the policies of NOW.

In 1950, the average American family with children paid 2% of its income in federal taxes. Today, they pay 25%, and if you include their state and local taxes, that swells to 38% of their income. But the average woman in a family earns about 34% of the total income of the family. That means that more than the *total* income of the average working woman with a family, is being used to pay taxes.

There are groups of women that do realize this.* The largest is Concerned Women for America (CWA), which has more than double the number of members as NOW (600,000 compared to 250,000). But you never hear of it. The members of CWA are mostly at home raising their families, whereas most of the women in the press and other businesses belong to NOW. Therefore, the press always calls NOW when it needs a comment on anything, but you won't read about CWA in your newspaper or hear about it on TV.**

An interesting survey was done for CWA by the polling company, Wirthlin Worldwide, of women who were *not* members of CWA. That survey showed that 67% of the women are aware of NOW, and 46% say they agree with what NOW stands for. Only 19% disagree.

The survey also discovered that these women wouldn't agree with NOW if they knew the goals of the organization. On most issues

---

* A list of these organizations is found in the appendix.

** An example is a *Boston Globe* story in which it said that NOW is "the largest women's rights organization in the world...." July 1, 1993, p. 25.

IT'S A CONFLICT AMONG WOMEN—NOT MEN

these women want something totally different than NOW does. For example, the survey showed:
- A surprising 80% of the women would like to stay home and be a full-time mother if they could afford it.
- As for abortion, 11% were totally against abortion, 13% thought it should be prohibited except to save the life of the mother, 30% thought it should be prohibited except in cases of rape, incest or to save the life of the mother, for a total of 54% who were against an unlimited right to abortion.
- As for homosexuality, 66% said that it was more important for the government to support traditional family values while 23% said it was more important to promote tolerance for alternative lifestyles and family structures. However, when asked whether sexual orientation should be added to civil rights laws, 59% answered yes. But only 31% favor homosexual marriage while 59% opposed it. And 58% opposed allowing homosexuals to adopt children.
- 76% favored voluntary school prayer.

There's no question but that this survey shows that the effect of the "elite," liberal media has been profound on American women. The women know about NOW and they believe they support it although if they only knew, they actually *dis*agree with most of what it stands for.

What are some of the things that NOW says it is working to accomplish?
- **Favors "Partial Birth" Abortions.** This type of procedure is used only in the last months of pregnancy and is accomplished by cutting the baby's neck as it is born. Congress passed a law outlawing this procedure but President Clinton vetoed it. NOW termed it a "grievous and hateful piece of legislation that accurately reflects the disdain the extremist Republican leadership has for women."[1]
- **Approves Other Extreme Positions on Abortion.** In other abortion matters, NOW is against notifying parents of minors before an abortion takes place. NOW favors providing abortions for women in federal prisons; requiring that *all* gynecologists *must* be trained to perform abortions; the use of fetuses in research including becoming pregnant just for that purpose; etc. The list goes on and on.[2]

- **Endorses Gay Marriages.** With Hawaii apparently on the verge of approving gay marriages, there was concern that every state would have to recognize a gay marriage that took place in Hawaii, which meant that any person could fly to Hawaii for a ceremony, and every state would be required to recognize it. Therefore, Congress passed a bill which said that other states could not be required to recognize a Hawaiian marriage. NOW called this a "hateful campaign against lesbian and gay citizens."[3]
- **Led Fight Against Colorado's Constitutional Amendment.** After Colorado amended its Constitution to forbid towns and cities from enacting laws that would favor homosexuals, NOW was the leader in the successful fight to nullify the decision of Colorado citizens. After the U.S. Supreme Court struck down the Colorado Constitution, NOW said: [W]e need to make sure Bob Dole doesn't get an opportunity to appoint any more homophobic, right wing justices to the high court."[4]
- **Against Welfare Reform.** Even though most agree that our welfare system needs a drastic overhaul, NOW opposed "Passage of ANY of the welfare dismantling proposals before Congress...."[5]
- **Favors Raising Minimum Wage.** They favored raising the minimum wage from $4.25/hour to $5.15 even though this will mean a loss of jobs for teenagers, particularly black teenagers.[6]
- **Attacked "Promise Keepers" as promoting "homophobia, patriarchy and misogyny."** "Promise Keepers" is a 600,000 member group of Christian men led by former Colorado University football coach Bill McCartney which is helping men to remain loyal and faithful to their families by following biblical teachings. "NOW activists in Colorado, Michigan and across the country have staged protests and conducted media interviews regarding Promise Keeper events."[7]
- **Favors Quotas (called "Affirmative Action").** NOW favors retaining all of the quota systems now in place.[8]

These are only a very few of the positions that NOW is aggressively working toward even though most women have no idea of it.

IT'S A CONFLICT AMONG WOMEN—NOT MEN

They Do Not Like Women At-Home

Betty Friedan, a "conservative" leader of the feminist movement, put it this way:

"[W]hen a woman defines herself as a housewife, the house and things in it are, in a sense, her identity; she needs these external trappings to buttress her emptiness of self ..."[9]

More radical leaders said it more bluntly: Bourgeois women are the "ultimate, useless parasite."[10]

But many woman would disagree with those conclusions. There are many women in America who, rightly or wrongly, would take issue with the fact that they are "parasites" because they choose to stay at home.

This is a conflict between those women who wish to stay at home and those women who for whatever reason, whether necessity or personal taste, would like a career.

There is no reason why both types should not be satisfied, but right now the entire thrust is to require *every* woman to work outside of the home.

When we hear someone say that they speak for "all" women, the alarm bells should sound. This is the type of talk that leads to the worst forms of racism and sexism. Will we never learn?

No large group of people is monolithic.

How can any intelligent person possibly say that they speak for "all" women? We have tall women, short women, smart women and not-so-smart women, aggressive women and placid women. All types and all shapes.

And yet there are highly aggressive women out there who are attempting to portray themselves as the leaders of all women.

But most American women who do not work do not yet realize that these changes are going to reach right into their home and affect them as well. They are the "parasites" in the present picture of things. If we have government day care centers and payments to homemakers, we can be assured that it won't be very long before there are 20 children assigned to a woman and the rest of the mothers will be out working "where they belong" instead of staying at home and taking care of just one child as the "parasites" do today.

These words of mine will sound just as "far-fetched" as the predictions that were made about the Civil Rights Act back in 1964.

FREEDOM WILL CONQUER RACISM (AND SEXISM)

Instead of promoting "sexism" and "racism" and trying to force everyone into a mold that suits the most verbal, aggressive people, why can't we give everyone the freedom to choose his or her own life style?

Who Speaks for Women?

We started hearing about the gender gap in the 1980s. A day after Senator Dan Quayle was nominated as Vice President in 1988, the usually fair Robert McNeil asked him on the McNeil-Lehrer News Hour how he could possibly close the "gender gap." All the "women's groups" were saying, according to McNeil, that Quayle was unacceptable to them.

Who were these "women's groups" that McNeil was throwing in Quayle's face? Would we agree that it was probably NOW? Do you think that McNeil asked Concerned Women of America what they thought about Quayle?

Probably the most important reason why McNeil didn't ask CWA is that the women who are working in McNeil's office and in the rest of the press are likely to be members of NOW. And those who write the news give all of their attention to NOW.

Another very important reason is that NOW is rich because it gets a substantial amount of money from our large corporations and also from the large foundations on which these businessmen and women also sit.

Is it a payoff? Do the contributions from the large corporations and foundations stop the EEOC from further punishing those corporations which give to liberal women's groups? We don't know why they give to these organizations, but they do.

We do know that the President's commission, the OFCCP, has forced government contractors to "donate" money to these liberal groups, according to a former director.

"Some officials even arm-twist business to make payments to activist political groups such as the NAACP, the Urban League, and the Mexican-American Legal Defense Fund. Says former director [Ellen Shong] Bergman: 'The OFCCP, on an individual basis...has at some time in the past pressured contractors to make contributions of one sort or another.'"[11]

IT'S A CONFLICT AMONG WOMEN—NOT MEN

Concerned Women for America gets absolutely nothing from them. The studies of the Capital Research Center, for example, show that in 1985 feminist groups got more than $472,000 from our leading corporations. And how much did they get from our foundations? NOW received $525,000, from the Ford Foundation alone; Steinem's group, the Ms. Foundation, received $600,000 from the Ford Foundation and at least $230,000 from other foundations.

The Ford Foundation also gave over $1.4 million to other feminist groups.

In 1994, NOW got $1.2 million in contributions.

So what appeared to be a grassroots agenda which Robert McNeil threw at the embattled Quayle is not "grassroots" at all, but is a program supported and financed by the big businesses of America and their foundations.

18

"SEXUAL HARASSMENT" LAW HAS CHANGED OUR MORALS AND DAMAGED WOMEN

The concept of "sexual harassment" was not written into the Civil Rights Act by Congress. It is another creation of the federal judges with the approval of the U.S. Supreme Court. The courts have interpreted the word "discriminate" in a manner which has 1) changed the morals of our country for the worse, and 2) made it more difficult for *hard-working, diligent* women.

The case that the Supreme Court used to approve this new idea involved Mechelle Vinson, a woman in Washington, D.C., who said she had sex with her boss. She was also promoted very rapidly.[1]

Did Vinson get her promotions because she went to bed with her boss? Or did she have a lot of ability? We'll never know the answer to those questions. (The U.S. judge who heard the case did not believe Vinson.)

That is not new to the world. Good looking, young women have often risen rapidly in business and social life because they were attractive to men. It has been happening ever since the world began.

So what's new?

"SEXUAL HARASSMENT" LAW HAS CHANGED OUR MORALS AND DAMAGED WOMEN

Who Should Sue?

If we're going to stop this type of conduct, who should sue and receive money in a case such as this?

- The other employees? The other employees might sue Vinson or the boss because an "unfair" element has been introduced into the workplace. Why Vinson received her rapid promotions will always be suspect to the other employees. How can they compete if a woman uses sex as a tactic?
- The bank? If this type of thing is going on, it's going to hurt the company in two ways. First, the most qualified employees will not be the ones who will be promoted, and therefore the business will suffer. Second, an excellent employee is not going to hang around a company very long if it operates in this fashion.
- Vinson or her boss? One of them could possibly sue the other. The career of each would be seriously damaged if this became known.

The story that you are about to read is true, according to Vinson. Her story became a landmark decision in the United States Supreme Court.

Who do you think the U.S. Supreme Court allowed to sue under The Civil Rights Act of 1964?

Vinson's Story[2] (As told by her)

Mechelle Vinson's story began in Washington, D. C., on a morning in September, 1974, on busy Rhode Island Avenue, N.E.

She was an eager young 19-year-old black woman with a high school equivalency degree and part-time work experience. She sat in a car in front of a dilapidated sidewalk and store front in Northeast Washington. Nearby was building number 2010, home to the Northeast branch of Capital City Savings and Loan Association.

Vinson knew that Sidney Taylor was the manager of the Capital City bank, which sits among two short rows of businesses that line both sides of Rhode Island Avenue.

Taylor was on his regular walk to the post office less than a quarter-mile down the street when Vinson blew her car horn and beckoned him to speak with her. When he approached the car, the petite, attractive Vinson asked about a job at Taylor's Northeast branch. The

FREEDOM WILL CONQUER RACISM (AND SEXISM)

40-year-old bank manager told her to come into the bank. She did and he gave her an application to complete.³

The next day, on Sidney Taylor's recommendation, Capital City officials hired Vinson and assigned her to Taylor's branch. It was the first steady, full-time job she ever held—she had worked briefly at a food store and a shoe store as well as an exercise club before that. In fact, this new job was perhaps a welcome symbol of stability in a life marked by turmoil.

A rocky relationship with her father had made her childhood a nightmare. She had repeatedly run away from home, lost her hair and her ability to swallow because of stress, and had visited a court-appointed psychiatrist. At one point, Vinson's mother tried to put her troubled daughter in a foster home. Vinson was 14 or 15 when she married an older man, a friend of her family's.⁴

When Mechelle Vinson reported to Taylor's Northeast bank branch on September 9, 1974, only teller Christine Malone and Taylor worked there. Under Capital City's system, Vinson would undergo a 90-day probation period. Vinson sailed through this period and earned the first of several promotions to $6,500 per year.⁵

Taylor took Vinson under his wing. He helped her through her work, gave her banking books to read so she could move up the ladder as he had, and encouraged her to succeed.⁶

But Taylor was not treating Vinson's new friend Christine Malone with the same respect. In front of Vinson, Taylor was fondling the married Malone—touching her buttocks, back and breasts. In the bank's back room, he was chasing her and making sexual advances. Vinson tried not to let Taylor's behavior diminish her high opinion of the boss. She ignored his advances to her friend Christine.⁷

Vinson had problems of her own. Her rocky marriage was disintegrating. By early 1975, she had moved in with her mother and was searching for a place of her own to live. Sidney Taylor was more than a boss during these trying times. He was a confidant.

In the meantime, the other teller, Christine, had left the bank because she had money shortages and trouble balancing her teller sheets.

On May 6, 1975, Vinson found a place of her own to live. Taylor was a big help; he gave her some cash to help pay for her apartment. That seemed in line with Taylor's general kindness.⁸ Previously, he

"SEXUAL HARASSMENT" LAW HAS CHANGED OUR MORALS AND DAMAGED WOMEN

had paid her overtime pay for hours she never worked. Vinson accepted the fraudulent money without protest.

However, Vinson began to notice a change in Taylor's attitude toward her.

With Christine gone, Vinson and Taylor worked alone together in the bank. About two weeks after Vinson moved into her new apartment, Taylor offered to take her to dinner after work. Vinson accepted. Taylor had often taken Vinson and Christine to lunch at a Chinese restaurant about a quarter-mile from the bank.

The restaurant was at the intersection of Bladensburg Road and New York Avenue, about a five minute drive from the bank. The small Chinese restaurant is connected to a large motel. In fact, the Chinese eatery is but a small portion of the motel. It is barely discernible among the bedrooms which surround it and its courtyard.

As the unsuspecting Vinson ate, Taylor made a surprising suggestion: that the pair finish their meal, get a hotel room and have sexual intercourse.[9]

"I have been better to you, more than your husband," Taylor told the unsuspecting Vinson.

"Well, Mr. Taylor, I appreciate that," Vinson responded.

"I don't want appreciation, I want to go to bed with you," an insistent Taylor replied.

"I don't want to go to bed with you," Vinson shot back.

"Just like I hired you, I'll fire you, just like I made you, I'll break you, and if you don't do what I say then I'll have you killed," was Taylor's blunt reply. A terrified Vinson agreed to accompany Taylor to a motel room because she was afraid she would lose her job.[10]

When Taylor dropped Vinson off at her apartment about 7:00 or 7:30 p.m., the still naive young woman hoped that would be the end of sex between Taylor and herself. She would not be so lucky. In fact, Taylor's torment of Vinson was just beginning. The next day at work, Taylor began the same treatment of Vinson he had perpetrated against Christine Malone. He felt her buttocks and breasts and verbally tormented her. Vinson felt sick inside but did not know what to do or who to tell about her problem. The touching and feeling occurred 20 times that day and every succeeding day.

For three years, the then 22-year-old had been forced to have sexual intercourse with Sidney Taylor 40 or 50 times—all on bank property except for the initial motel advance. He often raped her, once so brutally that it led to serious vaginal bleeding for which she required a doctor's care.[11]

Vinson's life was a walking hell. She had nowhere to turn. Fortunately, at least, her job was going well. Unrelated to the sexual harassment by Taylor, Vinson was promoted to head teller and then to assistant manager by 1977. All promotions and her significant increases in pay were the result of Vinson's outstanding abilities.[12]

At the start of 1978, Vinson found herself a steady boyfriend. At that point, almost as suddenly as it began, Sidney Taylor's sexual harassment of her ceased. In addition, Vinson was promised a bank branch of her own.[13] By the end of the year she would be a manager far away from Sidney Taylor. But for Vinson, it was too late. She could never forget the torment through which Sidney Taylor forced her to live. The nights of lost sleep caused by his actions were not easily erased from her memory. Vinson simply could not wait for her promised promotion. She searched for a way out.

So goes the story of Mechelle Vinson.

What Should Happen to a Rapist?

If the story of Vinson is 100 percent factual, what should be done about such behavior on the part of Sidney Taylor?

The answer is obvious.

We have criminal laws against assault and we also have criminal laws against rape. Taylor should be criminally charged.

But that was *never* done.

Taylor's Story

Sidney Taylor denies all of Vinson's story.[14]

Taylor portrays himself as "too good"; he is always looking to help other people. Vinson was a perfect opportunity for the church deacon and father of seven children, three of them girls. Vinson was from the neighborhood, seemed bright and ambitious, and sorely needed a helping hand.

He either did not know or did not care about her history of instability when he hired her.

So he had reason to feel good about himself when he drove the three-quarters of a mile to his modest brownstone that night after hiring Vinson. He had given another young neighborhood kid a

"SEXUAL HARASSMENT" LAW HAS CHANGED OUR MORALS AND DAMAGED WOMEN

chance at a better life. Banking had worked for Taylor; why not for Mechelle Vinson?

Sidney Taylor was himself a walking success story in his small world. He was a high school graduate with 12 years of U.S. Army experience under his belt.

Eight years earlier, he had been hired by Capital City as a janitor and messenger—his opportunity for a better life was laid out just as Vinson's had been that September morning. It took Taylor only a year and a half to begin his rise to the top. He attended a savings and loan school and progressed in the company. Eventually, Taylor worked his way up to manager of Capital City's Northeast branch—a significant achievement for a black man with no college education.[15]

Who Was Sued?

So who got sued as a result of all of this?

Mechelle Vinson never filed any criminal charges against Taylor. She filed a civil suit to try to collect $200,000 *from the bank*.

The Bank Is Sued—by Mechelle

Vinson called in "sick" on September 21, 1978, and filed her suit in the U.S. District Court on the next day alleging sexual harassment *by the bank*. She said this was a violation of the Civil Rights Act.

She told the Washington Post that she called in "sick" on a lawyer's advice once she realized that she could sue the bank.[16]

But when it finally came time for a trial, Vinson did not do very well in the courthouse just across from the Capitol. She called two other tellers who testified that Taylor had also harassed them. But neither did well on cross-examination by the bank's lawyer.

The first teller, Christine Malone, was the one who had been working at the bank when Vinson first started. She suffered under cross-examination in several areas. She said that she had quit the bank because of "the harassment by Mr. Taylor, the sexual harassment that he wanted in order to stay there. He wanted to have sex." But after cross examination it was clear she left because she had a significant shortfall and trouble in balancing her teller sheet.

The next teller to raise her right hand and swear to tell the truth was Mary Levarity, who at one point had been engaged to Vinson's cousin. She had worked at the branch for one month. She said that Taylor harassed her also, but she also said that she complained only to Vinson, who told her, "He don't mean it." Vinson said that this woman was fired for refusing to have sex with Taylor, but the bank's main office showed that she was fired because her teller sheets did not balance 33 times in her 90-day probationary period.

Another teller was called not by Vinson but by the bank. Vinson had testified in depositions before the trial began that this woman, Doretha McCallum, was also harassed by Taylor. But McCallum denied that. She testified that Vinson was the one who was always talking about sex (such as Vinson would wish she had some oysters and "come") and she was no more discreet when Taylor was present. McCallum said she had suspected there was something going on between Vinson and Taylor—their close working relationship and Vinson's provocative style of dressing raised the suspicion. Vinson would commonly wear shirts which revealed half or more of the breasts; her skirts were short.* When McCallum had raised the issue of Vinson's relationship with Taylor, she was confronted by an angry Vinson, who was upset about the "rumor." Vinson, according to McCallum, had strongly denied that anything was going on between Taylor and herself.

McCallum also recounted a fantasy that Vinson had told her: Her grandfather returned to life as a young man and had sex with her. Vinson had also told her that Mary Levarity was a prostitute who on one occasion charged Sidney Taylor $50 to have oral sex. McCallum testified that one male customer referred to Vinson as a "wild chick." Finally, McCallum said that Vinson thought very highly of Sidney Taylor.

And there was other testimony that hurt Vinson. Although she said she was in fear of Taylor, the bank revealed that she had turned

---

* A reviewer of this book tells me that what Vinson wears is *her* business. That raises some interesting points. 1) Everyone, including *every* woman, knows that *every* man will be distracted by an attractive woman who displays her body in a provocative manner; and any business will suffer when the employees are distracted from the serious business of the company in that manner. 2) If a woman says that she was harassed by her supervisor *against her will* and even brutally raped, would she be likely to keep coming to work in provocative clothing? Even the Supreme Court agreed with this reasoning at 477 U.S. at 69.

"SEXUAL HARASSMENT" LAW HAS CHANGED OUR MORALS AND DAMAGED WOMEN

down two transfers that would have gotten her into another branch of the bank.

The Judge Rules

A U. S. District Court judge sat in his courtroom and listened to this sordid tale for more than two weeks. When it was finally over, he held that an employer could be liable for "sexual harassment" under the Civil Rights Act. But this bank had never had any notice of what was going on. Even if everything that Vinson had said was true, how could the bank be at fault? Neither Vinson nor any other employee had ever made any complaint to them about any problems in the Rhode Island Avenue branch.[17]

How could the bank correct anything if no one had told them what was happening?[18]

And as to the important issue of whether Vinson was telling the truth?

The judge didn't believe her.* He said that *if* any sex was taking place it was purely voluntary on Vinson's part. He dismissed the suit, holding that Vinson was not a victim of sexual harassment.[19]

The Appeal

Vinson had lost her case. The judge did not believe her. And even if he had, he would not have held the bank liable because it didn't know that anything was going on.

But not to worry.

Vinson was becoming something of a cause celebre. Groups like Equal Rights Advocates, the Working Women's Institute of New York, the Women's Legal Defense Fund, and others began to take interest. Her attorney, Patricia J. Barry of California, stayed with the case despite great personal sacrifice.

---

* A boyfriend told the *Washington Post* that Vinson and the two tellers who testified for her were "totally" lying. The boyfriend was living with Vinson when she left the bank. He said the whole thing was premeditated. "It's a distorted operation that she is making up to make money. They're not little innocent girls. They are streetwise. I know the people they hang out with. I know that she's a very flirtatious person. I lived with her for two years. That's how she gets her jobs." *Washington Post,* August 12, 1986, p. C2.

FREEDOM WILL CONQUER RACISM (AND SEXISM)

And so an appeal was taken to the U. S. Court of Appeals.

A three-person panel of the court sat on February 16, 1982, in that low, white granite building on Constitution Avenue, just a few blocks from the U. S. Supreme Court, and heard Vinson's lawyers argue that the trial judge had made a mistake.

And three years later, in January, 1985, the judges finally announced that they had decided the case: The trial judge was wrong. He must hear the case again.[20]

On to the Supreme Court

By now the Capital City Federal Savings and Loan Association was bankrupt. But the company that bought it felt that it had to appeal the decision to the U. S. Supreme Court.

Whether Vinson and Taylor had ever had sex, and, if so, when and where, and who had instigated it was becoming a very important issue.

And so on to the U. S. Supreme Court went this case of alleged sex in the vault on Rhode Island Avenue.[21]

Many people were by now very much interested. Twenty-nine members of Congress filed papers in favor of Vinson, as did the AFL-CIO, the National Education Association, and many others.

And in June, 1986, the Supreme Court held unanimously that indeed there did have to be another trial because the trial judge had made some serious mistakes. Here is what the U. S. Supreme Court told the trial judge that he must do:

1. There was a new cause of action under the Civil Rights Act called sexual harassment.
2. The bank could be liable to Vinson even if it had no knowledge whatsoever about what was going on.
3. If Vinson did have sexual intercourse with Taylor, it wasn't important that she had voluntarily agreed to have sexual relations. The trial judge (and therefore any business in any future case where employees were having sex together) had to determine whether the sex was "welcomed" by her.
4. Even if her job wasn't in jeopardy at any time, the bank could still be liable. The question was, was Taylor allowed to create an "abusive working environment?" If so, then the bank could be liable to her.

"SEXUAL HARASSMENT" LAW HAS CHANGED OUR MORALS AND DAMAGED WOMEN

So now this U. S. judge had to decide if there had been sex in the bank on Rhode Island Avenue, and if so, who first had the idea, Taylor or Vinson?*

It Changed Our Moral Standards

We are *not* deciding in this book whether Vinson and Taylor ever had any sex or whether Vinson was at fault in any way. Let's not get side tracked on that. We have a much larger issue here.

Obviously, someone has decided that women are *always* the victim—that women have no control over their lives and are totally subject to the domination of men. But we all know that this is pretty unrealistic.

Everyone has seen it happen. We have all seen a young, attractive, and seductive woman get ahead solely because she was an attractive young woman.

What message does the U. S. Supreme Court send in this case? It sends a message that we are not going to end this type of unfair competition in our workplace. *We are going to reward sexual promiscuity.*

As a result of this case, any woman can continue to get ahead by using her sex. If she is successful, then she will be rewarded with good assignments and promotions. But if she is successful only in

---

* Let's stop for a moment and show how the public often does not get the information it needs to judge a case like this.

Every single court right up to the Supreme Court (and every newspaper story also) made it clear that Vinson's promotions were based solely on her merit. This would tell us that she was a very competent person. It would make us judge her case more generously than if she were merely using her sex to have an easy position.

How then can this book be telling you that we don't know whether that's true. And that we will *never* know if it's true.

How can I possibly be telling you that the Supreme Court does not know what it is talking about?

It's really very simple. A trial court does not hold an "investigation" like a detective would. It doesn't go around and try to decide what really happened. A trial judge can only sit in court and listen to the witnesses that the opposing parties present. And if the opposing parties agree that one piece of evidence is true, then it's "true" and there's nothing the judge can do about it.

having sex with her boss but doesn't get any promotions, she can now sue the company and say that it was all its fault.*

Or when she gets bored with the job, she can quit and sue the company and receive more money.

Do you think that "sex in the workplace" (that we all say we don't want) will increase or decrease in the United States as a result of the Civil Rights Act?

It Made It Difficult for Hard-Working Women

Hard-working women are the ones who have suffered from sexual harassment suits, according to a feature article in *Variety*[22], which said:

"Fear of costly—and possibly baseless—lawsuits has changed the way men and women work together in Hollywood, and may actually hinder a woman's rise up the studio ladder, some say."

It may hinder a woman's rise up the ladder.

There is no question about the fact that it is hurting the good, conscientious worker, whether it be male or female.

"It's beginning to cause a backlash against women," said attorney Karen Kaplowitz. "Men are becoming frightened of working closely with a woman. Men are becoming afraid of working behind closed doors, of having dinner, of traveling." And the article continued, "It is also putting another obstacle in the way of women trying to make their way in the workplace," said attorney Kathleen Dillon Hunt.

So let's look at this central fact: "Did Mechelle Vinson obtain her promotions because she had sex with her boss?"

—The bank is going to say, "No", to this question. They believe that she never had any sex at all with Sidney Taylor. So obviously, they say that her promotions were based on merit alone. They couldn't logically argue anything different.

—Mechelle is going to say that her promotions were based solely upon her superior ability. She would never argue that she got them because of sex.

So when the case came before the trial judge it was agreed by the parties that Mechelle's promotions were based solely upon merit. The trial judge never had a chance to make that decision himself.

And therefore, in all of the court opinions (and in every newspaper account you ever read of this story), it is said very clearly that all of her rapid advancement was solely on merit.

But we will never know if it is true. And many people will have their doubts as to why she advanced so rapidly.

"SEXUAL HARASSMENT" LAW HAS CHANGED OUR MORALS AND DAMAGED WOMEN

But those women who don't want to work like it very much. "Probably 80% of demand letters are bogus in my experience," said attorney Kathleen Dillon Hunt.

The article says that attorney Michael Robbins agrees. "'Ten years ago I settled cases for between $10,000 to $20,000. Five years ago it was around $50,000.' Now he says the average settlement of a case before it gets to court is anywhere from $100,000 to $250,000."

"Some attorneys who specialize in defending management in sex harassment cases go so far as to say that almost any harassment complaint, whatever its validity, will extract some financial settlement from an employer.

"'Sometimes it's just a good business decision,' says Jaffe Dickinson, a partner in....one of the largest employment law firms in the country.

"'It's blackmail,' said the head of an independent film company who recently settled a sex harassment complaint against himself." He learned later that the woman had also received a settlement from her previous employer, using the same lawyer.

Two Types of Harassment

Everyone knows about "harassment." We're never going to eliminate it. We see it all around us. Someone is harassed because they are shorter than usual, or bigger or smaller. Or because they just moved in from the East or the West. Or because they went to Central High. Or because they have a big nose or small ears. Or because they like ballet.

Some of this "harassment" is in good fun and enjoyable. Some of it is obnoxious and mean. And sometimes it is difficult to decide which type it is.

---

* The Polaroid Corporation had a similar case happen in a plant on Route 128 near Boston. A male computer operator was accused of rape by a female (who was fighting for the same promotion). In that case, he was the one who sued the company. He sued Polaroid Corporation for over-reacting and a jury awarded him and his wife $5 million which was reduced to $3.5 million by the trial judge. The Supreme Court of Massachusetts reversed much of the decision and sent it back for a new trial. The Vinson case and the Polaroid case show what a difficult time a corporation has when it is put in the middle—no matter what it does, there is someone on all sides ready to pounce. *Foley v. Polaroid Corp.*, 400 Mass. 82, 508 NE2d 72 (1987).

FREEDOM WILL CONQUER RACISM (AND SEXISM)

Some of this harassment will always be based upon sex. Sometimes women like the attention and sometimes they don't. What one woman likes will not be liked by another. And the sexual advances of a particular male will be welcomed eagerly by one woman and detested by another.

Some women will even initiate the harassment because they enjoy it.

Our courts have made the decision that harassment by sex is more important than other types of obnoxious harassment. They have declared there are two types of sexual harassment that are covered under the Civil Rights Act: 1) Where an employee is required to do something in order to get a promotion or to keep his or her job. 2) Where bad language or offensive behavior makes a job unpleasant or intolerable.

When the Mechelle Vinson case was argued before the U. S. Supreme Court, a group of women lawyers filed a brief in which they advised the judges that there is a difference between "harassment" and "courting." They told the judges: "[S]exual harassment is distinguished from the more innocent forms of social-sexual conduct which naturally occur in the workplace, i.e., flattery and dating or courting behavior."[23]

They're correct that it is easy for *each individual woman* to decide whether a man is "harassing" or "courting." But how will the *employer* know the difference? And who is going to advise the employer when the "lovers" have had a fight and the "courting" has suddenly changed to "harassment?"

Oh, that's easy, said the women lawyers in their brief. "[T]raditional evidentiary inquiries will resolve the question."[24] In other words, the courts will have no problem deciding *after it's over* and the business has been sued, whether it was "harassment" or "courting." But how was the business to know *while it was happening*? And, of course like the bank in this case, most businesses will have no idea there is anything going on if no one tells them.

Even The Women's Freedom Network appears to be a little naive on this subject. In one issue of its *Newsletter*[25], an article discusses sexual harassment and correctly points out the terrible hypocrisy in the way the militant feminists idolize Anita Hill (because she was accusing a conservative man) while giving Paula Jones a kick in the jaw (because she accused a liberal man). But the article also applauds the concept of suing for harassment, saying:

"SEXUAL HARASSMENT" LAW HAS CHANGED OUR MORALS AND DAMAGED WOMEN

"Sexual harassment is ... undoubtedly an achievement of feminism ... But that achievement remains a shaky one. Nothing is more certain to undermine confidence in public awareness and condemnation of sexual harassment than cynical abuse of sexual harassment statutes for *personal or political gain, or revenge...*"

But we know that these statutes will *always* be used for personal gain or revenge. A prime use of these statutes is to extort money—because the businesses will *always* settle.

"Sex" Has Always Been Thorny to Businesses

The problem of "sex" in a business has always been a thorny one. How do you eliminate the factor of "sex" when men and women work together? If a company doesn't eliminate it, there has always been a morale problem in that company.

There are cases where men have been very raunchy and disgusting and one wonders how such a business could continue to operate, and who the women were who put up with such behavior.

But now we see the leaders of the Movement using vulgar, disgusting language like "cunt," "pussy," "motherfucker" as though the use of this language* will make all women equal with men. Then when men use the same language, it is "harassment" and a business must pay its offended workers.**

---

*   A reviewer tells me that I should not use these words in the book. But they are taught in our schools, colleges and elsewhere. How can we hide our heads to it. We see most newspapers not printing what our children are listening to everyday.

**   Meanwhile, in another courtroom another activist U. S. judge tells a school board that, under the U. S. Constitution, it is *required* to allow its teenage girls to read the following:

> The city is:
> One million horny lip-smacking men
> Screaming for my body.
> The streets are long conveyor belts
> Loaded with these suckling pigs.
> All begging for
> a lay
> a little pussy

FREEDOM WILL CONQUER RACISM (AND SEXISM)

A Final Thought

A lot of reviewers have told me to delete this final thought," but we cannot deny the obvious and put our heads in the sand.

We are all concerned because there is no industry in the ghetto areas. Jack Kemp and other people keep talking about "enterprise zones" in order to bring in more businesses. Will it be more or less difficult to get investors to put their money in a business in Vinson and Taylor's neighborhood as a result of this case?

Would you invest your dollars in a ghetto neighborhood where men are accused of raping young women, the women don't complain to anyone, and *the whole thing is going to be <u>your</u> fault*?

As a result of this case, will Jack Kemp find it easier or more difficult to attract a business if the business knows that it will be held responsible for this type of conduct—even if it has no knowledge of it?

Are we helping or hurting the poor and the disadvantaged?

---

a bit of tit
a leg to rub against
a handful of ass
the connoisseurs of cunt
Every day, every night
Pressing in on me closer and closer.
I swat them off like flies
but they keep coming back.
I'm a good piece of meat.

The local school board was not allowed to take that off their library shelves and away from their children because of the Constitution, said the U. S. judge.

But *their mothers* must be *protected* from such language.

The judge quoted with approval from another case which said, "If...the students must be protected from such exposure, we would fear for their future." These teenage girls do not need to be sheltered from this type of language but their mothers do?

No one can disagree that no person should be subject to harassment, whether it is sexual or otherwise, *at any age*.

See *Right to Read Defense Committee of Chelsea v. School Committee of The City of Chelsea*, U.S. District Court, District of Massachusetts, CA77-2318-T.

19

THE "GLASS CEILING" IS WOMEN'S CHOICE

It is women themselves who *choose* to make less money.

U.S. government data shows that women as a whole earn less than half as much as men, but this narrows to the vanishing point—and in some cases is even reversed—when corrections are made for marital status, full-time as against part-time employment, and continuous years of work.

For example, in 1971 women's median annual earnings were only 40 percent of those of men. But when the comparison was restricted to year-around, full-time workers, the figure rose to 60 percent. When the comparison was between single women and single men in the same age brackets (thirty to forty-four) with continuous work experience, single women who had worked every year since leaving school earned slightly more than single men. according to government data for the economy as a whole.

What are called "sex differences" are largely differences between married women and all others, and the origin of these differences is in the division of responsibilities in the family rather than discrimination in the work place. The increasing proportion of married women in the work force (who are not as "career-oriented") has been a major factor in the decline of the earnings of women relative to men.[1]

A similar study in 1996 by the Independent Women's Forum shows the same:

- Women earn 95% to 98% of what men earn if experience and life situations are constant.
- The glass ceiling is a "misnomer" when you factor in career and family aspirations, employment experience and education.[2]

The new study continued:

"Unfortunately [there is] an image of women as victims of widespread discrimination. Such a portrayal of women overlooks an important factor: the possibility that many women do not want to reach the top of the corporate ladder. The mass media uncritically accepts as the standard of equality the requirement that women's achievements be statistically identical to men's achievements in all areas. That standard is insidious: it suggests that something is wrong if the highest salaries are not earned. That is insulting to all workers who choose flexibility, a friendly workplace environment, and other nonmonetary factors in the course of their careers.

"Challenging these long-held assumptions about women is a perilous exercise, particularly because many groups have an investment in maintaining myths such as the wage gap and the glass ceiling. Both the wage gap and the glass ceiling are rhetorically useful but factually corrupt catch phrases. As we have demonstrated, those myths are harmful to women and do little to accurately describe the complex factors that determine a woman's place in the labor market. Important elements like education, consecutive years in the work force, and field of employment are not taken into consideration by those who generate pessimistic statistics about women's lack of progress. In addition, those who constantly point to the existence of a wage gap and a glass ceiling ignore one of the most important (but least statistically measurable) factors: personal choice.

"The heterogeneity of the female population in this country guarantee that there will never be a consensus among women on all issues."

THE "GLASS CEILING" IS WOMEN'S CHOICE

An Interesting Debate

An interesting debate took place in New York City between feminists and neo-feminists as a result of *Women's Figures,* as reported by columnist Maggie Gallagher.[3] One feminist shot out:

"Forty percent of male partners in law firms have stay-at-home wives. Those women are single mothers; the men are just sperm donors and ATM machines!"

To which appreciative laughter burst through half the room. But another scholar shot back:

"What about the women law partners who work 60-hour weeks? Would you refer to them as egg donors?" And applause burst forth from the other half. To which, Ms. Gallagher commented.

"In the end, the two sides were closer than either would like to admit. The differences that remain are less about gender politics than economic theory. Betty Friedan, while chiding the neo-feminists, conceded their main point: The battle for equality of the marketplace has been won....Ms. Friedan now improbably wants us to pour our energies into building a Euro-style socialist welfare state. Meanwhile neo-feminists urge less taxes and regulation to spur economic growth."

But I disagree with Ms. Gallagher.

The "battle for equality of the marketplace" is not something that "has been won." It has always been there for women to take whenever they decided they wanted it. But that is *not* what the feminists have *ever* wanted; they have *always* been after a socialist welfare state. Therein lies the conflict between them and the rest of us.

I also disagree with Ms. Gallagher over another point.

I agree with the feminist who said that men partners in law firms are just "sperm donors and ATM machines." I agree that many men (and now women) spend too much time at work and too little with their families. How we solve that problem, I do not know. But I know that any attempt by the government will only make it worse. It is only individual men and women who can make those decisions. Betty Friedan said in an article in 1988:

"Superwoman goes to the office, then she comes home to be Supermom—just like the woman of the past whose only power and responsibility was the perfectly run home, the perfectly controlled

FREEDOM WILL CONQUER RACISM (AND SEXISM)

children, and who had all the time in the world to do it. Masking guilt becomes impossible for her. So with a little extra flagellation, she becomes an even *more* perfect mother—teaching her child computers before the age of 3!—but she's got just 24 hours a day to do it and keep her head above water in the office. In her own mind she is never doing enough, and she's isolated by her double burden, without even the time to go to a meeting to talk about it."[4]

Friedan is correct in the above and that we need change in this new world. But her coercive methods of flagellation from big government are exacerbating the problem, not correcting it. Can you imagine an employer even thinking of suggesting that a woman might want to spend more time at home with her child?

If you believe an employer would consider that, please read the later chapter about what happened to John Silber, when he was President of Boston University.

20

NO MORE HATE FROM FEMINISTS

> *Modern feminism, until recently at least, promised not to intensify sexual warfare but to bring about a new era of peace in which men and women could meet each other as equals, not as antagonists.*
> Christopher Lasch in *Women and the Common Life: Love, Marriage and Feminism.*

There have always been and always will be intelligent, competent women. But the women of America in the late 20th century have allowed their good names to be used by a radical, hateful group of people.

This will change. It is only a matter of time.

But how the change will occur is not yet clear. Either it will be violent, with a total moral and spiritual collapse of our country, with the men from somewhere like China or Iran conquering the men of the United States and imposing total totalitarian control. This, of course, will mean a total loss of everything that women have gained over the centuries since the birth of Judaism and Christianity.

FREEDOM WILL CONQUER RACISM (AND SEXISM)

Or we will return to a more reasoned discourse to solve the problem of how we can arrive at an intelligent answer to the tremendous possibilities that lie ahead.

There is going to be "change" in our society. It's necessary because the world is becoming more technological.

But it can't be driven by "hate," or everyone will suffer.

The problem is that, about 20% of the people are driven by hate and anger; and they are always the loud, vocal ones who appear to dominate the scene.

Our society can't pretend that the females of the world are the only ones with problems. I didn't go to law school at night when I was thirty years old because I enjoyed working day and night. I loved the outdoors and active physical work, not sitting in an office. But I had found that there was no way to work for me in the outdoors.

Betty Friedan realized that. She said, "[M]ore and more boys cannot find images in our culture—from their fathers or other men—to help them in their search. The old frontiers have been conquered, and the boundaries of the new are not so clearly marked. More and more young men in America today suffer an identity crisis for want of any image of man worth pursuing, for want of a purpose that truly realizes their human abilities."[1]

She's right.

How do you tell a 250 lb. young man that he should learn to keyboard a computer? Only a few years ago he could have shown how strong he was by working on a farm. But today, one man on a tractor can do it all by himself. Or he could have used a pick and shovel on a road job, but today it's all done by machine.

I went through that. Life in a suburb is sterile and barren to me. I need to be able to plow a field, tend some cattle, look at a sunset.

Yet almost all of the women of my generation wanted a home in the suburbs. And then when they were given their home, they said they were unfulfilled.

Although Friedan seems to have some realization that it is tough for men also, she returns to egocentricity saying: "But why have theorists not recognized this same identity crisis in women?"

She ignores the fact that we've spent much of the twentieth century debating the "identity crisis" in women.

The Lies Are Believed

No woman under 50 years of age can remember what it was like to live as an adult before the Civil Rights Act was passed.

A young woman reporter on my newspaper wrote a feature story in 1996 about sexual harassment in the law office. She told about an older lawyer who had harassed a paralegal and then she asked this question:

"Is this a case of an old-time lawyer who simply hasn't kept up with what is—and what is not—acceptable office behavior in the 1990's? Some in the bar say that this isn't an isolated example—and argue that harassing conduct doesn't just come from 'old timers' who are living in the dark ages."

The "dark ages?"

Obviously, this reporter is a victim of feminist propaganda. She has been told, and believes, that before she was born, men used to harass women as a matter of course. But, that is simply not true. It was not until the 1970s that you began to see and hear about this type of thing. No one would even have thought of it in the "dark ages."

A life would have been destroyed by that type of behavior.

In another example, a columnist for the *Boston Globe* wrote about the retirement of Helen Gurley Brown as Editor of *Cosmopolitan* magazine. In the column, she recited a story from a biography of Brown that had been shown on the Art and Entertainment television channel.

"When [Brown] was very young she worked in an advertising agency where the office 'sport' involved the 'boys' ganging up on one or another of the more attractive 'girls' and stealing her panties." According to the A&E account, Brown was hurt because she was never the chosen victim in one of these raids."

They did what!?

This *never* happened.

The columnist says the story "seems bizarre—if not criminal—by 1997 standards..." The story is bizarre and criminal from *any* standards, much more so from those of the 1940s when it was supposed to have happened than of 1997. This simply did not happen.[2]

Men Have Also Been Misled

It's also amazing to hear many of the young men of today. They often talk about the "great problems" that women face. Even the rhetoric of Promise Keepers is suspect. There was a cover story in their magazine entitled, "Why We Need Feminism."[3] It was written for them by the Managing Editor of the well-known and respected magazine, *Christianity Today,* which is an excellent magazine; but the editor obviously has very little historical background on this issue. Let me give you a few quotes from his article. (If you've read my book, you don't need me to tell you where he has been misled.)

"Many Christians now take for granted what feminism fought hard to win—even the recent victories. Do Christians, even in the most conservative camps, still believe women should not vote, go to school or be able to own property? I don't know any. Nor any who think women should have to put up with sexual harassment at work, and yet it was not until the 1970s that this violation was recognized by the courts. Should the victims of rape be the ones tried and harassed by the legal system? Feminists lobbied for and won new guidelines making it easier to protect the dignity of rape victims.*

"And we still need feminism. Why do women receive 70 percent of what men receive for comparable work? Why does a woman's mental health and life expectancy go down when she marries while a man's mental health and life expectancy go up? Why are the faces of those living in poverty overwhelmingly female? Is this what God desires?"[4]

He rambles on to say that in Jesus' time women were "thought to be sources of temptation." Of course they were thought to be

---

* Although you can answer most of his confusion, I must say something about rape. This is a very serious, complex problem and one that is not suited to slogans or cliches. It used to be taken very seriously with the death penalty being a possibility for the rapist. Because of that, a defendant was allowed to show that the intercourse was not rape but consensual. For example, suppose the woman were a prostitute; one must wonder whether it was really rape as she said, or a failure to pay for the sex, as he said. Therefore, he was allowed to show her reputation in the community. A man's life could be in the balance. What we have done with the "new guidelines" is to make it much more difficult for a man who is falsely accused. I do not have enough experience in these cases to know the answer, but I do know that the old rules were not to "harass the victims of rape." It is a very difficult balance we must make in this area, and while the "elite" liberals always want to protect the rights of the criminal defendant, this does not apply to a man falsely accused of rape. We must remember that all of the accuseds are not guilty.

"sources of temptation," because they *were* and they *are*, at least for most of us.

JFK

It will be very unpopular to say it, but John F. Kennedy was the man who popularized this type of sexual harassment.

Everyone who worked in Washington knew in the late 1950's that this Senator from Massachusetts was chasing any young, attractive woman he saw. His behavior was not usual, that is why it was so well known.

Although other presidents may have been involved with women, they were involved with only one woman and it was done with discretion. It was probably true that Franklin Roosevelt had a mistress. There were rumors that Eisenhower had a mistress during the years that he was overseas, but many people dispute this vehemently. Even if true, these actions would pale next to the sexual escapades of JFK. He was the first of the "movie-screen presidents" and the majority of women loved it. He saw women solely as sex-objects; yet they adored him.

In my lifetime we have had twelve presidents. Two of those twelve men were promiscuous, Kennedy and Clinton. Only two of those twelve presidents saw and harassed women as sex objects. (Probably Lyndon Johnson also.) Yet those are the only two of those presidents that women have adored. For most men and any thinking woman, this is a great riddle.

Bill Clinton saw how Kennedy operated and learned well. It is clear to everyone that Clinton uses women to his own personal advantage, and yet women were the ones who elected him president in 1996. Bob Dole actually won the vote of the men (by one percentage point, 44% to 43%); it was the women who elected Clinton by a vote of 54% to 38%.

It has been pointed out by David Frum that married women went for Clinton by a small margin of 48%, but unmarried women gave him 62% of their vote. He points out that there are 40 million unmarried women. (Of these, 10 million are widows, 10 million divorcees, 5 million unmarried mothers, and 15 million are single, childless women.) Frum says:

"These 40 million women form a new American proletariat. They are more likely than most Americans to be poor. They are more likely to depend on government for help, either directly (welfare, Social Security, food stamps, Medicaid) or indirectly (government collection of child support, subsidized day care). They are most hostile to or alienated from the institutions of American society than are their married sisters; while polls find that married women are very nearly as conservative in their politics as men, unmarried women veer sharply to the Left.

"And American society seems to be producing more and more unmarried women all the time. In 1970, nearly 70 percent of adult American women were married. That proportion has since fallen dramatically: to 63 percent in 1980, 60 percent in 1970, and 59 percent today. And divorce is by far the most important cause of this social transformation....

"What constituency can there be for Social Security reform and reductions in the welfare functions of government in a society where an ever-rising proportion of the female electorate—which is 52 percent of the total electorate—has come to depend on Social Security and welfare?...[T]he worse the distrust between women and men, the better the Democrats do."[5]

David Frum is only partly correct.

It also appears that many women are also attracted to a man who is unfaithful and disloyal to his wife and children. This somehow makes those men "exciting."

This is bad, but it is even worse if women use this criteria for picking the leader of our nation.

The "Scorched Earth" Policy of Feminism

A professor of Yiddish literature at Harvard, Ruth R. Wisse, is scathing in her denunciation of what feminism has done.

She says that when the Republicans took over Congress in 1994, they faced the same problems that were faced in the Soviet Union at the end of Communism. There was only a "scorched earth" remaining.

"Women's liberation, if not the most extreme then certainly the most influential neo-Marxist movement in America, has done to the American home what Communism did to the Russian economy, and much of the ruin is irreversible. By defining relations between men and women in terms of power and competition instead of reciprocity and cooperation, the movement tore apart the most basic and fragile contract in human society, the unit from which all other social institutions draw their strength.

"Cooperation between men and women is enormously painful and difficult, depending as it does on the ability of unlike individuals to accept lifelong responsibility for one another and for the children that will issue from their union. Of the two sexes, women may stand to gain more from domestication and have more to fear from its erosion, which is why our culture—and Jewish culture certainly—has tried so strenuously to define what husbands owe their wives. But like all revolutionaries, the ideologues of the women's movement did not calculate the value of what they wanted to destroy when they sought the liberation of their gender from the domestic 'mystique.' They may not be solely responsible for the collapse of the American family, the rise in domestic violence, the proliferation of undisciplined young men, and such related items as the decline in education, but none of these conditions can be improved unless and until women reinvest their energies in nurturing and sustaining families as their most cherished and vital preserve."[6]

It's Becoming Embarrassing to Watch

It is becoming embarrassing to watch some of what is happening today among the feminists. The *Lawyers Journal* of the Massachusetts Bar Association had a large, banner headline in its June 1996 issue:

"Panelists say bias remains a problem for women lawyers"[ ]

The *Journal* then recited the following instances of "bias."
• The first "problem of bias" reported in the article was that the press reported on the dress of Marcia Clark during the O.J. Simpson trial. "Some participants blamed the continued discrimination, in part, on the media's fascination with highlighting obscure courtroom incidents directed at female lawyers. For example, O.J. Simpson prosecutor Marcia Clark's hair style and attire often made more headlines than the real issues each day in court in the double murder trial in California ..."

This shows discrimination against women lawyers?
• The next complaint was about a woman who was the first woman attorney at a large firm in Springfield. "Although she did <u>not</u> experience any discrimination in her law firm, there was speculation

elsewhere that she got the job because she is a woman, she said." [emphasis added]

Of course they speculated and people are going to *continue* to wonder why she got the job as long as we have the Civil Rights Act. No matter how much we punish people, we will *never* be able to stop what they think.

The lawyer opined that she "should be recognized for being a 'trial lawyer' not a 'female trial lawyer.'"

We will say "Amen" to that. So let's start talking about lawyers, not women lawyers, and get on with our lives. Then people **will** think of her as just another excellent lawyer.

She also said, "Early in her career at the law firm ... there were occasions [sic] when other male lawyers in the courtroom would assume she was a paralegal and not an attorney because there were so few women attorneys at that time." Well, that was a logical conclusion, wasn't it, if there were "so few women attorneys at that time?" I will wager that most paralegals also believed she was a paralegal.

• Another lawyer "shared her experience involving a criminal trial early in her career when a judge told her she tried the case 'just like a man.' At the time she took the judge's remark as a compliment, although today she understands the subtleties of discrimination and would probably react differently..."

If *she* thought it was a compliment and the judge intended it as a compliment, who in the "elite" educated her to change her mind.

At this point, I am sure that someone will think I am leaving something out; something important that was discussed in the article. But I have not; that is what was discussed in this article about "bias" against women.

Let's Give Thanks

These women lawyers are apparently excellent, successful lawyers. Why are they not on their knees every day, along with the rest of us, that we were born in a country where a woman can become a successful, prosperous lawyer? Why are they not celebrating? It is sad to see such a demonstration of victimization.*

---

* One of the very few lawyers that I would recommend enthusiastically, without reservation, is the woman who was my employment lawyer when I

NO MORE HATE FROM FEMINISTS

It is sad because the women in America have many momentous decisions to make in the coming years. If we continue to trivialize them and never get to discussing the very important issues that face us, men and women, we will continue to be in serious trouble.

---

owned a business. (However, she will probably disagree with most of what I wrote here.) I even wrote to her Managing Partner a few years back to tell him of her excellence.

Section V

IT'S A SERIOUS THREAT TO OUR FREEDOM

Our freedom is under serious attack by the Civil Rights Act. But *no one* seems to notice or else they're afraid to say so.

21

CENSORSHIP OF A UNIVERSITY

The speech of the president of a large American university was censored in June, 1987. Even a U.S. Court of Appeals agreed that this resulted in a "chilling effect" on academic freedom. But the censorship went unnoticed. In fact, it was cheered and applauded by the media and most of the academics in America. It is merely *one example* of what happens many, many times, over and over. The president was charged with sex discrimination. One of the counts against him was as follows... *(and this is a true story)*.

<u>John Silber. You are charged with saying: "A child will do better if the father or mother is at home to care for it."</u>

<u>That speech is a violation of federal law.</u>

<u>You are charged with the high crime of "sexism."</u>

* * * *

Those aren't the exact words that were hurled at the President of Boston University in a courtroom in the United States Courthouse in Boston in June, 1987, but they accurately summarize the charge.

And he was found: "Guilty."

It happened during the trial of *Julia Brown vs. Boston University* in a suit under the Civil Rights Act of 1964.[1]

We have always believed that a strong family is the bulwark of American society. It is essentially a *crime* to believe that today.

How did this happen?

Listen to this tale about a great *private* American university. (This school has no affiliation with the government, local or federal.) Its president made a speech.[2] In it, he worried whether we are providing a satisfactory nurturing system for our children while their parents are out working. And, he expressed his concern that this is a basic cause for the tremendous drop in the educational levels of our children.

This would seem to be an appropriate topic for the president of a university.

However, when a woman professor was not given a lifetime position, the speech was used to show that Silber was a "sexist." Therefore, the university could be 1) subject to payments and penalties that could amount to over two million dollars and 2) required to appoint a professor to its faculty that it did not want.*

Censorship At A Great University

As you read about this true story, please keep in mind: we are <u>not</u> concerned with whether Prof. Brown should have been promoted. She may be the best teacher in the world. That is not important.

What is important is this:

(1) Should six ordinary people off-the-street be deciding who should be on the faculty at Boston University?

---

* The trial judge noted that the higher courts had warned him to be very careful about forcing a college to reinstate a faculty member it did not want, "[b]ecause of the special responsibility of university trustees and the lifetime span of academic tenure..." But this federal judge was confident that he knew how to run a university. He said, "There seems little risk that Boston University will be stuck with an unqualified person on its faculty, judging from the evidence in the case, *although there was some dispute as to the quality of her scholarship."* [emphasis added] See 674 F. Supp. at p. 394.

FREEDOM WILL CONQUER RACISM (AND SEXISM)

(2) Should a faculty member of a private university be allowed the freedom of speech to state his opinions on American families without being ordered to a federal courtroom before a federal judge to explain his speech?

The Case of Professor Julia Brown[3]

When John Silber, the president of Boston University, learned in 1981 that Assistant Professor Julia Brown had sued the university for sex discrimination because she hadn't been offered a lifetime position on the faculty, he wasn't surprised.

After all, practically every college in America had such suits filed against them all the time. It was almost impossible to make any decision about hiring or promoting a faculty member without someone cautioning, "You're going to be sued."

Still, he was a little angry.

But not worried. The worst part was that he knew it would cost the university many thousands of dollars in lawyer fees to fight this unfair charge. This was money that could be better used for faculty salaries and other improvements that were so badly needed. He also resented the time and attention that would be taken from the many important matters that a university must face every day.

He had cause to be angry. After all, Prof. Brown had known when she came with the University that she would have six years after which she would either be appointed to a lifetime "tenure" position or be dismissed. That's the way it was in every college in the country.

Moreover, she had received an additional benefit because President Silber had been concerned that six years wasn't always long enough to judge a teacher. Some of the judgments had been made before a professor had a full chance to mature. As a result, Silber had started a new system which gave some professors who were not yet qualified an additional three years in which to prove their ability.

Prof. Brown was one of those. Although the University had not awarded her a lifetime contract, it had offered her one for three additional years. But Brown had refused it in a huff and resigned from the faculty.[4]

Now she was suing.

CENSORSHIP OF A UNIVERSITY

What the B.U. Lawyers Were Told

When the lawyers arrived to talk with President Silber, he was impatient. There really wasn't much to discuss because the case was obviously absurd, he thought. Since he had arrived at BU in 1970, Silber had recommended tenure for three women and five men in the English Department and he had dissuaded a fourth woman professor from leaving. It was obvious to him that there was no discrimination at BU. Even the Chairman of the English Department was a woman.

Besides Prof. Brown had *not* been fired. She had been offered a contract for an additional three years when she would be evaluated again.

But the lawyers for BU pointed out that you never know what a jury is going to do. When you go before a jury, it is always like playing Russian roulette. If the same case is tried before different juries, you would usually get different answers. One juror might have a child who didn't get admitted to BU. Another might be a militant feminist who would always vote for a woman plaintiff, and so forth. This is particularly true in a six-person jury where a strong person can dominate all the others. The University had to be careful.

After all, the faculty in the English Department had recommended unanimously that Prof. Brown be appointed, as had a committee from the College of Liberal Arts.

However, the University's case was powerful. As President Silber told the lawyers, only four other persons besides Prof. Brown had been reviewed for tenure between 1979 and 1985. Of the four other candidates, only one had received tenure; she was a woman. Of the other three, which accepted the three year extensions, two were men and one was a woman. The woman received tenure when reviewed a second time.

Prof. Brown wanted to be special. She was the only person from the College of Liberal Arts who had ever rejected a three-year extension.

Also, at least five male professors in the College of Liberal Arts this year had also been denied tenure even though they had also been recommended by their departments, sometimes unanimously. In addition, four women had been granted tenure even though they had gotten negative recommendations.

FREEDOM WILL CONQUER RACISM (AND SEXISM)

Also, the volume of writing that Prof. Brown had done had been small. She had published one book, which was merely a rewrite of the dissertation she had prepared for her PhD. And that book had gotten mixed reviews, including some strong praise but also criticism: "platitudes and weak generalizations," "inconsistencies and many careless errors," "arid and artificial," "erratic" and "weak."

She had been given a leave for the entire school year beginning in September 1979 for the purpose of finishing another book by the following June. But here it was 1981 and she still hadn't submitted anything at all, not even a first draft.

It's true that her friends and fellow workers in the English Department and the College of Liberal Arts had recommended her, but the Dean had not been so enthusiastic. Although he also recommended her, he had qualified this by saying he would understand if she were given a three-year extension so that she could be re-evaluated later on.

Both the Assistant Provost and the Provost of the University recommended to the president that she *not* get tenure but be given a three-year extension to evaluate her better. The Provost wrote: "It is clear that Professor Brown has the promise of becoming a significant critic of nineteenth century literature, but needs time to complete her first independent project and establish herself as a mature scholar."

A special outside committee of three had recommended by a 2-1 vote that she be appointed although each had "some reservations" about her. They said that they really didn't know enough about her. They said, "We all regret that we had no further work on which to judge Professor Brown."

Professor Brown was having personal problems during this period. She was suffering through an unhappy marriage that would end in divorce; she sought therapy from an analyst. She had her first baby, and she would later blame her "unsatisfactory relationship" with that child on Boston University.

Therefore, most observers would agree that President Silber had done exactly the right thing by giving this person an additional three years in which to finally write the book she had promised. And although some would disagree with his decision, it would be difficult to question his motives.

It was not surprising that President Silber looked at all such positions with care. Each position usually obligated the University to a contract for 40 years at a cost of over $2 million in salary, benefits and pension.

Silber knew about those financial problems all too well. When he came to BU in 1970 it had a projected deficit that year of almost $9 million. Since then, he had balanced the budget and taken the school out of debt.[5]

The Trial

Was the jury still listening?

The attorney for Professor Brown was concerned. She had been warned by the judge that she would be "foolish" to make a long closing argument to the jury; and it was, indeed, a long one. And it was boring. It was a comparison of those professors who had gotten tenure at BU and those who had not.

But now she was getting to a more interesting part. She could put some excitement into it. She could talk about a speech that President Silber had made a few years ago down in Washington. Her voice rang through the courtroom.

"He bemoans the deterioration of three branches of society: the family, the church and the school."

She looked up and down at the six jurors before her.

"Who is to blame for the deterioration of the family? Well, women of course, single mothers and working mothers because mothers are out working instead of staying home with their children. Children watch too much television and children are not properly educated.

"At trial President Silber tried to excuse the speech as a plea for day care, not a criticism of working parents, working mothers, but in cross-examination he admitted that the speech, which is in evidence, does not make any mention of day care at all."

Was that juror on the end still listening? This was the important part. The lawyer for Professor Brown went on:

"It is hard to say just how this attitude about working mothers affects his tenure decisions, but it is clear that women and not men carry the burden of being seen as wives and mothers and not just as scholars."

That wasn't true, of course. He did *not* say that.

But suppose it were true. Suppose President Silber did believe that women have a unique role in raising children—a role that only a mother can fill. *__When did it become a "crime" to believe that?__* Does anyone doubt that we have a problem in America with our young people? Is there anyone who has not seen the test scores going down and down? Is there anyone who has not seen the drug use going up and up? How do we solve those problems?

Do we not need a great public debate on those issues? And if that debate is not to be engaged in by a president of a university, then who is to debate those problems? And if anyone believes that a mother (or father) is the best one to take care of a child, should that person no longer be allowed to state that view?

What type of mind-control do we have?

The Truth About What the President Said

The lawyer for Prof. Brown was not telling the truth. President Silber did not say that in the speech he made down in Washington. What he did talk about was "Citizen Responsibility." He worried about the many students who do not feel any obligation to help the society of which they are a part and which has given them so much.

Silber blamed this on a deterioration of family, church and school. He talked about the decline of the family in great detail, but the part that Professor Brown's lawyer gave to the jury and which she used to attack him was just a few paragraphs (out of the long speech) where he had said:

"It is essential to note, moreover, that in a two-parent family where both parents are at work, there is less likelihood of providing an environment that encourages education—much less than in a two-parent family in which one parent remains at home for the nurture of the children, to devote himself or herself full time to their care, feeding and education. Over the past decade, the proportion of our children who benefit from living with two parents, whether their own two parents or a parent and a step-parent, has declined by 10 percent. During the same period, the number of working mothers—that is, the proportion of children who do not have even one parent at home during the day—has increased sharply. Reliable national statistics on this are hard to come by, but between 1960 and 1981, the proportion of working wives—as opposed to working mothers with children under 18—rose from 26 percent to 46 percent. Lack of parental supervision associated with both parents working explains in part that children typically watch 24 hours of television a week."⁶

At the trial, President Silber was asked by the lawyer if he meant by this small portion of his speech that women with children should not work.

"I sure don't," he answered. "If women with children had not worked, my brother and I would have starved. Our mother had to work."

And he noted that he had also called for a national day care center for all children who do not have adequate family care from age 3 to age 12.

"My point in this thing," he testified, "is not to blame the working mother for anything, because most women who go to work have very good reasons for working. It is rather to say that there is no way they can have a career outside the home, leave no one at home to care for the children, and account for the essential responsibility society has for nurturing of the children. Someone in society has to step in and say if the women had to work and there is no one at home to take care of the child, then we have to have a day care center or some other national institution to overcome this national loss of the decline and disappearance of the traditional American family. It is not to blame anyone. It is to call for correction of a bad situation."

But even the trial judge, who is never supposed to interject his own feelings into a jury case, questioned Silber after he had finished:

"Some of those career women are in the universities, including your own?

"That is right," replied President Silber.

And then the trial judge did something that no judge is ever supposed to do. Because he is a figure of great authority who will have immense influence on a jury, he is not to get personally involved in the trial. But this judge asked this inflammatory question which isn't close to what President Silber was saying. The trial judge asked President Silber:

"And I suppose one way to get them back in the kitchen," and the judge paused, "is to get them out of the university; is that so?"

The jury and judge went on to award Professor Brown over $200,000 in damages plus a lifetime position at Boston University.

FREEDOM WILL CONQUER RACISM (AND SEXISM)

Is It A "Crime"?

Suppose someone does believe that a child should have a mother who will stay at home with him or her. Is it against the law to believe that in America today?

Did you know you are breaking the federal law by having those thoughts in your mind?

The judge told the jury in this case,

"...you [the jury] have to get inside people's minds..."

But we have a great problem. Many experts were questioning whether a young child must be with its mother or suffer as a result. The famous Harvard scholar, Dr. Burton L. White, was distributing a booklet in 1980 which began:

"For more than 20 years my work has been with babies—how they acquire skills and knowledge as they grow, how they develop personality, what makes them happy, sad, eager, indifferent, obedient, creative and confident. Most of this work, naturally, involves the environment in which the baby lives and the people who share that environment. Usually that means the baby's home and the baby's family.

"But over the last ten years or so, I and many of my colleagues in child development have become deeply concerned over a growing trend in society: the placing of very young children in full-time substitute care.

"I am concerned by this trend. I'm worried most about the effects on children, but I'm also disturbed about the pressure being put on parents, especially mothers, who want to raise their babies themselves.

"I'm also saddened by the thought that many adults, by choosing full-time substitute care, stand to miss some of life's sweetest pleasures.

"This pamphlet is an effort to state the other side of the case. Its theme is simple:

"What's best for your baby?"

The question was so important that the federal government gave grants to many colleges to study the problem. Prof. Jay Belsky of Penn State was one of the leading researchers in the area. He started his famous research in the early 1970s and was constantly updating it. It is certain that a leading academician such as President Silber was well aware of this research, and of Dr. White and others.

In an update published in 1988, Prof. Belsky cited the *Handbook of Child Psychology* in order to show that it was certain that there was a difference between children raised at home by their mother and those raised in a day care center. The only question was how you view the difference. There was a lot more work needed to be done in this important area. Belsky said:

"Some people can—and undoubtedly will—read my pronouncements to mean that mothers should not go to work during their infants' first year. Others can—and conceivably should—be led to conclude in view of the poor state of day care in this nation [citation] that the current evidence demands that more effort be made to provide parents with affordable, quality care and with greater freedom and choice regarding their day care decisions. It remains for each reader to infer then, what the implications of this review are—to families, communities, and to policy makers."[7]

It remains for *everyone* to infer . . . except for the President of a large American university, who is probably one of the most logical persons to be making such a decision. Silber's choice was that there should be more day care available.

What is the correct answer?

The studies showed that day care centers did not provide the love and nurturing that these young people need. Should we relieve the tax burden on parents who stay home with their children? Should we abolish the labor laws that don't let mothers work at home? Should we *encourage* employers (by leadership, not coercion) to have more flex-time, good part-time employment, job sharing, and "take-out" work?*

---

*   The debate still goes on today.

In 1996, Dr. Mark Genuis pointed out many errors in a recent federal study which claimed that infant day care was harmless to the development of children. Dr. Genuis criticized the federal study with the following:

"Over the past decade, an accumulated pile of evidence has lent support to the fear that working mothers can inflict real harm on their infant children by placing them in someone else's care, and especially in a day care center. The [federal] study only tracked children up to the age of fifteen months—years before the damage (if any) done by day care is expected to show up.

"Worse, the [federal] team studied only one possible ill effect of day care: poor mother-child bonding. The team declined to test the effect of prolonged exposure to day care on children's intellectual development or their physical health."

FREEDOM WILL CONQUER RACISM (AND SEXISM)

Court of Appeals Was Concerned . . . Or Was It?

After an appeal by the university, the U.S. Court of Appeals agreed that the trial judge had erred. He was wrong to allow the testimony about Silber's speech. It said:

"To our minds this evidence is far afield....It is an untenable leap from such a speech [by President Silber] to the inference that the author would deliberately deny tenure to a qualified faculty member. Its relevance, if not quite zero, is close to that. While one would hope that jurors would see them for what they are, there is the danger such red-herrings, skillfully manipulated, could cause a jury to stray. We fear, moreover, the chilling effect that admission of such remarks could have on academic freedom. Use of such evidence in a court of law could cause a university president, dean or teacher to avoid topics of this kind altogether for fear that one or two sentences might later be used as evidence of alleged discriminatory animus. It was error to admit these remarks."

It was error, said the Court of Appeals.

But it was unimportant.

Unimportant?!

That's what they said.

"While we hold that the evidence should have been excluded, we do not believe that it effected [sic] the outcome of the trial."

The Women's Quarterly, Summer 1996. Dr. Genuis reported many other faults with the study.

Another recent study has shown that male children in white, middle-class centers were likely to be bitten by another child nine times. As reported in the *Journal of the American Medical Association* and quoted by columnist Maggie Gallagher. *Washington Times,* March 31, 1997, p. 1.

At the end of 1997, Bill and Hillary Clinton held an urgent White House Conference to discuss the "silent crisis" in day care. They had to call it a "silent" crisis, because apparently no one knew about it except them. And it was to be a large portion of the President's State of the Union address in 1998. Those who favor this expansion of the government into the care of our children argue: 1) there is a shortage of child care facilities, 2) the ones that do exist are not affordable, and 3) unregulated day care is harmful to children. However, recent studies show that 96% of parents are satisfied with their child care arrangement, child care fees have not changed in real terms since the late 1970s, and the number of child

CENSORSHIP OF A UNIVERSITY

If it was not crucial to the decision, then Prof. Brown's lawyer would never have mentioned it or talked about it in her summary to the jury. Of course it was important. And our interviews with the jurors, as you will see in the next section, bear that out. They did *not* believe that Prof. Brown had been treated differently because of her sex, but *they had been convinced that President Silber was a sexist.* The judges in the Court of Appeals said that this type of evidence would have a "chilling effect" on "academic freedom." Yet, they allowed Prof. Brown to get away with using it. The great notoriety of this case means that it could not help but have had a "chilling effect." Everyone saw what happened to John Silber in the federal court in Boston.

Who Was The Jury?

Who were the six people on this jury who made this important decision?

The trial judge didn't have great faith in their abilities. He told the lawyers in his chambers before the trial started that the workings of a university were "as foreign to these people as growing oats on Mars."

There were five women and one man on the jury. We interviewed some of them for this book to determine why they decided the way that they did. There was a secretarial temp, a homemaker, a retiree, two financial analysts and a man who worked for the state.

We were told that the man was skeptical at first, but after things were pointed out to him, "he came around."

Some members of the jury also told us that they decided Prof. Brown had *not* been treated differently because of her sex. Therefore, they should, under the law, have held for the university. But they held for Prof. Brown anyhow. Why? Because they didn't like President Silber. He was arrogant, they didn't like his mannerisms, and he was a "sexist." They believed that he thought that a woman must always stay home and take care of the kids.

And they thought Prof. Brown was a nice person, who was well qualified to be teaching 19th Century English literature and should have been given tenure.

---

care providers has kept pace with the swelling demand. Darcy Olsen, *The Advancing Nanny State, Why the Government Should Stay Out of Child Care.* Policy Analysis No. 285 by the Cato Institute, October 23, 1997.

FREEDOM WILL CONQUER RACISM (AND SEXISM)

What Does It Mean?

Boston University and President Silber are not unique. Every major college and university throughout the country has numerous suits brought against it all the time.

And that's true of every major business. But it's not just the businesses which are being sued. Any person in the company can be sued from the president right down to the foreman. Nobody can speak out on the issues without fear of being sued *personally*.

Low-level supervisors can be sued personally if a person has a grudge against him or her.

Even a fellow worker who is not a supervisor can be sued. Although fellow workers have always been dismissed from the suits so far, they have been successfully harassed and have had to hire lawyers to defend themselves from a lawsuit.

The central figure in this case, John Silber, was a well known, controversial figure in Boston. An old-time liberal, he also had many conservative values, particularly on social issues. He had rescued Boston University from the chaos of the '60s but he had also angered most of the liberal faculty at the same time. He was to run against Bill Weld for governor of Massachusetts in 1990, almost winning the election with many of the conservative Republicans voting for Silber and many of the liberal Democrats voting for Weld.

This trial became a great rallying cry for the liberal faculty and others in Boston, including the *Boston Globe*. They were unable to see any threat to freedom of speech, even in a university setting; they were set only on using this event for another attack on a person they disliked. The *Globe* wrote glowing stories about the trial, with Prof. Brown as the heroine.[8]

If the president of a great university can no longer speak out on the issues of the day and exercise his free speech without being hauled before a Court of Inquisition, who can?

22

CIVIL RIGHTS ACTIVISTS: WHERE ARE YOU?

In June, 1965, Lyndon Johnson made a commencement speech.[1]
He said: "[W]e seek ...equality as a fact and equality as a result."
This speech was made at the black university in Washington, D.C., Howard University. Most of us didn't notice it. But it marked a major change in American society.
Why is it important?
With that speech, the president changed the goals of our society from individual liberty to the goals of the socialists. And most of us never noticed.
That statement of mine will sound stark to many, but it is true. The principal advocate of the new thinking was Michael Harrington, a leader in the Socialist party, whose avowed purpose in life has been to push the agenda that he believed was best for America, the Socialist one. It is his book, *The Other America,* which was read by Presidents Kennedy and Johnson and many others, which helped to motivate the change.
As a result of his book, we abruptly switched from the "rights of man" that had been taught by Locke, Paine, Jefferson and others.

FREEDOM WILL CONQUER RACISM (AND SEXISM)

These "rights" had stimulated our independence from England and had led our country on the road to individual liberty and freedom.

Our civil rights leaders had always agreed with the "law of nature" as expressed by Locke that, "[N]o one ought to harm another in his life, liberty, or possessions."[2] We believed that the reason that individuals create "societies" is for the sole purpose of protecting their natural rights. But, since no one possesses the right to invade the rights of others, he cannot bestow upon society the right to invade the rights of others. Therefore, we had always believed that a society acts in accordance with natural law only when it scrupulously observes the sanctity of the rights of each individual.

As Thomas Paine said, "Man did not enter into society to become *worse* than he was before, nor to have less rights than he had before, but to have those rights better secured."[3]

But all of this thinking which had sparked America ever since its beginning was scrapped in 1965.

At that point, we embraced the values of socialism. We went from "equal opportunity" to "equal results." We went from protecting the rights of individuals to protecting the rights of the group.

Under the values of Locke, Paine, and Jefferson, a person could work as hard or as little as he or she wished. It was his choice. But under the values of Harrington, this was no longer true. According to him, we must see that everyone had the same result. Harrington would not recognize the right of a person to be a hermit or a "failure." Everyone had to receive the same amount of food and housing. It was not the beginning point that mattered for Harrington; it was where everyone ended that was important.

In our schools today, we see it in "outcome-based" education.

The only problem with having everyone end at the same point, of course, is that this cannot be accomplished without coercion. There has to be a giant dictator sitting somewhere who will decide exactly how we are going to accomplish the goal of distributing equally to everyone.

As one prominent philosopher says, "[T]he only way to place [everyone] in an equal position would be to treat them differently. Equality before the law and material equality are therefore not only different but are in conflict with each other; and we can achieve either the one or the other, but not both at the same time."[4]

CIVIL RIGHTS ACTIVISTS: WHERE ARE YOU?

But no matter. Michael Harrington's goals were embraced by the powerful in Washington. And President Johnson noted the change in his speech.

The change shocked old liberals such as Justice William O. Douglas who wrote in a Supreme Court case where a black had been preferred over a white, "There is no constitutional right for any race to be preferred....Whatever his race, [the white applicant] had a constitutional right to have his application considered on its individual merits in a racially neutral manner."

And when Justice Douglas expressed these concerns to the other members of the Supreme Court at its Conference, all of the Justices sat in silence except for Thurgood Marshall. He said, "You guys have been practicing discrimination for years. Now it is our turn."[5]

Justice Marshall had forgotten what he had argued for the NAACP before the Supreme Court in 1953 in the case that ended school segregation, *Brown v. Board of Education*. Then he had said, that the ideal was to "prohibit all state action predicated upon race or color," and "that the Constitution is color blind is our dedicated belief."[6]

In the old days of racism, the supporters of slavery used to defend that terrible system by saying that white people needed to "provide for, and take care of the Negro." In the new era of racism, Michael Harrington says that the blacks still need someone to take care of them. He ridicules those who say, "[T]he Negroes will rise in the society like the Irish, the Jews, the Italians, and all the rest."[7]

Where Are Those Who Support Civil Liberties?

As we have seen, the president of Boston University is no longer allowed to state his views on the care of our children. If he believes that a parent should stay home and take care of the children, should it be *"against the law"* for him to say that?

Where are our civil libertarians?

Have not all of us lost a part of our liberty when this is done to President Silber?

How about a businessman? How is he supposed to prove that he loves black people or women? It is very difficult to prove something like that, and yet he must prove it in America today. He has lost a great amount of the freedom that we have always held so precious.

FREEDOM WILL CONQUER RACISM (AND SEXISM)

Or how about a business which is supposed to watch the morals of its employees? We have gone through a period in our legal history where our nation and our children have been exposed to tremendous amounts of porn and filth in the name of Freedom of Speech. And yet this Freedom of Speech does not extend to our businesses. They are supposed to act as arbiters of the morals and the speech of all of their employees. If a male supervisor is ever speaking to a female employee, the company has a duty to go running over and find out what he is saying. If it tries to clean up the language in the workplace and it disciplines an employee for saying a bad word, it will undoubtedly have a suit from the union. If it doesn't, it will have a discrimination suit. Its role as "chaperone of the workplace" is not an enviable one.

We need a new awakening of our civil libertarians in the United States.

They need to stop the stifling of civil rights that has occurred under the Civil Rights Act. And they need to open up the avenues of entrepreneurship that are being denied to our minority citizens.

Why can a young person not contract for his or her labor at any price that he deems to be beneficial for him? Why is the state allowed to block the entry of young people into so many occupations today? These are the types of concerns that the civil libertarians of today should be embracing.

As Professor Walter Williams says, our civil libertarians should be promoting our right to work:

"The broad solution to exclusion for all Americans is for the United States Supreme Court to interpret the right to work as it now interprets the right to speech. The Court has all but said that there is no compelling [government] reason for limiting freedom of speech. Similarly, there are very few compelling [government] reasons for limiting the freedom to work."[8]

23

WHO IS GETTING TOO MUCH?

When we give more to our "minorities," who are we going to take it from? Who is getting too much in our society?

The number of Anglo-Saxons is only 14% of the population. Are we going to take it from them?

Who are the "over-achievers?"

The Jews and Asians are two of them. When we have a quota system, are we going to have to cut back on the numbers of these races, who have succeeded, in order to make a balance?

One person who is concerned about this is Harvard sociologist, Nathan Glazer, who says that we are Balkanizing our country. Up until the 1960's we all considered ourselves to be Americans. And we were proud to do so.

But this began to change in the 1960's. As we started to treat the blacks differently, we began to raise other questions.

"[T]he effort to make the Negro equal to the *other* Americans raised the questions of who *are* the other Americans?"[1]

This is not to minimize the problems that the blacks in America have faced. But we must be careful when we perform such drastic surgery on the culture of America that we do not kill the patient in the process. That would not do anyone any good, whites or blacks. We still have one of the best civilizations in the world, and we must maintain that and include everybody in it, not destroy it.

It always used to be assumed in the past that each ethnic group would have to struggle for a while. But after a time, they would succeed.

What was unique about a very large percent of the blacks was that they were immigrants who came not from without the country but from within it. They came from the farms of the South to an urban culture which required education and skills they did not possess.

As we attempted to push these people beyond the point of their skills and education levels without first changing those skills and education, the other groups who had just struggled or were still struggling had a legitimate complaint.

As Professor Glazer says, "Was it true that the only way the great national effort to overcome discrimination against groups could be carried out was by recording, fixing, and acting upon the group affiliation of every person in the country?"[2]

What has happened as a result?

Sociologist Glazer says that the tone of black political rhetoric shifted from emphasizing, "We are like everyone else and want only integration," to "We are, of course, different from anyone else and want our proper share of power and wealth."[3]

This changed the whole landscape of America. And other groups began to make similar demands.

"This was a very striking change," says Glazer.

"It legitimated the raising of similar demands among such distinctive groups as Mexican Americans and Puerto Ricans. It helped create a Native American movement. And it helped, too, to legitimate the same kind of demands among white ethnic groups. These groups had emphasized: 'We are like all other Americans, and even more so. We work harder, we are more patriotic, we are more anti-Communist.'"

"What the rise of a distinctive black political movement meant was that inevitably the question had to be raised, 'Are we *indeed* like all other Americans only more so'? Or—another form of the question—'Is it to our *interest* anymore to emphasize this kind of identity rather than a separate identity as ethnics?' If we are like all other

WHO IS GETTING TOO MUCH?

Americans, then we bear the responsibility for slavery, exploitation, and imperialism. If we are, however, Poles, Italians, Jews, and the like, we have our history of being exploited to refer to in protecting our position or extending it."[4]

And thus we saw in 1988, presidential candidate Michael Dukakis traveling around the country to Greek neighborhoods and saying, "Vote for me, I'm Greek." Why should that possibly be of any importance to anyone? And yet this racist expression was never noted, much less criticized, by any commentator that I ever noticed.

Are We Balkanized?

Is our country becoming Balkanized? Are we to become another Lebanon or Bosnia with each race fighting and clawing for its "share?"

In the latest introduction to his book, Professor Glazer says that some of the worst things that he fears have not happened. But don't be too sanguine. *The Fort Worth Bank* case shows that the use of quotas is very much on the march.

We are not going backward in our use of race. We are still going forward. And where we will end, no one knows.

One of the most popular presidents in our history was unable to accomplish anything in eight years. This whole intellectual concept has a life of its own. Congress has given up. It doesn't want to know what is going on. It is afraid to act or it will be branded and tarred as Senator Goldwater was. Even the conservative judges now seem uncertain as to what they should do.

Where it will finally end is anyone's guess.

One justice on the Supreme Court who can hardly be counted as an extremist, John Stevens, sends a very strong warning. He says that if the government is serious about defining by race, it must look at what happened to Nazi Germany:

"If the National Government is to make a serious effort to define racial classes by criteria that can be administered objectively, it must study precedents such as the First Regulation to the Reichs Citizenship Law of November 14, 1935."[5]

This law defines a Jew as "anyone who descended from at least three grandparents, who were racially full Jews," etc.

Is Justice Stevens' comment an exaggeration? Do we want to find out? Do we want to find out where this will stop in our country?

FREEDOM WILL CONQUER RACISM (AND SEXISM)

We do know that Jews are only 3% of the population, but they are 9% of college faculties, 19% at prestigious colleges, and 24% of faculties at law schools and medical schools. They have been over 50% of the students at Yale Law School.

There have been reports that so many Asians are getting into colleges that there have been restrictions put on them. Harvard denied this in 1985 after its college newspaper reported a study which showed that the number of Asians had remained frozen at 15%. But the author of the study, Arthur Hu, remained adamant.[6]

Where will this end if we keep up our emphasis on race? No one knows.

Section VI

MUCH OF OUR INDUSTRY IS RUSTING ... EVERYONE'S AFRAID TO TALK ABOUT THE CAUSE

Much of our industry is rusting.

The men who used to work in many of those factories are struggling. Their wives have been forced to work. Many blacks have given up any hopes of getting a job.

There's a major cause that everyone is *afraid* to mention.

The Civil Rights Act is a forbidden subject in this regard. Although many economists worry about the regulations that are hampering our businesses, we hear almost nothing about one of the most intrusive regulations of all, the Civil Rights Act. President Kennedy did not include any regulations about employment in the Act that he first presented to Congress. He had reason for concern. We have put a tremendous burden on our businesses.

And we've been told that all businessmen in the United States are sexists and racists. This is quite an accusation to make against anyone. But we have done it. And we wonder why many of our businesses are not doing so well anymore.

24

WHY DO WE INSIST ON DRIVING OUR BUSINESSES OVERSEAS?

During the debate in 1964, Sen. Tower worried about "keeping America competitive."

He was very prescient, saying:

"Whether we like it or not, our American economy is engaged in a worldwide competition with the economies of other nations. All of us must be concerned with maintenance of a strong American position with regard to this economic competition."

He continued:

"And yet here we are today attempting to legislate still further harassments upon American employers and American workers and American unions. Here we are talking about the addition to our laws of a so-called equal employment requirement that is not only unconstitutional but also would operate as a massive depressant upon our economy."[1]

His fears have become true.

These fears were repeated in 1982 by the general counsel at the EEOC, Michael Connolly, who said that jobs were being lost to other countries where the businesses were able to produce more

WHY DO WE INSIST ON DRIVING OUR BUSINESSES OVERSEAS?

economically. He opined that minorities and women were not being helped by this overregulation.[2]

But Connolly's remarks were said during a very short window in the early 1980's when some people dared to be critical of the Civil Rights Act. But that window lasted only a very short time; the Reagan administration was pummeled so badly by the "elite" and its minions in the press that it had to withdraw.

Has It Hurt?

Were Tower and Connolly correct? Has the Civil Rights Act affected our workers and consumers? Has it contributed to the rusting of our industries?

In 1965, the Civil Rights Act made its effect on business for the first time.

Two years later, in 1967, our "team" peaked relative to the rest of the world. Our industrial production was more than 34% of the world total.[3]

From then on, it has been largely down hill.

Even Pat Buchanan who usually appears to relish any controversy is afraid to discuss this issue. When he was running for President in 1996, he was at a debate in Atlanta and was questioned by Cynthia Tucker, the "elite" liberal writer of the *Atlanta Constitution* what he was going to do about the "glass ceiling." He responded by assuring her that it was a terrible thing and he would certainly do his best to eliminate it.

It was at this point that I rolled my eyes and realized that someone had to write this book because *everyone* was afraid to discuss the issues and tell the truth.

However, Buchanan did strike a chord with many of the people whose jobs have gone overseas. After the elections were over, Buchanan wrote in a column that our trade deficit in 1996 went up to $170 billion in red ink, with Japan selling us $47 billion more than it bought and China now in second place with a $41 billion surplus over us. The real wages of our workers rose in 1996 to $11.98/hour so that the N.Y. Times ran a graph titled, "End of a Drought?" But these wages were only at the level of 1965 and they were $2/hour lower than our best year, 1973.[4]

There is no question that some workers in our country are hurting; no one disagrees. I do not know enough about economics to argue whether we need tariffs or free trade. (But common sense would seem to dictate that NAFTA and GATT have not given us free trade if we must have foot after foot of regulations and rules.)

But I do know that our basic industries are having a difficult time competing on the world market because they can't have the best workers on their teams.

How Much Is It Hurting?

How much of our decline is because of the Civil Rights Act?

The "elite," of course, would say there has been none. They believe that only a racist or sexist would even *ask such a question*. But John Hunter, an industrial psychologist at Michigan State University and Frank Schmidt at the University of Iowa have done some studies, which show:

<u>*Our total output as a nation would be $150 billion higher each year if our businesses were free to use tests and select on merit*</u>.

That's about 2.5% of our Gross National Product.

Schmidt and Hunter believe that our productivity stall of the 1970's was caused by the effects of the war against testing.

In addition, this does not count the tremendous costs to business of complying with all of the government red tape at $16.5-$19.7 billion for direct costs and another $95 billion for indirect costs.

Not Surprising

These numbers from Schmidt and Hunter are not surprising.

Running any business is just the same as running a sports team.

Suppose that our Olympic hockey team is getting ready for the next Winter Olympics. Will they pick a player from every section of the country?

"That's absurd," you'll say. Of course, they won't do that. They need the best players they can possibly get.

Think what it would do to the morale of the team if they insert a "*qualified*" player as determined by the EEOC or a federal judge, instead of the person that the coach believes is the very best. Instead of having an "edge," with every player putting out his very best, the team would start to "ease up" just a bit. They won't skate quite so hard if their teammate might miss the puck. The pride would be gone.

We spend billions of dollars a year trying to motivate workers, trying to get them to pull together as a team. If a business is successful

WHY DO WE INSIST ON DRIVING OUR BUSINESSES OVERSEAS?

in accomplishing that, it will be successful. If it is not, then you can write it off as a doomed failure.

It is a constant struggle to keep that winning spirit. But when a business executive is able to accomplish this, then he or she will have a fine business or a hockey team.

And, of course, this is also to the workers' benefit; because if an executive can't pull it off and get the workers working together as a team with the best player in every slot, then there's going to be no money for increased salaries. And that's what we're all interested in.

We can't argue whether or not that increase in money will actually be distributed "fairly" with the workers. That's the subject for another book. But we do know that if there is no increase in the amount and quality of production, then there won't be any increase in profits to argue over.

Or, to the contrary, if the productivity actually becomes worse, then the business will fail. And the jobs will be gone.

And the consumers will be suffering also. They may even start rooting for a Japanese or German team.

If we in the United States continue to damage our entrants in the "Olympics of the Marketplace," we mustn't be surprised if we do not do well.

What Is a "Qualified Worker?"

What does the EEOC mean when it says that a business must be satisfied if it is told to hire a "qualified" worker?

It means that it cannot require that a black or a woman be more qualified than the lowest "qualified" incumbent.

This is what the president's OFCCP specifically mandated in its famous "Revised Order No. 4," which was later endorsed by the EEOC.

A professor, Sidney Hook, pointed out how this would damage his college, or any organization. "It opens the door to hiring persons who cannot meet *current standards of qualification* because, forsooth, a poorly qualified incumbent was hired by some fluke or perhaps years ago when the department was struggling for recognition."[5]

Even though every organization is always trying to upgrade its members, such a regulation makes it impossible to do so because it will always be bringing in people at the *low* end.

But this is what American business was told to do. The chairman of the EEOC was asked what a business must do if there were two applicants for a job: a fairly well qualified woman and a man who was somewhat better qualified. "If it's just a question of 'somewhat better,' you should probably hire the woman," he said.[6] And of course, the even more important question which was not asked of him, how will a business decide whether he is "a lot better," "somewhat better" or "about equal?"

As a result, rather than going to the extremely expensive task of hiring lawyers, industrial psychologists and statisticians to produce studies that the courts wouldn't accept anyhow, the businesses just gave up. "The result was a well-documented decline in the quality of employees hired and the rejection of the merit principle. Applicants were hired who previously would have been considered unqualified."[7]

As just one example, when the U.S. government was forced to give up its test for hiring professional employees, it cost the government about ½ billion dollars a year according to the Office of Personnel Management. Just one government agency, the IRS, estimated a yearly loss of $115 million in its department owing to reduced efficiency.[8]

Does this affect _you_? . . . When you go to a hospital for expert care, consider this. _Every_ employee in _every_ hospital in the country—whether a doctor, nurse or other professional—is covered under the Act.

You may be treated by a "qualified" doctor or nurse. Or if you are not that lucky, you could be treated by someone who isn't even at the "qualified" level. He or she may have been hired simply because the hospital was tired of always trying to determine who is "qualified" and then being taken to court, second-guessed, and having a judge decide who they should hire and how much they should pay in damages. So they gave up and started to fill their quotas by hiring anyone who was marginally "qualified."

If you have children, their teachers may be only "qualified," because every school in the country is also covered.

This is very important to everyone in many areas of our lives.

Why Are Our Basic Industries Suffering?

"Okay," you'll say, "maybe the productivity of our 'team' and our world competitiveness isn't as good as it used to be. But you can't _prove_ that the Civil Rights Act did it."

WHY DO WE INSIST ON DRIVING OUR BUSINESSES OVERSEAS?

There were undoubtedly a lot of other causes contributing to these facts, but the timing would make a person suspicious that the Civil Rights Act did indeed have an impact.

Many readers will be saying that all of the problems in American business were the result of poor "management." But don't make the mistake of thinking that the Civil Rights Act affects only the lowest levels. The "quota" provisions apply to promotions as well as to hires. The "quota" provisions apply to the highest levels of management, engineering and every aspect of American business.

And don't forget that if a business has to stop requiring high school or college diplomas or stop its testing of employees, it does so for everyone. Even if it were considering two white males for a job, it could no longer use diplomas or tests in judging who was the better person.

We all know that the Civil Rights Act became effective in 1965, and it took a few years before the bureaucracy was able to make its impact felt. We also know that this nation peaked as an industrial leader of the world in 1967.

Any independent researcher would certainly be suspicious of those factors.*

Certainly, I must agree that the late 1960's were the beginning of an important "business bashing" period that has ebbed somewhat but continues today. The 1960's began a period when we would regulate, control and hate our businesses almost to death. We have

---

* Historian Paul Johnson puts it in perspective with the following:

But the anti-business climate was not the creation of politics alone. It was also the work of the courts, which in the 1960s entered a period of aggressive expansion—part of the movement towards a litigious society—led by the Supreme Court. Chief Justice Waite had laid down the correct principle in 1877: "For protection against abuses by legislatures, the people must resort to the polls, not the courts." But in the 1950s and early 1960s, liberal America had appealed to the court to remedy the refusal of Congress to pass effective civil rights legislation. The courts responded and, having acquired the taste for power, indulged it long after the essential civil rights battle was won. They eroded the legitimate sphere not only of Congress but of the presidency, not only in the area of rights but in the conduct of the economy. Thus the early 1970s saw the birth not only of the "imperial press" but of the "imperial judiciary."

The animus of the court was directed particularly against businessmen, notably when the judiciary, by an extension of the civil rights concept, embraced the

FREEDOM WILL CONQUER RACISM (AND SEXISM)

treated our businesses as though they are not "us." And then we wonder why we lose jobs to Japan and the rest of the world.

We had seen the goose who laid the golden egg and we were determined to take the goose apart and put it back together in the way we thought looked nicer. We never considered that we might kill or cripple the goose in the process.

At the end of the 1980's, we were seeing some good news. The competitiveness seemed to be returning. In 1986 and 1987, our productivity per worker rose more than in Japan.[9]

Why did it start to rise? The experts say our management improved as we involved the workers in more of a team effort. We also increased our automation by replacing workers with computers and new machinery. And, of course, many workers took a cut in pay, which would boost the dollar volume per worker. But a big reason was that the U. S. dollar dropped in value, thus making our products much cheaper for the rest of the world to buy.[10]

Our exports to other countries were booming.

But this good news was not across the board. Most of the jump in exports was coming from small companies. It was not the large giants that were exporting. Much of their manufacturing had already been shifted out of the country. They were manufacturing in other countries.[11]

Is it merely a coincidence that large business, which has been hit the hardest by the Civil Rights Act was doing poorly or moving out

---

principle of "affirmative action" (that is, discrimination in favor of "underprivileged groups") and began the process of imposing "race quotas." This was only one aspect of "rights": the rights of women, homosexuals, the handicapped and many other collective entities were interpreted by the courts as enforceable against powerful institutions, such as business or government. The Supreme Court in effect reinterpreted the constitution to sustain the particular political and legislative preferences of the judiciary, which were liberal. Hence constitutional principles, and the legal practice derived from them, changed with frightening speed. A growing proportion of business resources and executive time was devoted to responding to litigation: in the 1970s, America had four times as many lawyers *per capita* as West Germany, twenty times as many as Japan....The cumulative effect of these and many similar decisions was to make it exceedingly difficult to reverse the growth of government expenditure and create room for a revival of business confidence and efficiency.   From *Modern Times*, p. 663

WHY DO WE INSIST ON DRIVING OUR BUSINESSES OVERSEAS?

of the country? Can I prove that it wasn't just cheap labor that made our largest businesses move out of the U. S.? No, I can't.

But there has always been cheap labor in Mexico and other parts of the world. Why did this rapid flight from our shores *suddenly* happen at this time?

And there's no question but that when the conditions became right, it wasn't the large corporations that started exporting goods to other countries.

It was the small businesses that started to put America ahead again; the ones that hadn't yet felt the full impact of the Civil Rights Act. It was also the high-tech industries which have a less difficult time proving to a judge that they need the brightest and most capable person.

In 1996, manufacturing again rose to 19% of Gross Domestic Product, but the number of workers in manufacturing dropped from 20 million to 18.5 million and the percentage of workers in manufacturing dropped from 22% of the workforce to only 15%.

Education and Training Are The Answer

Everyone agrees that if we are going to improve our "team," we need a lot more education and training. It's the answer to a better work force, a more productive work force. It's always been our "ace in the hole."

And that's why all of America is telling our young people, "Stay in school." "Get the best education you can."

Everybody except, of course, the persons who enforce the Civil Rights Act.

The U. S. Supreme Court has said in its opinions about the Civil Rights Act that education is not important. It has talked about the foolishness of any business which requires a diploma as a requirement of getting a job. It said in the *Duke Power* case:

"History is filled with examples of men and women who rendered highly effective performance without the conventional badges of accomplishment in terms of certificates, diplomas, or degrees."[12]

In other words, the youth of America needn't bother getting a high school diploma or a college education. It's not important.

The U. S. Supreme Court said that a business can no longer require a diploma of its employees unless the business goes to court and proves to the judges of America that there is no other way for them to hire or promote.

FREEDOM WILL CONQUER RACISM (AND SEXISM)

What message does this send to the youth of America? The message is out on the streets that "they" can't make you graduate from high school anymore. Or college either.

What does this do to a business which is competing in the "Olympics of the Marketplace?"

Does this mean that Supreme Court judges will no longer require that a person who wants to work for them have a law degree? Can a teenager walk in off the street and start working as a clerk for the judges? No, that's different; those people need to graduate from Harvard, Yale and the finest law schools and be tested to death before they start to work for a judge. But for the "rest of you out there," you don't need to be so "picky" about the people who work for you.

We could cite many thousands of examples. But you get the point. If blacks or women do not have as many college degrees or if they have been convicted of more crimes, then you can not use those criteria when you hire anyone, even if a business is deciding between two white males. All businesses have lost much of their ability to decide who to hire.

What does it mean in practical terms to American business and its workers and consumers? Here are just a few sample cases out of many thousands that have been decided:

- A college degree was always required by one company to enter its "management training program," but this is now against the law.[13]
- Although a social worker (who investigates cases of child abuse and similar problems in families) was always a college graduate, this is now unlawful.[14]
- Where a physical education professor at a college is required to have a Ph.D., this violates federal law.[15]
- Even though a job applicant has a conviction for criminal fraud and has made false statements to the employment office, a company cannot just refuse to hire him as head of "security."[16]
- An employee with 15 misdemeanor convictions in four years could not be discharged for that reason.[17]
- A school board's policy of putting a "stopper" on all applicants who had been convicted of a felony past their 21st birthday was illegal.[18]
- Where a family business for 73 years had over one hundred family members who were shareholder-employees, all of Italian descent, who were given preference in driver positions or management, this violated federal law.[19]

WHY DO WE INSIST ON DRIVING OUR BUSINESSES OVERSEAS?

- The makers of Ivory Soap could no longer require 20 years of service for people considered for management level positions.[20]

This list of examples could go on and on.

And of course practically most of any testing is illegal. Never mind that this had been used for the entire century as a fair and scientific manner of picking a person for a job at which he or she would do well. It is now in any practical sense, "illegal."

Has It Helped?

Does anyone believe that the Civil Rights Act has helped the "productivity" of America? No one could argue that it has helped. The only question is, "How much has it hurt?"

Please do not misunderstand. There is no question but that a business is improved when it hires the best employee, regardless of that person's race, color or sex.

That has always been true. A business that hires anyone but the most qualified person is going to suffer. The plain, simple law of economics will make that come true sooner or later. And it is much better for our country now that we have broken down some of the old barriers and have a larger pool of people to draw from, regardless of their race or sex.

But when we set a law into motion such as we did in the Civil Rights Act, we have given a fantastic amount of power to some people in Washington to remold our society the way they think it should be.

John F. Kennedy spoke out against quotas and was very cautious about even putting Civil Rights at all into the business community. He was much more inclined to use the leadership of his office than to use the compulsion of a law. And he did have many, many meetings with business leaders, pointing out to them that they must take the lead in this endeavor. It was Lyndon Johnson who really pushed the law to its utmost as he tried to prove to the world that he, Lyndon Johnson, was not a bigot and that he was a "leader."

What had started as friendly cooperation under Kennedy's "Plans for Progress" changed when it suddenly became antagonistic and unfair. Companies that had proudly publicized their minority employment suddenly became reluctant to make any comments about them (as we saw with Sears).

FREEDOM WILL CONQUER RACISM (AND SEXISM)

In 1982, a survey showed that the 500 largest companies were spending a total of close to $1 billion a year just to fill out the reports.[21] Just to fill out the reports.

And would you like to know how we picked the contractors for the space shuttle? A vice president of the Rockwell International Corporation says that when his company was awarded the $2.6 billion space shuttle contract, "a definite factor" was their success in filling their quotas.[22]

The telephone company had always resisted its unions' demands that workers should be promoted on seniority, and it retained the right to promote the best qualified person. But this changed under pressure from the federal government, sometimes to a black but usually to a woman who was "basically qualified." No longer "the best" but someone who was "basically qualified." The company revealed that a decline of one second by its operators cost $20 million annually[23] and that adding one day to its training program for telephone operators costs over $1 million a year.[24]

Probably the most ironic fact is that while many members of our society drive in Toyotas and Hondas and condemn our American business, they do not realize that Japan is still one of the most insular and therefore one of the most racist and sexist societies.

Very few in Japan were surprised in 1986 when the Prime Minister of Japan said that our intellectual standard is low because of our blacks and Hispanics.[25] But many in this country were shocked.

Prime Minister Yasuhiro Nakasone said: "We have become quite an intelligent society, much more than the United States. In America there are quite a few blacks, Puerto Ricans and Mexicans. On average [the intelligence] is extremely low."

It is extremely ironic that many of those who support the Civil Rights Act say that America is no longer capable of producing a good product (they don't wonder why this may be true today); therefore, they drive in cars from a country that will not tolerate any outsider, much less a black. Meanwhile, many of those who believe that the Civil Rights Act is damaging our country's manufacturers are still loyal to the workers of this country, both black and white, and drive in domestic autos.

Even the crude remark by the Prime Minister has apparently had no effect on car purchases in the U.S.

The most popular hire in the U. S. is a black, Spanish-surnamed female engineer. The personnel director of one aerospace company

WHY DO WE INSIST ON DRIVING OUR BUSINESSES OVERSEAS?

complained bitterly in 1975 that it was just as though they were bidding for seven-footers in basketball or 25-game winners in baseball. They were offering salaries $200-$300 per month higher than for white males, stock options, and they even offered to place the engineering student on the payroll six months before graduation.[26]

What Happens in the Real World

When I was just a new lawyer, a judge dismissed a case where I represented the defendant. It was so obvious that he did not even allow it to go to the jury. But then he turned to me and said, "How much will your insurance company pay?" I was naive and shocked. The judge had already dismissed the suit. The other lawyer and his client had brought a frivolous suit, wasted the court's time and yet the judge was instructing me that I should telephone the insurance company and recommend that they give something so that the lawyer and his client would have something for their time.

This is what happens in almost every suit, *including those under the Civil Rights Act*.

Therefore, if a business has an incompetent employee and has to fire him or her, it will have a lawsuit on its hands if that person is female, over 40, black, gay (in many states), alcoholic, overweight, etc. etc. If you fire one of those protected persons (and that includes almost everyone), you're going to have a lawsuit. And if you have a lawsuit, the lawyer will quickly say, "You'd better settle." The saddest thing is that the lawyer will be correct. So the smart thing is to give the employee the extortion money when they are fired and obtain a written "Release" so that they cannot sue.

You do this almost regardless of the circumstances. Of course, this hurts the hard working, conscientious employee, but we don't seem to worry much about those persons today anyhow.

"Go Home and Put on Some Clothes"

Every executive in America has had this problem. When a beautiful, high school girl was working at a hardware store near my home one summer, the manager was having a difficult time keeping the store employees working. The girl's skirts were up to the top of her thighs, as is true with most young women today; and her top was form-fitted, which is also usual. She was a captivating creature and she was captivating the entire store away from their work. But there was nothing the manager could do about it without getting into potential trouble with the federal government.

He could only wait until the summer was over and she would go back to school.

I used to feel sorry for some of my male employees who had to sit there all day and watch the young women parading by in their clothes that are worn solely for the purpose of getting the attention of men.

Everyone knows that women are the seductive gender while men are aggressive. (The feminists haven't change that yet.) And yet the U.S. courts have made it so that an employer can dare to say almost nothing to a female employee, no matter how outrageous her conduct or her dress.

But if any male employee is foolish enough to respond to the invitation, the employer is liable for the "harassment." The employer is a chaperone even though he has no control over the situation.

We live in a world of "instant sex" where women go to bars and wander home with anyone they meet (or even have sex right in the bar[27]) and arrive at work with clothes that are meant to seduce. Yet when these same women get to the doorway of the workplace, the whole culture of society must be changed and it is the employer who must do so. He is required to be a strict chaperone—but only with the males. He has no control over the females.

As one woman commentator says:

"Thus have young women been convinced to play the whore for their male peers. In the United States today, an adolescent high school male can find at the desk next to him a young girl equipped by their high school clinic with the latest birth control device ready to provide him with the sexual services that, in an earlier time, he would have received, if at all, from a prostitute."[28]

And yet when these people arrive at the workplace, the employer must change that culture for a few hours. How wonderful it would be to see women again arriving at work in dignified and professional dress.

Who Is Protected?

Who is protected from discrimination if we include all of the federal laws? It covers a vast majority of the population, well over 75%, including:
- Females.
- Blacks.

WHY DO WE INSIST ON DRIVING OUR BUSINESSES OVERSEAS?

- Those of Spanish, Asian, Pacific Island, American Indian, or Eskimo ancestry.
- Vietnam-era veterans.
- Handicapped, which might include alcoholism, drug addiction, over weight people, etc.
- Almost everyone over 40.
- Members of religious and ethnic groups, such as Jews, Catholics, Italians, Greeks, and Slavs.

And there are probably more that I have not included.*

---

*   Even many young white males are included in a "protected" class because of the many other laws that Congress has been passing. For example, the Americans With Disabilities Act, while noble in purpose, has caused many more land mines for employers, of which the following are just a few. I could cite many, many other cases.

As you read these cases, you will understand why I say we should make the Civil Rights Act a *criminal* offense. It is obvious that no one knows what this new law covers, but if a business doesn't follow it, it will be in trouble. The law is obviously too vague to be obeyed.

—This employer was compassionate. The employee was receiving psychiatric treatment for "post-traumatic stress disorder," and a number of employees under him complained about his temper and volatile personality. Even though he may not have actually been "disabled," a judge held that the employer was liable because it *regarded* him as having a disability. The judge said it would have been permissible to fire the employee for his irascibility alone; however, the employer tolerated his irascibility for some time and only fired him when his boss became afraid that he was capable of a shooting spree. This was discrimination based on a perceived handicap, and the employee was awarded $790,000 for economic damages and $75,000 for mental anguish and loss of enjoyment of life. The response of expert lawyers to this case was that employers can no longer be compassionate. "One of the biggest traps that employers can fall into is trying to be 'compassionate' toward troubled employees rather than strictly enforcing the rules, experts say," was what *Lawyers Weekly USA* reported. And employers have a double burden because if they don't act against a violent employee, they could be sued by an injured employee because the federal law OSHA requires that they maintain a "safe workplace." *Lussier v. Runyon*, U.S. District Court for the District of Maine, March 1, 1994. 94 LWUSA 504.

FREEDOM WILL CONQUER RACISM (AND SEXISM)

—This employer was also compassionate. It tried to help a disruptive store manager who was throwing food off the shelves and "manhandling, berating and threatening" the employees. The company asked him if he was having any "problems" that they could help him with, and they referred him to an employee assistance program. This, said the court, was evidence that the company regarded him as having a mental disability. Therefore, when they later fired him, the jury could use this to infer that the real reason they fired him was because they believed he had a disability. Therefore he was covered by the disability act. The company was liable even though the court held that the employee was not disabled. *Holihan v. Lucky Stores, Inc.*, 87 F.3d 362 (9th Cir. 1996).

—A depressed employee was fired after she called her boss a "bitch" and said she wanted to kill her. The federal judge order her to be reinstated with back pay and attorney fees. *Collins v. Blue Cross of Michigan,* 916 F.Supp. 638 (E.D.Mass. 1995).

No one is saying that we should not be compassionate in our dealings with people. But the government cannot intelligently make those individual decisions. And a business cannot be totally responsible for every person they hire, no matter how long the person has been with them. In the case of the store manager above, this was the consensus of lawyers, according to *Lawyers Weekly USA,*

"The bottom line is that employers can no longer be 'compassionate' toward a troubled employee, experts say."

"'What this tells employers is they're better off going through an investigation and possibly terminating the employee rather than first referring him to an assistance program and giving him a chance to work out his difficulties,' says Portland, Maine, attorney Rick Finberg."

"'The employer should just terminate then and there,' says Washington D.C. attorney Jonathan Mook. 'If you're out the door, you can't be regarded as disabled.'"

"Brian Bulger of Chicago says, 'If you just go in and address the misconduct and don't worry about the reason for it, you're safer.'" (See 96LWUSA 721)

To put the above into simple language. Because of this federal law, an employer can no longer afford to be compassionate to its employees.

According to *The Wall Street Journal,* employers are winning 90% of the lawsuits filed against them under the Americans with Disabilities Act. This may sound like good news, but don't forget that the real cost to these employers is the time, energy and money spent in going to court to fight these unfair suits. And most employers do not go to court, they pay the extortion money and settle. Also, don't forget that as a taxpayer you are paying the burgeoning cost of providing judges and courtrooms to hear these tales of woe. *The Wall Street Journal,* February 18, 1997, p 1.

25

WE'RE *PUNISHING* OUR BUSINESSES

The most damaging part of the Civil Rights Act is that it's being used to *punish* our businesses.[1]

This is best illustrated by an award that was given to the Chicago office of the EEOC in 1988.[2] The head of that office was Kathleen M. Blunt, formerly an Associate Director of "Women Employed," an advocacy group for women. She is a zealous advocate for women, not the neutral person who should have been hired to work in cooperation with business to achieve a more balanced workforce.

We were assured when the Act was passed that the EEOC would be cooperative. But most people would laugh today if they were told that the EEOC should work hand-in-hand with business and unions in a joint effort to help to eliminate discrimination.

And what was Blunt's proudest accomplishment? She obtained over $3 million dollars in 1987 in settlements from area companies, and over $5 million after suit was started. That was a total of $8 million in 1987. It's much like a sales effort; how much did you make this year?

Blunt said proudly, "We have the commission's most active litigation program, particularly in class action cases."[3] One of her main contributions is a SWAT program where high profile cases are identified and pushed.

Her office of the EEOC is doing well in policing the businesses in its part of the country.

In other words, we assume that all of business is guilty and we measure our success by how much we are able to collect in fines each year.

You know about one of the companies that was harassed by Ms. Blunt and the Chicago office of the EEOC. The case certainly raised her statistics for the year. She was praised by the head of the EEOC who said the case was the "latest of many instances of the Chicago office's excellent work."[4]

Guess who was the target of Blunt's SWAT program?

It was the big glass company of Libbey-Owens, about whom we have already read.

In the last twenty-five years, we have seen a lot of our smokestack industries moving overseas. There is a lot of unemployment in the Midwest. How much has the Civil Rights Act caused the decline and the flight of these industries? Nobody knows.

But one thing is certain. There no one in the world who enjoys pain or tension. We go to great lengths to avoid that in our lives. And if the people who run the businesses in our country are constantly being attacked and vilified, they will find a way to avoid that pain in their lives. You can be certain of that.

We also see a lot of consumers in America who believe that the workmanship in America is not up to the standards of foreign countries. There is one thing you can be certain about. We do not tell the coach of our hockey team who to put in as goalie.

Will we ever allow "excellence" again in the U. S.?

Business Is To Blame

There is no question but that big business is also to blame for allowing this to happen in America.

A former executive at Ford Motor Company has written how cowardly the large corporations of America are. When he was working at Ford, the company believed, he says, in "cooperating with institutions that ... could hurt us if they were angry, even if this meant sacrificing company interests."

The executives at Ford are typical of other large companies and are merely out to keep their salaries and bonuses going for just one more year, he said. These people "have few incentives to stand and fight even in connection with public policies that damage the entire economy, provided they can attach riders or create loopholes that make individual lines of business relatively lucrative amid the general economic chaos," he says.

A Justice on the U. S. Supreme Court agrees that the large corporations are not unhappy with what is happening. They just adjust their business or they simply move out of the country. According to the judge, "[T]he cost of hiring less qualified workers is often substantially less—and infinitely more predictable—than the cost of litigating [civil rights] cases ..." But it's not as easy for an unemployed worker to "adjust."

In other words, it's easier for big business to pay its extortion than to fight. And if it's being extorted, it wants everyone else in the same boat.

We've seen that these big corporations are even going so far as to provide much of the funding for the NAACP, NOW and the other organizations which are harassing them. They believe that it is easier to buy peace than it is to fight for what is right.

U.S. District Attorneys

What we have done is to turn loose a network of U.S. "District Attorney" offices which are prosecuting any American businesses that they can get their hands on, *just to set an example.*

We call it the EEOC, but it is a "District Attorney."

It prosecutes any business that it wants to. Before 1972, it had to go to the Justice Department and request the Attorney General to sue a business. But now it asks no one. It just starts suit.

And if a business is "guilty," the fine that it will have to pay could run into the millions. But unlike other criminals, there are no protections to make sure that a trial is fair for a business which has been accused of "discrimination." In fact, a business is presumed to be guilty before it even starts its side of the case—if it doesn't have the proper numbers of blacks or women.

FREEDOM WILL CONQUER RACISM (AND SEXISM)

When an agency like the EEOC is established, it is not neutral people who are put in charge. These are always zealots, who are out to reform and change the world in their image.

But it's not just the EEOC. A class action suit by a private group can be very costly. One U. S. judge got so angry at the NAACP Legal Defense Fund that he took the very unusual step of imposing $83,000 in penalties against it and its clients. That organization had brought a suit against the U. S. Army at Fort Bragg claiming racial discrimination. But seven years later with 13,000 pages of testimony, 1200 exhibits, 149 statements from witnesses each over 50 pages long, and 95 Orders written by the judge, the NAACP lost. The case had cost us taxpayers millions of dollars. And this was not a case brought by a beginner, but by seasoned civil rights attorney Julius Chambers. The judge said, "No reasonable attorney could possibly have hoped to prevail in this case."[5]

But they don't plan on winning, don't you see?

They just plan on wearing you down. *And then you settle*.

Any reasonable person would settle. As the EEOC itself said: "Court ordered compliance with Title VII often results in large expenses to the employer, usually exceeding the cost of effective voluntary affirmative action."[6]

Let's put that in our language. "It costs a lot more for a business to fight the EEOC than it does to just give in and 'settle.'"

It's only the fools that will spend their lives fighting a case such as this. Not to mention the money in lawyers' fees and the time that would be better spent on improving the business.

Not Unusual

The *Sears* case is not unusual. It is typical of what happens to U. S. businesses every day.

A U. S. judge out in Michigan issued a blistering opinion and socked attorney fees against the EEOC for a suit against the Union Camp Paper Company.[7] An employee had been disciplined 22 times by 11 different supervisors, and had been suspended for his behavior a total of 37 days, and then had been discharged. The Michigan Civil Rights Commission dismissed his claims of discrimination three separate times and he also lost five times before an arbitrator.

But after all that, the U.S. government brought a suit against the company anyhow, saying that the employee had been discriminated against because he was Hispanic. After 19 months of court proceedings, it lost. The U. S. judge was so angry at the EEOC that he wrote:

"[T]he charging party cries discrimination and the EEOC, despite an utter lack of evidence, sympathetically files suit, hoping that defendant will surrender rather than go to trial. When, as here, defendant refuses to knuckle under, EEOC goes to a lengthy trial, tries the case poorly, loses, and hopes a lesson has been taught."[8]

A lesson has indeed been taught.

Sure, Union Camp won that case. But every time it wanted to fire a Hispanic or a woman, was it worth it to go to court? Could it afford the bad publicity in the newspapers that Union Camp is back in court "because the federal government has caught it discriminating against minorities again." Do you believe that some Hispanics and women are going to stay employed at Union Camp even though they may not be the best?

Is Union Camp allowed to put the best players on its team that's going to compete with the Japanese and German teams?

Discrimination Cases Are Increasing Rapidly

The number of discrimination cases are increasing rapidly in the federal courts which are already greatly overloaded. In a typical state, Missouri, this type of case is attracting many more lawyers because of two events that are resulting in more settlements: 1) ongoing efforts by the court to streamline the process and increase settlements, and 2) a change in the law in 1991 which allowed for greatly increased damages (and risk to employers) by allowing for punitive damages and emotional distress.[9]

Judges are expressing frustration. At one meeting of federal judges in Missouri, one complained about the "overabundance" of these cases, which caused another to quip, "You mean you have other kinds of cases?" In one of its federal courts, 30-35% of all its cases are discrimination cases and the number is rising.

Not many race cases are being brought. The hot areas are age discrimination (which is under its own law, separate from the Civil Rights Act) and sexual harassment.

The Radicals Like Big Business

When my wife attended a program at radical feminist Wellesley College, her alma mater, they were decrying the formation of so many small businesses.

They said that it was easy to work with big business. They had gotten control over big businesses. But the small businesses (which kept our economy going and produced all the new jobs) were too independent. They did not do what they were told.

These members of the "elite" are not happy unless everything is controlled from Washington, with them in charge.

When Hillary Clinton, the most famous alumna of Wellesley was chairwoman of the President's Health Care Task Force, she was told that her plan would devastate small business, but she replied, "I can't go out and save every undercapitalized entrepreneur in America."[10]

This, despite the fact that women are starting their own businesses at twice the rate of men. In 1972 there were only 400,000 women-owned businesses. Today, there are 8 million women-owned businesses in the U.S., employing 15.5 million people with $1.4 trillion in sales.[11]

A Discouraging Story

Although it's always been tough to start a business, this story illustrates how much more difficult we are making it today.[12]

There was a plumbing company in Virginia which did work for the government and was found by the President's commission to be below its quota during one month in its use of minorities. Only 18% of the hours worked were by minority workers, whereas it was supposed to be 25%.

The reason? There were only five employees in the company and the one black male had taken seven days off to go on his honeymoon. Never mind that the owner of the business was a woman of Filipino-Mexican-Spanish origin, who went to the government office to explain the situation even though she had pneumonia and the government worker didn't show up. The next day she was hospitalized; and soon after, she gave up her business.*

---

* For an excellent book that discusses how all the laws, including the Civil Rights Act, are damaging American business, see Walter K. Olson, *The Excuse Factory: How Employment Law is Paralyzing the American Workplace* (New York: Free Press)

26

ANOTHER SMALL BUSINESS IS HARASSED BY THE U.S. GOVERNMENT

"I don't care what it costs! I want justice!"

Every lawyer has heard that from a potential client. The lawyer gets all excited about this poor person who has been so terribly wronged. He replies:

"I'll do all the paperwork as soon as I can. It'll be ready by tomorrow. I'll need $15 to pay to the clerk of the court."

"You'll need $15 ... well ... maybe I'd better go home and think about it a little more."

This is where the hard decisions start and a person decides whether it really is worth it to bring a suit. This potential client doesn't even want to pay an initial filing fee, much less a lawyer's fee or all of the other costs. Without such a safeguard, *everyone* will be suing *everyone* all the time.

Congress removed those safeguards at the end of the 1960's when it made the legal services free to poor people across the entire country. While everyone would agree that this is a noble goal, it obviously must be watched very carefully because it can easily get out of control.

Here's what it did to one small businessman.

FREEDOM WILL CONQUER RACISM (AND SEXISM)

He could have settled a discrimination suit for $3,000. Should he have done so? Or was he right to spend $80,000 to prove that he is not a "racist."

He wasn't sued by the EEOC. It was the federal poverty lawyers who sued him.

Should Lamar Have Settled?

Lamar Perlis was having trouble sleeping during September 1981. Those government poverty lawyers were taking him to a U.S. court up in Macon for being a "racist."

He knew it was hurting his truck stop because he had to spend so much time with lawyers who wanted to know everything that had ever happened in his business. He didn't have much time to think about the business nowadays.

And those articles in the papers. Did his neighbors really think that he was a racist?

Maybe his friends were right. He could settle the case for only $3,000 and forget the whole thing. But that wouldn't be honest.

But it would sure be a lot easier.

Perlis Truck Stop

If you've ever driven down to Florida along Interstate 95, you've passed by the flat, dusty fields of Central Georgia and past Perlis Truck Stop.

Most people wouldn't jump at the chance to move down there and get a job. But to Lamar Perlis it is something to be proud of. It's a very successful business where the truckers come 24 hours a day and seven days a week—to fill their big trucks with diesel fuel, get a meal, take a shower or sleep for the night. They can even have repairs made to their rigs.

But it's tough to keep a busy place like that staffed for 24 hours a day.

It's about the closest thing to running a dairy farm that Lamar Perlis could think of. You have to always be there.

Unless, of course, you can hire good help. But Lamar, like every other businessman always had a problem getting good help. And he had a special problem because he had to have four shifts in order to be open around the clock.

ANOTHER SMALL BUSINESS IS HARASSED BY THE U.S. GOVERNMENT

And that's why he had been reluctant to fire Carlton Whitehead. Carlton had been with him now ever since he opened the truck stop 6 years ago. But he had become convinced that Carlton was a thief, in addition to being a bad mechanic and an alcoholic.

And so Lamar had fired Carlton.

That's no big deal. It happens every day. The employee goes out and gets a new job, and the business gets a new employee.

But that's no longer true when the employee is a minority or a woman. Carlton was a black man.

Lamar knew something about discrimination himself. His family had come to Georgia in 1904 when the Polish Jews were immigrating to America. His father was 12 at the time. They had worked hard. And they were prosperous.

When he opened the truck stop in 1971, Lamar was pleased when Carlton, who was almost six feet tall and muscular at about 200 pounds, had come by. Lamar liked Carlton instantly. He was congenial and quiet and he could drive a bulldozer to help build the new business.

When the business opened, he became a tire repairman. In 1975, he started doing some simple mechanical work.

But even though Lamar liked Carlton, the managers in the shop did not. One of them fired him, but Lamar overruled it. And then another manager told Lamar that he should be fired. But Lamar still didn't do it.

A big problem was that of theft. With so many people having access to the inventory all the time, they were stealing everything in sight. Now, over $20,000 in inventory was missing. Lamar had used lie detector tests in the past to try to solve this problem. Carlton had had problems on these tests before. Lamar decided he had to use them again.

Carlton didn't want to take the test this time, but after finally doing so, the test examiner thought he was not telling the truth. So Lamar decided he finally had to fire Carlton.

"Carlton had done this a number of times before," says Lamar. "He had been reported to me as a potential risk by practically every supervisor that I ever worked with."

FREEDOM WILL CONQUER RACISM (AND SEXISM)

The Trial

Lamar never thought that the federal government would go after a little truck stop down on the plains of Georgia for discrimination—particularly when over 40% of his employees were black.

How could he be discriminating against blacks when he hired so many of them?

But the federal "poverty lawyers" weren't impressed by anything he said.

It took the "poverty lawyers" only a few weeks to file a complaint, although they represent only indigents. They also got the court to waive normal fees for filing a suit because Carlton claimed he was a pauper. But when they took his testimony at the end of 1978, Carlton was making $200/week after taxes, and he also rented out his 125-acre farm for more than $2,000 a year. Lamar's attorneys thought the land was worth a half million dollars.

Lamar quickly found that it would be expensive for him to defend himself against this attack by the federal government. He couldn't just go into court and tell his story. He would not only have to hire a lawyer, but also a statistician who would have to classify all of Lamar's workers since 1971 and compare them with all of the blacks in the surrounding area.

That was the hardest part. It took weeks and weeks to go back and find all the old records that the statistician needed. It had kept him and his bookkeeper really busy.

When it finally came time for trial, one mechanic, Dave Dugger, testified for Carlton. But another, Lansing Mays, testified that Dugger had promised that he'd testify for Lamar if he gave his fiancé a $2,000 loan and a job.

Albert Tookes was a 54-year-old black mechanic who had worked for Lamar for four years and was the highest paid mechanic at the truck stop. He said that blacks were treated fairly and that Carlton was a poor mechanic.

And the statistician, a professor from the University of Georgia, had found that Lamar not only had as many blacks in his work force as were available in the general population; he had *more* than he should have.

For every one of the 28 levels of employment, from "truck washers" to "manager", there were more than enough blacks. In fact, there was only one small deviation; in the 9 years that were studied,

ANOTHER SMALL BUSINESS IS HARASSED BY THE U.S. GOVERNMENT

during one year there were too many *whites* in the *lowest* category of workers, "truck washers."

The Judge Decides

At the end of the trial, the "poverty lawyers" told the judge that Lamar was guilty of racism even though he hired a higher percentage of blacks than there were in the general area. They said he had no "objective standards" to evaluate mechanics and give them raises.

But the judge disagreed. (Under the Fort Worth Bank case, Lamar would probably lose today no matter how kind he is to blacks or no matter how many he hires.)

So Lamar had won.

But had he? It cost him over $80,000 in fees to lawyers and statisticians to defend himself. It cost Carlton absolutely nothing. It cost Lamar in time and emotional drain. "The personal drain on me was significant," says Lamar. "Earnings went down in part due to my lack of attention to the company." Would he have been smarter just to pay the $3,000 to Carlton?

If you are in a small business in America today, you'd better be ready to answer that question, because you will be getting it sooner or later. It's only the small businesses that are so outraged that they will fight a case such as this. The big companies all know that it makes more business sense to pay a settlement than it is to fight a case in court.

Section VII

HOW CAN WE CONQUER RACISM & SEXISM?

What has happened in our country because of the Civil Rights Act has happened _everywhere around the entire world_ when any type of preferential policy is implemented.

Professor Sowell discovered this while studying many countries. We are not different. (He gave special attention to India, Nigeria, Malaysia, South Africa, Sri Lanka and the U.S.)[1] He found the following:

- **Strife increases.** Strife and polarization increase among the races after preferential policies are implemented. (This varies from political backlash to mob violence and civil war.)

- **Helps Only the Rich.** If any benefits do occur, they go to those members of the protected group who are already more educated and more prosperous; while the lower members of the group see their conditions deteriorate.

FREEDOM WILL CONQUER RACISM (AND SEXISM)

- **Never Ends.** Once these programs are begun, they not only persist but continue to expand and include more groups, even though they were initially defined as "temporary."*

- **Fraudulent Claims.** Fraudulent claims of belonging to the protected group are widespread.

- **Results Unknown.** There is a dearth or even total absence of data as to the outcome of these programs and their impact on society.

---

* Here's an example of this phenomenon.

In 1973, the top officials of the Nixon administration were saying that the quotas they were imposing were only temporary and would be limited to certain trades in certain cities. This was discussed at the time in an article in *Fortune* magazine.

"It seems reasonable to speculate that at some point the Administration will abandon goals and timetables, conceding that they lead in practice to preferential hiring and even quotas. Indeed, some of the program's senior officials regard the present format as temporary. [J. Stanley] Pottinger [head of the Office of Civil Rights at Health, Education and Welfare] who has spent a lot of time in recent years arguing that goals don't mean quotas, nevertheless says, 'I sure hope they're not permanent.'" March 1973 at p. 168.

27

TOO IMPORTANT FOR LAWYERS AND JUDGES

A definition of "discrimination" is much too crucial to leave to lawyers and judges. It is not because they are not capable, but because this is not their function.

They are not the ones who are expected to decide questions of "policy." They solve specific disputes between individuals.

Questions of "policy" are to be decided by Congress.

Congress has the power to hold hearings and to listen to a great debate from many different people and groups; whereas the courts must decide each case on its own merits.

What we have done is to have the important issues of "racism" and "sexism" being determined without any coherent strategy in little courtrooms around the country. The judges, while hearing their individual cases, have no concept of what effect, if any, their decisions have upon our society as a whole across the entire country.

It's Congress' Fault

But the ultimate responsibility is that of Congress.

When Clarence Thomas (now a Supreme Court justice) was head of the EEOC under President Reagan, he pointed out the problem

FREEDOM WILL CONQUER RACISM (AND SEXISM)

very clearly. He was appointed to enforce the Civil Rights Act; but he had great frustrations, as have all of us.

He says that Congress had a reason when it left the law very vague. It said only that we cannot "discriminate." Why was it left so vague? Because when the law is so vague, Congress can have it both ways.

"[Congress] can be insulated from a hostile public, when public policy has little popular support. When laws are administered or interpreted in dubious or controversial ways, the bureaucracy or the courts get the blame. On the other hand, by strategic intervention, members of Congress can get credit from those who benefit from the law or its implementation."[1]

This is not the way it used to be, says Thomas.

"Courts have played a small part in policy-making, until recently, precisely because they were not thought to be suited to the task of policy-making, or policy resolution. When they have made important political and social decisions, in the absence of majority support, they have only exacerbated the controversies. Despite the supposed neutrality of the courts, few would suggest that judges are better suited, merely because of their training, to make *political*—as opposed to judicial—decisions, than are elected officials."[2]

Do we want our courts to make "political" decisions? Of course not. That is not their purpose. A conservative moderate judge has difficulties when newly appointed because the opinions from a court are supposed to have a continuity so that the citizens will know what is lawful and what is not. It is very deleterious to have the courts continue to change the law. Therefore, although a moderate judge may wish to change the course abruptly, he or she will be much more reluctant to do so than a liberal, activist judge.

Allowing the courts to make political decisions has affected the Civil Rights Act which Thomas enforced.

"Let us look once more at the Civil Rights Act of 1964 as an example of the way in which this process has worked. We note that Congress passed a general law in relatively clear language. Subsequently, as in the case of Title VII of the Act, it was interpreted in a very different way. Does this cause great concern to members of Congress? Not really. Congress is not held accountable by the general public for the manner in which a law is implemented or

TOO IMPORTANT FOR LAWYERS AND JUDGES

interpreted. Rather, Congress, as a body, was generally credited with passing a reasonable law, which had the support of the majority."[3]

Why does Congress do this?

"The net effect is to insulate Congress, as an institution, from accountability for unpopular decisions, while preserving for Congress credit for choices that prove popular."[4]

Let's put the burden back on Congress where it belongs.

Let's not fall for the line that when the courts say something, it is from God and all good citizens must never question it. The judges of this country were never meant to make political decisions. Let's force Congress to take back that power and make those hard choices so that we as an electorate can have an intelligent choice at election time.

Is this one of the reasons why many people are becoming cynical about their ability to change anything by their votes?

"The people are becoming increasingly aware that their votes no longer reflect an ability to influence the vital centers of power,"[5] says Thomas, who continues:

"[C]ongress prefers to leave the questions of moral and social significance to the courts or bureaucracy. Perhaps this helps explain ... the greatest mass movement of our time, the movement of the American people away from the polls."[6]

Congress Agrees

Although they won't admit it, Congress agrees with this book. That's easy to prove.

Nothing in the Civil Rights Act ever applied to Congress until the Republicans took over in 1995 and changed that.

In 1978, a survey showed that out of a professional staff of 3,200 for the Senators, only 33 were black. By 1983, this had changed to 35 out of 4,660.

In the House, seven percent of the employees were blacks, mostly in clerical, restaurant and custodial positions. In 1983, only 90 were black in the House out of the 1,266 highest professional positions. And 44 of those 90 people were on the staffs of black congressman, who had mostly black staffs.[7]

The same statistics could be shown for women employees.

FREEDOM WILL CONQUER RACISM (AND SEXISM)

The "elite" had spoken wonderful words, provided great "leadership"; but they saw to it that none of it applied to them. Their staffs, after all, are confidential. These Congressmen and Senators are important people with important things to do. And they couldn't have just anyone telling them who to hire for their own personal staffs.

It is only "you other people" out there who needed to be taught a great moral lesson.

There have always been great, wonderful words that are spoken to us about civil rights. There has always been the wonderful posturing that goes on in Washington. But none of it applied to the "elite."

As Mark Twain said, "To do good is noble. To advise others to do good is also noble, and much less trouble."

This was foreseen by the men who wrote our Constitution. The father of that document, James Madison, wrote in the Federalist Papers (when he was urging the people to approve the Constitution) that we had a great safeguard. This was that Congressmen would also have to live under the laws they enacted, the same as any other citizen. Therefore, we could be assured that they would write laws that would be fair. Madison wrote:

"There can be no law [passed by Congress] which will not have its full operation on themselves and their friends, as well as on the great mass of society. This has always been deemed one of the strongest bonds by which human policy can connect the rules and the people together."

But Congress has seen fit to abrogate this rule and to pass laws which applied to everyone except themselves. No wonder we have such bad laws as a result.

You Can Understand This As Well As Any Lawyer

There is nothing that angers me more than to hear an intelligent person say, "I'm not a lawyer and I can't speak with authority ...." You do not have to be a lawyer to understand these issues. Any intelligent person knows what the Civil Rights Act says. There is nothing magical about being a lawyer.

The liberal experts will tell us, "You can't change what the courts have said. *You don't understand* the "rule of law." *You don't understand* the constitutional process."

This is not true.

TOO IMPORTANT FOR LAWYERS AND JUDGES

The judges disagree all of the time. A large number of the cases that get to the Supreme Court are there because the lower judges are in total disagreement. And the Supreme Court Justices disagree with each other much of the time.

The Supreme Court itself has changed its mind many times over the years, even on very important issues of the Constitution.

Back in 1857, the Supreme Court held that a black man had no right to sue in our courts. This was the infamous *Dred Scott* decision. And in 1896, the Supreme Court held that the state could require separate railway facilities for blacks. That was *Plessy v. Ferguson*. And in 1908 it held that a *private* school could be told by a state that it must remain segregated. That was *Berea College v. Kentucky*.

Does anyone believe that the Supreme Court should not have reversed those opinions which concern the meaning of the Constitution itself?

So don't believe this talk that the U. S. Supreme Court is some sort of sacred institution that was sent from God. It is only as good as the men or women who serve on it. And sometimes, they are great and sometimes they are not. But they are all human; none of them is a god.

If we disagree with any of the Supreme Court's decisions, we have not only the right, but the duty, to change the law. We have the obligation as members of a democratic society to work for that change.

28

WHAT DO YOU THINK?

If I have stimulated your thinking, then you must decide what you believe to be right for the country.

The choices were spelled out very crisply back in 1973 by Daniel Seligman in an article in *Fortune* magazine.[1] There are four policies that a business could use to eliminate discrimination:

1) **Discrimination is not allowed.** This is a simple policy. Everyone shall be treated alike in all decisions about hiring, promotion and pay.

2) **Affirmative Action.** Under this policy, a conscious effort is made to increase the pool of applicants to include everyone. However, when the company hires (or promotes) it picks the most qualified person, without regard to race or sex.

3) **Affirmative Action . . . *plus* Preferential Hiring.** The company not only ensures that it has a large labor pool to draw from; it systematically favors women and minority groups in the actual decisions about hiring and promoting. This might be thought of as a "soft" quota system, i.e., instead of establishing

targets that absolutely must be met, the top officers of the company beef up employment of women and minority-group members to some unspecified extent by indicating that they want those groups given a break.
4) **Hard quotas.** No two ways about it—specific numbers or proportions of minority-group members must be hired.

When we passed the Civil Rights Act in 1964, we thought we had approved #1, but we've been given #4 by the U.S. Supreme Court. Almost all of us would agree on #2, and if it were not imposed unfairly, possibly even a portion of #3 (without any involvement by the government), although that would probably be a dangerous, slippery slope.

Prof. Sowell's research and our common sense tells us that if the government is involved, it is inevitable that we will have disastrous results.

What do you think?

The President's Commission

The other problem that you must consider concerns the many businesses that are selling products and services to the federal government. Should the president alone have the dictatorial power to establish the OFCCP and exert this vast control over a large part of our businesses?

We know from past experience that any government program will grow and grow and gain more power. And we have learned that the OFCCP is no exception.

We have not discussed much about the OFCCP in this book because it is not a creation of The Civil Rights Act (nor is it governed by its law), but you cannot ignore it in your discussions.

It Will Be Difficult to Hold A Debate

It will be extremely difficult to hold a debate.

When I was researching the history for this book, I naturally went to the *New York Times* because it is known as the definitive source of news. However, I was surprised to find that much of what it had reported over the years was inadequate, inaccurate or even biased. It would have been impossible to know what had happened by using

FREEDOM WILL CONQUER RACISM (AND SEXISM)

only it as a source. Of course, the television news would be even worse.

So it will be difficult for you to obtain the facts as to what is happening in Washington and across the country.

Another reason it will be difficult is because everyone is afraid to talk, and with good reason. I would not write this book while I still owned a business. It would be equivalent to committing suicide.

The "elite" would have *buried* me with baseless lawsuits, the same way that they did Sears Roebuck, the president of Boston University and thousands and thousands of other businesses and people. Certainly, I could win most (but not all) of the baseless suits that would be brought against me, both by the federal government and by private individuals. But at what cost? No one in his right mind will attempt to speak against "Civil Rights" today.

When the "elite" see this book, they will attempt to twist the truth. They won't report that I am the one who declares that blacks and women *can* make it, because they *do* have the ability. The "elite" will never admit that; they will try to say that I am a bigot. Anyone who opposes the "elite" will be labeled "bigots" and "racists." And it will be vicious. We know that the "leading" colleges such as Smith College will not even allow people such as Jeanne Kirkpatrick to speak without shouting her down and even putting her safety in danger. Clarence Thomas is not allowed to speak.

When Ward Connerly, the black leader of the California Civil Rights Initiative, Proposition 209, was campaigning for it in 1996, the windows of his office were shot out and the premises was sprayed with graffiti. Students from the University of California at Santa Cruz vandalized his home. *The Oakland Tribune* published an editorial cartoon showing a dry cleaning shop, "Connerly and Co. Ethnic Cleansers," with a Ku Klux Klan robe hanging inside. *The Sunday Examiner and Chronicle* in San Francisco had a cartoon of two men labeled, "California Rights Initiative," carrying a gas can and fleeing a burning church labeled "affirmative action." The opponents of Connerly even went so far as to invite former Ku Klux Klansman David Duke to come from Louisiana to California to debate in favor of the subject in an effort to make it look as though it were racists who were supporting the proposition.[2]

All of the establishment politicians, including Bob Dole and George Bush, told us why the Civil Rights Act is so important,

WHAT DO YOU THINK?

because they do not want to go the route of Barry Goldwater. Other persons, particularly those in big business, are in favor of it because they are terrified of the EEOC. And well they might be. They have good cause to be terrified. Also, their businesses are overseas by now, so they really don't care. Others will be for it because when the liberal press says things over and over again, you begin to believe them even though you know they're wrong. Another problem is that most of the country is too young to remember 1964 so that they believe the distortions they have been told all of their lives.

The Press Will Not Help A Debate

The press will not help in formulating a debate. They are totally staffed by the establishment liberals. They will not even understand the issues. If you want to understand why all of the press is so liberal today, you must realize that the owners of these newspapers are "buying peace" the same as all of the other businesses. They must watch very carefully what they print and whom they hire, including their editors and reporters.

This was illustrated recently when the new head of the OFCCP, Shirley Wilcher, volunteered during an interview with *Newsday* in 1994, "We're taking a look now at Time-Warner," the publisher of *Time* magazine, *People*, *Sports Illustrated*, etc.[3] What would possibly cause Wilcher to single out and *publicly* name this one company during an interview? Is this merely an ego-trip in which she is trying to impress the world with how important she is? Or is she sending a warning to *Time*?

We don't know the answer, but if you were the CEO of *Time*, you would certainly wonder why this behemoth is after *you*.

And you would make sure that the radical, liberal, feminist point-of-view is well represented in *Time* and your publications. You would really have little choice.

This will make an honest debate a very difficult task. You will read or hear about only one side of the debate in the liberal press.

Why Our Newspapers Are Prejudiced

A tremendous struggle has occurred within our newsrooms ... because that is where the __power__ is.

It *is* worth fighting about.

FREEDOM WILL CONQUER RACISM (AND SEXISM)

In New England, almost all of our information comes from the liberal *Boston Globe*. Our lives are dominated by what it allows us to know. Many people are angry and upset with it, but there is nothing they can do. There is no viable competition. When I was in college there were four or five newspapers in Boston, with different points of view. Now there is just the *Globe* and a tabloid.

The paper is, in effect, run by the EEOC and the federal judges.

Every once in a while, we ordinary mortals get a peek at what has been going on behind the scenes at that powerful institution.[4]

About two dozen of the women employees were complaining bitterly at the beginning of the '90's because the men (and any women who wished, but only one joined in) would play basketball during their lunch hour. This was an historic tradition. One editor said:

"The basketball game has attained ridiculously high symbolic status in the newsroom. All it really is is a bunch of people who want to get exercise and play a game. In the current conspiracy that's abroad, it's me and the other editors perhaps cutting secret deals and giving the boys the best stories."

The women complained to the senior editors. One of them even made a chauvinist remark about the "hormones that are running around here." The games continued, but some of the editors were forced to quit.

One of the best known columnists at the *Globe*, David Nyhan, is as liberal as a person could possibly be. But when a male reporter would not join the game one day when Nyhan needed a sixth player, Nyhan teased him as being "pussy-whipped."

A woman overheard his remark. Nyhan immediately apologized. He even put a memo on his door and went around the newsroom, apologizing to any women he could find. He says his apologies were immediate, profuse and groveling. But he was not to be forgiven. To make it worse, the *Globe* had just spent thousands of dollars on "sensitivity" workshops to prevent this type of sexism.

A senior editor said, "Coming off of [the sensitivity workshops], I for one am all the more saddened by today's experience," and he warned, "[R]emarks that are racially and sexually offensive to co-workers will not be tolerated here. Those who utter such remarks will be subject to disciplinary procedures." Nyhan was fined

WHAT DO YOU THINK?

$1,250, with a suggestion that the money go to a charity to be named by the women who had heard him.

It's unclear why the women were so upset.

Apparently it was not because the word "pussy-whipped" was used. This vulgarity did not bother them. They were upset because they believed that Nyhan was showing "disrespect" for the women editors who were giving that male reporter his assignments.

So, there was a fight between women who wouldn't allow the poor guys to have some fun and play a little basketball during their lunch hour and a man who lectures us about women's rights while he describes them in such coarse terms.

Nyhan is obviously frustrated by what is happening in his newsroom.

What does Nyhan really believe? Does he believe his own columns? Is David Nyhan the one who is "pussy-whipped?"

There are many businesses in our country where men and women *do* work together with full respect for each other, but it isn't at the *Globe*. They don't get along at all; they only tell *us* to do so. As one commentator said, the *Globe* is "too distracted by civil war to turn its full energies to the news wars."*

And what do the owners of that newspaper go through? There is an EEOC right in their offices, watching every single word that is said by anyone.

---

* It's ironic but typical. The editor who had to quit playing basketball because two dozen women complained had just finished using the enormous power of his editor's position to help defeat President Silber of Boston University in the very close battle against Bill Weld for the governorship. The editor had even told *Newsweek* that Silber was "Archie Bunker with a Ph.D." Even some newsmen questioned in public whether the editor had been fair with Silber. But the ironic part is that Silber was a man who respected women and still had his wife of many years, but he does not accept the radical feminist theory. In contrast, the chauvinism of the editor was much in evidence as he was on his third wife. It appears that he was the real Archie Bunker, but he gives lip service to the feminist theory. Therefore, he is tolerated by the feminists. Perhaps he was so angry at Silber because he realized that that man did have courage.

It was reported at that time by Columbia University that the *Globe* had one of the "worst records" for putting female bylines on page one. This means that someone is sitting and counting the stories in the major newspapers across the country. If you don't have enough female bylines, the EEOC will be in to see you.

It does not matter that the vast majority of women want to be at home with their children. If you own a newspaper, you had better find the women and get them into your business.

Some of the reporters at the *Globe* thought that the punishment against Nyhan was too strong. The feminist columnist, Ellen Goodman, said, "You do not want to get to the point where everybody feels every sentence is being monitored."

But that is exactly what she does want, although she will forgive Nyhan if he apologizes sweetly enough.

It would be great if we could get David Nyhan to tell what he really believes about what is happening at the *Globe*. Why does he believe the reporters are pussy-whipped? Does he *secretly* object to the newsroom being controlled by the EEOC and the radical feminists?

The Globe Helps the Radical Feminists

When Bill Clinton was charged with having sex with an intern at the White House and no one knew whether or not it was true, many of the radical feminists of America defended him, regardless of the facts. The *Boston Globe* helped to disseminate the message with an article by a columnist, Patricia Smith, that was *prominently* featured on the newspaper's website on January 23, 1998, as if to proclaim that the paper agreed strongly with the following:

"[W]hat makes the leader of the free world any different from the millions of other redblooded males who can't keep their willis from wanderin'....

"You've really done it this time, Bill. They're talking public humiliation, impeachment, perhaps a beheading. If you indeed did woo the lovely maid, Monica, we don't fault you for being human, even less for being a guy. As the song goes, all the world loves a lover."

And yet . . .

And yet if any *business* is unlucky enough to have a man like Bill Clinton as an employee, it will be sued for thousands or millions of dollars for sexual harassment. And this punishment will be cheered and applauded by both Ms. Smith and the *Boston Globe*.

WHAT DO YOU THINK?

Have they forgotten that Gennifer Flowers, Paula Jones and Monica Lewinsky were all employees of Clinton's, and young, impressionable ones at that (or that a black woman lost a promotion because Gennifer Flowers was hired instead of her or that Kathleen Willey was seeking a job when she was attacked)?

We've been instructed by Ms. Smith and the *Boston Globe* for the past 30-plus years that this type of conduct is outrageous. They say that we businessmen are required to chaperone the sexes.

In contrast to Bill Clinton all that David Nyhan did was to utter one remark to a friend and the *Globe* itself was within an inch of having a sexual harassment suit against it for "hostile environment."

These "elite" will always laugh and giggle at the Puritans and the Victorians, yet they want our *businesses* to be much more puritanical than the Puritans ever were.

One Person At The Globe Is Not Afraid

There is a recent arrival at the *Boston Globe* who is *not* frightened. He is also a columnist.

To understand his story, you must realize that the *Globe* operates under two civil rights laws, the Civil Rights Act and a similar state law. Under the state law, homosexuals have the same rights as do blacks and women. The last chairman of our Commission Against Discrimination was a very outspoken homosexual activist who even sent homosexual "testers" to stores to see if they would be employed as sales clerks.

The recent arrival at the *Globe* is Jeff Jacoby, an articulate, intelligent, courageous, conservative young man, who was hired as a columnist by the *Globe* a couple of years ago (to its obvious regret).

In the fall of 1997, Jacoby wrote a column about Harvard Law School where signs were torn down by homosexual activists after a Christian group of students announced that a young man would speak who had stopped practicing homosexuality after he discovered he was HIV positive.[5]

The signs were replaced with others such as, "For those struggling with Judaism, there is hope in the truth. You can walk away. (To the gas chambers.)." (Jacoby is Jewish)

Jacoby wrote: "There is no hate in [the young speaker's] story. He doesn't berate gays, or mock them, or demand that they renounce homosexuality. He knows that many gays are content and happy with their lives. He also knows that many are not ..." Jacoby continued:

"How was inviting this man to speak at Harvard analogous to sending Jews to gas chambers? Isn't his experience also an element of human 'diversity?' What does it say about gay advocates, who so loudly champion tolerance and freedom of sexual choice, that they are so poisonously intolerant of people who make a choice different from theirs?"

Because of this column, Jacoby was publicly attacked by the *Globe's* Ombudsman a few weeks later.[6]

The Ombudsman revealed that there had been great conflict in the newsroom as to whether Jacoby's column should even be printed. He also revealed that both of Jacoby's editors are "gay activists," who were overruled in their zeal that the column should not be printed. The Ombudsman opined that Jacoby had written "homophobic" columns before. He chastised Jacoby for "rhetorical devices" which "left some readers with an impression the meeting had been unruly." Here's what Jacoby said that allegedly gave that impression.

"When the [event] took place, gay activists thronged the entrance, many wearing T-shirts or holding signs demanding, 'Stop the hate!' But why is it hate to propose that people 'struggling with homosexuality' may be able, with the help of friends and religious faith, to live a non-homosexual life? 'Because it isn't possible!' shout the activists."

That was the entire paragraph with "rhetorical devices." The Ombudsman went on to make much of the fact the event itself was "noisy" but "peaceful." Everyone should be very appreciative of the fact that the activists allowed it to take place, according to him.

Jacoby reported that what had happened at the *Globe* did have a "chilling" effect upon him.

The Ombudsman concluded that the editor was correct in running the column even though it was "offensive," and even though it's a "high price to pay for freedom of the press." In the future, "Jacoby's columns about homosexuality will be judged case by case."

There is no question but that this had a "chilling" effect on Jacoby as he stated.

But think about the owners of the *Boston Globe*.

What does this do to the *owners* of the newspaper? They are under great pressure under Massachusetts law to hire homosexuals in every area of their business, particularly the newsroom. Is it merely coincidence

WHAT DO YOU THINK?

that both of the editors of Jeff Jacoby are "gay activists?" Were they chosen for their merit or solely because they are homosexual?* We may wonder about that, but we can not doubt that the pressure to conform is huge.

Boston Globe Grovels

We've seen the *Boston Globe* grovel at the feet of the government censor. That newspaper apologized emphatically by stating publicly that Jeff Jacoby is "homophobic." It's not necessary for the government censor to sue the *Globe* because the *Globe* "knows" it was "wrong." Not only has it apologized profusely, it has hired those homosexual editors to watch Jacoby very carefully. Such remarks will not be allowed to be uttered again.

You can hear the top management telling its editors: "Get more women and minorities down there. We can't afford to be sued!"

The liberal "elite" will be asking us why we're so worried if we're not "guilty." After all, we can go to court and prove that we are not sexist or homophobic. But why are we being dragged before a court? Isn't that what our Constitution is supposed to protect us from? Can anyone be dragged before a judge to explain our speech? Must we grovel like the *Boston Globe* is doing? When did this happen in America?

The *Globe* also groveled in the case of David Nyhan, who says he immediately apologized profusely. If it hadn't groveled, the *Globe* could have been ordered before a federal judge in that case.

---

*   Because I will surely be attacked as a "homophobe," let me state the following.

I have a good friend who is a farmer. He is outdoors everyday working in his fields, breathing in the fresh air. Yet, for some reason he chooses to smoke cigarettes. He says he has tried many times to quit. I believe he has a stupid habit, and he knows I believe that. But I try to never "bug" him about it, although it is hard. I don't dislike him because he smokes, but I believe he is foolish, and I would not want him teaching my grandchildren. They might come to believe it is "cool" to smoke.

I have also had many homosexual friends and employees. But their behavior is much more dangerous than smoking. I believe that they are also very foolish. I do not want my grandchildren exposed to a message that the homosexual lifestyle is an attractive alternative.

FREEDOM WILL CONQUER RACISM (AND SEXISM)

It is evident that it will be extremely difficult for our newspapers (or radio or tv) to help us have an intelligent discussion of any issue involving race or sex. They will follow the official EEOC agenda.

Where Will It End?

At the end of 1996, the U.S. Senate came within one vote, 49-50, of adding homosexuals to the federal Civil Rights Act. The bill was sponsored by Sen. Kennedy and supported by President Clinton.

Senator Bill Bradley said, "[O]pponents of gay rights have rooted their opposition in religion....These individuals also sometimes use Scripture to perpetuate blatant discrimination, hiding behind scripture to cover up an underlying intolerance."[7]

Senator Chris Dodd said, "Over our entire history, this Congress and this nation embarked on a quiet but monumental revolution, and that was to realize the full aspirations of our Founders that all men and women are truly created equal....But today, one group of Americans continues to be left unprotected in the workplace. That is gay and lesbian Americans."[8]

In the spring of 1997, President Clinton met in the Oval Office with Rep. Barney Frank and his companion, Herb Moses, to support the bill. The President said, "It is about our ongoing fight against bigotry and intolerance." In November 1997, he addressed 1500 homosexuals at the first annual Human Rights Campaign dinner and again called for passage of the bill.

A brilliant advertisement has been prepared by a homosexual group, the Human Rights Campaign, which proclaims in big letters, "Republicans and Democrats Agree, No One Should Lose a Job Merely for Being Gay." And then in smaller letters, "That's Why 'The Employment Non-Discrimination Act' Equals Basic Job Fairness.'" And then in small letters at the bottom, "In a bipartisan poll, 68 percent of registered votes—Republicans, Democrats and Independents from every region of the country—said they support the Employment Non-Discrimination Act, a bill to protect Americans from workplace bias based on sexual orientation."[9]

Most people would agree that gays and lesbians need to live and play in America, the same as other persons—the *same* as other persons, not with extra rights.

WHAT DO YOU THINK?

This law would give them extra rights and it would also mean that no one, under the law of the country, would be allowed to even discuss the morality or prudence of homosexuality.

Make It Criminal.

If we won't repeal the Civil Rights Act, we should at least make it criminal. There is no reason why the pimps, drug dealers and the like should have the passionate protection of our federal judges while our businesses are given the heel of the shoe. It's obvious to anyone that no one knows what is required under these laws. It's like walking through a minefield.

If we won't repeal the Act, then let's at least give our businesses the same protection as our criminals. Let's make the Act criminal.

Strive for Excellence and Eliminate Fear

I personally believe that a type of affirmative action is good. I believe that American business has an obligation to help us to create a truly color-blind society. And in doing so, it should help to train and motivate more black people so that they can and will succeed.

But this should be a matter of leadership, not a matter of coercion. It is always easy to hate someone and to blame them for all of the problems of the world. It is always easier to pass a law than it is to be a true leader. And this is what happened to us in the 1960's. The problems of the blacks were never caused by business. But it was much easier for the politicians to pass a law, lay the blame on someone else, and then forget about the problems.

And business, just as any other good citizen, does have a very vital role to play.

Before his death, President Kennedy was trying to use his leadership to help the improvement of blacks in the workplace. But the floodgates opened after his assassination.

In the current atmosphere of an Inquisition, everyone is afraid. There is no business that would talk to us while we were writing this book. Not Sears Roebuck, not Union Camp. No one. That was not always true. As we pointed out, there were many businesses that were happy to talk about their record in the 1960's. But not today. We have poisoned the entire atmosphere.

FREEDOM WILL CONQUER RACISM (AND SEXISM)

We must do away with the whole feeling of hate and race that has permeated our country.

If I were black, I would say that I would want no Title VII at all. I believe that most whites want the blacks to succeed even more than the blacks do, if for no other reason than that we can get beyond this issue and talk about something different for a change.

I would resent it greatly if someone told me that I needed special help to succeed.

If we have a great debate in the 1990's and finally put this matter behind us, we are certainly going to ignite the passions of racists on both sides. We are going to have the white supremacists who will tell us that the blacks are an inferior race with low I.Q. scores to prove it. And we're going to have the black supremacists who want to discriminate against all white males by putting everyone except white males into a Rainbow Coalition. No matter what you call it, that is discrimination in its purest form.

I am constantly amazed at the people who tell us with great shock that this country is run by white males. To the best of my knowledge, China is run by Chinese males, India is run by Indian males, and Africa is run by black males. Why should it come as a shock that this country is run by white males? To the best of my knowledge, the white males of this country are doing as well, if not better, than any group in the entire world in trying to incorporate others into the leadership of the society.

America must once again strive toward becoming a color-blind society, where a person's color or sex is unimportant. We may never reach that goal, but we should never stop striving for it.

And we must once again strive for "excellence" in our schools and our businesses. Until we are allowed to look for "excellence" once again, we will continue to have a trade deficit, a rusting industrial base and a decaying society with drugs and immorality.

Epilogue

"THE AMERICAN INQUISITION"

When historians look back upon the end of the 20th century will they refer to it as the period of "The American Inquisition?"

The "American Inquisition" is so much like the Inquisition that occurred in Europe a few hundred years ago that it is eery. Back then a man was asked, "Do you love God". Today he is asked, "Do you love women?" "Do you love blacks?" And if some of the "elite" have their way, "Do you love homosexuals?"

How does a person prove that he loves God? Or that he loves blacks, women, or homosexuals?

In both cases, his guilt is assumed.[1] In America, the Inquisitor need prove only that the "numbers" do not add up.

We probe the psyche of the accused. The head of the EEOC said, "We need this power to prod those...who honestly do not believe that they discriminate."[2]

And our defendants are urged, almost threatened, to salve their consciences by settling the case, just as they were encouraged to recant during the Inquisition in Spain.

It was only a few years ago that we saw a great reeducation taking place in China and Cambodia with millions of people being marched into the countryside to learn what the Communist leaders had decided were to be the purposes and goals of their lives. We don't see anyone being marched into the countryside in the United States; we see them being taken to comfortable auditoriums where they are then given "sensitivity" training sessions and told that their deeply held beliefs about their lives and their religion are totally wrong. If they do not agree, they are not shot or tortured; they are demoted or fired.

We have undergone a tremendous loss of freedom in the last fifty years, during The American Inquisition, but we don't realize it yet.

Freedom will *not* eliminate racism and sexism. But it will help us to conquer them. Although we are not perfect, this country has done extremely well over the last two hundred years with the help of freedom. Let's not abandon it now.

WOMEN'S GROUPS

A few of the new women's organizations that are fighting the radical left.

Clare Boothe Luce Policy Institute, 112 Elden St., Herndon, VA 20170. Telephone: 703-318-0730. This group is heavily involved in training young women "to counter the feminist propaganda".

Concerned Women for America, 370 L'Enfant Promenade, SW, Suite 800, Washington, D.C. 20024. Telephone: (202) 488-7000, Website: www.cwfa.org

Eagle Forum, P.O. Box 618, Alton, IL 62002 or 316 Pennsylvania Ave. SE, Washington, D.C. 20003. E-Mail: eagle@eagleforum.org Website: www.eagleforum.org This group has 80,000 members and is principally the agent of its founder, Phyllis Schlafly, a Phi Beta Kappa graduate of Washington University, a lawyer with a Master's in Political Science from Harvard University and the mother of six children. The foil of the radical feminist movement since her first book, *A Choice Not An Echo* in 1964, she almost singlehandedly defeated the Equal Rights Amendment. She founded the Eagle Forum in 1972 and has pictures of herself with Ronald Reagan, Rush Limbaugh, Robert Bork and other conservatives on her Internet site. Its mission is to "enable conservative and pro-family men and women to participate in the process of self-government and public policy making so that America will continue to be a land of individual liberty, respect for family integrity, public and private virtue, and private enterprise."

Independent Women's Forum, 2111 Wilson Blvd., Arlington, VA 22201. Telephone: 800-224-6000, E-Mail: iwf@iwf.org Website: www.iwf.org Founded in 1992 by Washington D.C. area professional women to battle the left-wing monopoly on "women's issues." It believes the following. "The IWF provides a voice for American women who believe in individual freedom and personal responsibility. Since 1992, the IWF has been taking on the old feminist establishment-and winning. 'The IWF has a profile almost unheard of for a group that is the new kid on the block,' says the *Boston Globe.* 'In the marketplace of ideas, from the national news media all the way down to local radio, the IWF has shown its real strength...[The] IWF is well on its way to becoming the foremost media nemesis of the feminist movement.' Why has the IWF been so successful?—Because the women who make up the IWF are not radical ideologues. They're businesswomen, economists, lawyers, truck drivers, police officers, teachers, and homemakers.—Because the IWF promotes individual responsibility, strong families, more opportunity, and less government-policies that help *all* Americans.—Because the IWF, a nonpartisan, nonprofit organization, sponsors public speaking events noted for provocative and open debates." Last year they took up the cause against human slavery in Africa where women are snatched out of their villages, enslaved and bred. "What particularly appalled us is that the Beijing conference, which was supposed to be a platform for women, said nothing about this," says Executive Vice President Anita Blair.

Women's Freedom Network, Suite 179, 4410 Massachusetts Avenue NW, Washington, D.C. 20016. They cite with approval the following quote about them. "...Unlike the women of the far right, these women have careers and call themselves feminists. They clearly want to appropriate and incorporate feminism into a free market, conservative politics. Don't be surprised if you wake up one morning and wonder how conservatives, who so successfully seized the language of family values, also reinvented feminism as a necessary ingredient of a deregulated free market economy. Who stole feminism? I'd bet on the Women's Freedom Network." President, Rita J.

WOMEN'S GROUPS

Simon, American University; Vice President, Cathy Young, *Detroit News*; Treasurer, Judith Simon Garrett; Board of Directors, Christina Hoff Sommers, Clark University; Jean Bethke Elshtain, U. of Chicago; Mary Ann Glendon, Harvard Law School; Joanne Jacobs, *San Jose Mercury News*; Jeane Kirkpatrick, American Enterprise Institute; Judith Kleinfeld, U. of Alaska; Elizabeth Fox Genovese, Emory University; Edith Kurzweil, *Partisan Review*; Barbara C. Lydick, B&A Associates; Rikki Klieman, Court TV; Virginia Postrel, *Reason*; Anne Mitchell, Attorney, Palo Alto; Jennifer Roback Morse, George Mason University; Mona Charen, *Washington Times*; Abigail Thernstrom, Boston University.

WHO WROTE THIS BOOK?
or
WHAT WAS IT LIKE IN THE 'GOOD OLD DAYS?'

My life has been much more diverse than the average person. I have had many different experiences in my 70 years. Let's take a quick look to see what it really was like in the "old days" before 1964.

I was born 15 years after the sinking of the U.S.S. Titanic when all of those men went to their deaths in order to save the women and children.

What "sexists!"

But no one complained.

My father was born shortly after his parents emigrated from Germany in the 1880s. He learned to speak German before he did English. Because his father died when he was 13, he had to quit school to support his mother and three younger children. Somehow, he managed to put himself through technical school and become an engineer with AT&T. However, his advancement was limited because he did not have the credentials of a college degree, which is necessary in such a large organization. My father was very limited because he was the son of immigrants, but he still had more opportunity here than in any other country in the world.

My mother's mother came from Ireland as a maid. My mother's father was a silversmith from Belgium.

When I was born in 1927 in an upper middle-class, suburban town, South Orange, New Jersey, we were still being taught the sexist creed, which was that the boys were to protect and cherish the girls in our

WHO WROTE THIS BOOK?

society. And even if the girls wanted to go "further" when we were on a date, it was our moral and *legal* responsibility to see that it didn't happen. It was *our* responsibility.

Was some of this extreme? And from an older era? Of course it was. And as our times changed, some of it also needed to be changed. But the main message was solid.

A large part of the message was implemented by women. In my suburban town, practically all of the men would disappear in the daytime. The teachers and principals in our grade schools were women, and most of those in the junior high schools were women. We existed in a women's world in the daytime, and we were constantly told not to be "mean" to the girls. Most boys really had no idea what their fathers did in New York City.

The classes in our grade school were divided into groups by academic ability. We had three different groups in my age category. In the highest group we had an equal amount of boys and girls. Everyone knew that there were very smart girls and very smart boys. It was not a big deal. We would have laughed if we could have looked ahead and seen how the people of today say that girls are not taken seriously.

The girls of our era were smart in other ways too. They knew that if you jumped off a 4-story building, you would hurt yourself. They also knew that if you went to a bar at night and took a man home to sleep, you were going to end in trouble by being beaten, raped or something similar. Maybe not that particular night, but the chances were that you would soon end up in trouble. Therefore, the possibility of a girl doing that was zero. They knew better. If they did get themselves in trouble, they didn't blame anyone else, the same as any man who got drunk in a bar in the wrong part of town.

While I was in the Boy Scouts, it was discovered that our Scoutmaster was a homosexual who was having relations with one of the Scouts, who was about a year older than I. The Scoutmaster was dismissed, but it was not a big deal. I believe that no one believes that a young male should be a scout leader for teenage girls; and by the same logic, no one believed that a homosexual male should be a leader for teenage boys.

There were a few slums in our town, and the black people lived there. We had a big high school and I never knew any of the black kids well; but I am certain they were treated with respect and courtesy, although they did not have all of the advantages that many whites had.

My life was mixed. Although raised in suburbia, I became a seaman in the U.S. Navy in 1945 during the final days of World War II. This was much different than suburbia. It was my belief, and I was told that I was in the Navy to protect my country, namely the women and children. If I had been born one year earlier in 1926, I might not be writing this book, because that high school class saw combat and some did not come home.

Some of the men and boys who returned from protecting our women and children came from Japanese prison camps looking like prisoners from the concentration camps of Europe. If you saw the emaciated faces from either place, you would be unable to tell the difference. Yet many people complain today about the fact that we dropped atomic bombs on Japan, killing innocent women and children. It's difficult for me to understand why I and the 500,000 or more 17-year-old and 18-year-old American boys who would have died (plus the million or more Japanese who would have died in an invasion) were not "innocent." What were *we* "guilty" of?

Off to College

After the war, I went to the prestigious, Ivy, all-male Williams College. My brother had entered there in 1941 right before Pearl Harbor because my father was determined that we would receive the best education that was possible. We were part of the first group (largely because of the G.I. bill) to go there that was not part of the rich, prep-school crowd from Exeter, Andover, Choate, etc. Although everyone was nice, you knew there was a difference and that we came from an entirely different world. There were a few blacks on campus. I can well imagine how isolated they must have felt, even when they arrived there a few years later in larger numbers. I can also imagine why they could have thought that the division between them and some of the other students was a racial issue. Some of it may have been, but for the most part I don't believe it was. It was just that the preppies had many more life experiences than we poorer students did because of their money and their family history.

They had yachting, Europe, Bermuda, excellent secondary educations, etc.

I did well and was Managing Editor of the prestigious college newspaper. But I could not reach my full potential because of an unknown combination of diabetes and low blood sugar that made it impossible to function at any level of my true ability. My physical problem was undiagnosed because the only way they tested for diabetes in those days was with a urine sample, and about 10% of diabetics do not secrete sugar in their urine. Although *I* knew I had a physical problem, its cause was not discovered until I was 32 years old.

There were campus-wide, weekend-long house-parties about four times a year, which would go on until the wee hours of the night, totally unchaperoned, with the parties being held in the various fraternity houses. There was plenty of beer and liquor, but no woman was afraid to come for the weekend and stay in Williamstown. The amount of consensual sex that occurred was minimal if not non-existent. Such a happening was looked upon with a jaundiced eye by everyone. There was no date-rape or

WHO WROTE THIS BOOK?

rape of any kind. (Some reviewers have told me that you can never say "never," but I say that here with confidence.) We went to many other parties at other colleges, particularly Amherst, Smith and Mt. Holyoke and the same was true there.

While at Williams, a good friend of mine was a homosexual. He was very talented, creative and well liked, but he died in his early '40s, as do most of that community.

I left Williams after three years because I knew I was not performing well because of my unknown physical problem and I also knew I did not belong in the New York City, country club setting towards which a Williams education was sending me. I was not to be a member of the "elite." I knew I wanted to escape that pattern. My mother had died and my father remarried, so I was on my own. I was lucky to find a poor New Hampshire farm where I boarded for a year and sold Fuller brushes door-to-door in order to support myself. Those people on the farm were very poor but as kind and honest as you could find. I discovered, to my surprise, that the many French Canadians in that area remained totally aloof from the rest of the people and were thought of as a lower class, both socially and economically. They even had their own, separate Catholic schools. I am sure they would say they were discriminated against, and probably they were, although they were white and French.

I then enrolled at the University of New Hampshire to study agriculture which was at a totally different societal level than Williams, yet the mores were identical.

You hear people complaining today about the poor college girls who were "locked up" at night back in those days. But, in a sense we boys were too. When you took the girls back to their dorms, there wasn't much else to do except go back to your dorm also.

I worked on farms during and after graduating from UNH, sometimes with migrant laborers and found little difference there. One of the finest men that I met was a black man named Ben who worked as a mechanic on a farm in Colts Neck, New Jersey.

In 1952 during the Korean War, I again found myself being ordered to go defend the women and children of my country, this time as a 25-year-old private in the infantry of the U.S. Army. I could have obtained a commission in the Navy but that would have been at least a three year commitment. So I became a private in the infantry. When you hear a man talk about the military, ask if he was an officer or an enlisted man. If he was an officer, he has no idea what it is like to be in the service.

Although you hear only about Vietnam, this war in Korea was also a "poor man's" war. It was fought mostly by poor teenage boys who were ordered there by the liberal "elite" because Harry Truman's administration

FREEDOM WILL CONQUER RACISM (AND SEXISM)

had foolishly and mistakenly told the Communists that we would not defend Korea. When the Communists responded to that declaration by invading the country, we were caught totally by surprise with an army which had been demobilized after World War II.

You could avoid the war if you were rich enough to stay in college or get married. While at Indiantown Gap, Pennsylvania, I was a guard at the prison stockade for a short period. The prisoners were mostly poor white teenagers from the hills of Kentucky and Tennessee or young black men, all of whom had gone AWOL and only wanted to go back home. They couldn't quite understand why they had been snatched away from their families. Anyone who saw that stockade would not want to be an inmate. It was not pretty. There was close-order drill and other "in your face" activities starting at 4 a.m. There was a solitary cell for those who did not conform; with no windows it was literally a wooden box and was called the "black box."

While we were training at Indiantown Gap, we were constantly told by the Drill Instructors that we were not going to a "soft life" in Europe; we were going to Korea. But *all* of us hoped that was not true. *None* of us volunteered for Korea.

This was the forgotten war where our young men were sent into the midst of bitter winters with summer uniforms because the liberal "elite" did not like the armed forces (even then) and therefore did not adequately equip them. Even as late as 1952 we would go out for days at a time in a foot of Pennsylvania snow with summer uniforms. Meanwhile, life on the civilian front of America went on as usual with not much notice of what was happening to the lower-class young men in Korea. The army had recently become integrated and had not yet become heavily black, and therefore what happened to poor white boys was not noticed.

We were very thankful on our troop ship in the Pacific to learn that President Eisenhower was able to end this war within a few months after his inauguration. Although no one knows exactly what he did, most people believe that he promised the Chinese that if it didn't end, he would no longer allow young American boys to be fodder for the Communist guns. Perhaps he would even use an atomic weapon. We didn't know what he did, but we were thankful that he saved our lives.

Because the fighting had stopped, I was chosen by the Public Information Office of the forces in Korea to write human interest stories about the Army for *Stars and Stripes, Army Times* and other publications. I did well and had many stories published but we had a very tough Master Sergeant who was a photographer. He did not like the fact that we "college boys" would take him on an assignment and tell him when and where to take a picture. So he trumped up some charges against me so I would be

WHO WROTE THIS BOOK?

sent up to the front-line infantry to learn some "discipline." Again, if I had had a different skin color, I would have thought that was the reason he chose to send me to tough duty. However, I went next door to the colonel at the Troop Information Office and he was happy to put in a request for me to work for him and critique all of the newspapers printed by the various regiments and divisions in Korea and help to improve them.

Although most G.I.'s in Korea saw only the barren portions of Korea, I was lucky to be able to travel over a large part of the country. It was very pretty and I admired the people. At night after duty, a group of Korean newspaper people paid me to help them publish an English-language newspaper. I was impressed how they managed to keep their society intact with strong families despite the war.*

While there, a person would look back at the United States and wonder why we were fighting so hard in our country to always earn more and more money. The people in Korea appeared just as happy. Was it the men in our country who were pushing this syndrome or was it the women?

The enlisted men in the U.S. Army are not exactly high-society and I had an opportunity to see a good example of life, both in the states and in Korea. Two of the better officers I had in the Army were both black, Master Sergeant Horace T. Dorsey, Indiantown Gap, and Capt. Hatfield in Korea. I never saw anything that indicated to me that anyone noticed the color of anyone's skin. The only time I remember was on the troop ship coming home and dozens of blacks would gather in the hold to play crap. They seemed to be there shooting their dice for 24 hours a day. I do not believe I would have been welcome if I had intruded into that gathering. My roommate from Williams never came back from Korea. He was always doing more than his share and he volunteered to be a reconnaissance officer in a small L-19 airplane over Communist lines and tell our artillery where to train their weapons. He never came back from one flight. The Defense Department has confirmed recently that it is true that many of our men who were reported as missing in Korea are probably still alive. However, some were used in medical experiments both in Korea and China. These experiments were as brutal as any used by the Nazis in Germany. One wonders if my roommate was captured when his plane went down and if he is still alive somewhere. What would he think of our world today and of our society which would abandon its young men?

While these boys were going through terrible hardships in Korea, Betty Friedan was writing about the poor housewives in their warm, suburban homes who were struggling so hard to find themselves.

You may wonder how I survived in the Army with diabetes and low blood sugar. All I can say is that there were many days when I thought I would not. Somehow I did, but it was not easy. Many chocolate bars were consumed on maneuvers (which, I now know, was the wrong thing to do) while trying to keep up my strength. But I was lucky to never see any combat.

Although the Army was tough and often nasty, I had a lot of respect for it. It has a miserable mission and it performs it quite well. I could not say the same for the U.S. government in Washington where I worked for a few years later while at law school. It was a bureaucratic mess.

Worked for Cornell

After the Army, I went to work for Cornell as an Assistant County Agent teaching farmers and then I worked for a trade association, the New York Farm Bureau. At age thirty it became apparent that I must go back to school if I were going to achieve my goals. So I matriculated at George Washington Law School in Washington, D.C. because they had a night school. I remember during that period driving from Washington to New Jersey one evening. We were always warned not to hitchhike or pick up other hitchhikers, but most young men did in those days. I remember stopping to pick up three young black guys and driving them for three hours to Newark, where I dropped them at Pennsylvania Station. Sadly, I would never dream of doing such a thing today.

I worked in the daytime and went to law school five nights a week, winter and summer, for three years.. I lived in a house in Georgetown with a group of other guys and somehow, intuitively slipped into the perfect diet for my diabetes and low blood sugar. Therefore, I did extremely well at George Washington and was accepted at Yale Law School, which has the reputation of being the best in the country. I did very well at Yale also, although I knew that I was again operating below my ability. I stayed at Yale for one semester, living at the Law School, eating dormitory food. This was terrible for my health. Because I was running out of money and my health was making it impossible to function, I returned to George Washington. Upon arriving back in Washington I finally found a doctor who discovered my diabetes and low blood sugar.

I had now been to two "elite" schools, Williams, the "elite" conservative school and Yale, the "elite" liberal school. At least Williams was honest. Yale talked the liberal "talk," but upon graduation, they all wanted to work for the big Wall Street firms, which represented General Motors, et al. One of the most prominent examples is Lloyd Cutler, who gained publicity recently when he filled in as the lawyer for President Clinton after Bernie Nussbaum left. I worked for Cutler's firm while in my first year at law school. While professing to be a liberal, he always appeared to be working for the wealthy and the famous. I wanted to help the ordinary person, not the big corporations.

WHO WROTE THIS BOOK?

While in Washington I lived in houses in Georgetown with groups of other guys. Women were still treated with respect.

My present wife graduated from Wellesley College in 1957, and she reports the same experience. She spent time at various men's schools, particularly Dartmouth, which had a reputation as a big "party" school with a lot of "animal houses;" but she never had any trepidations and never heard of any problems.

The Practice of Law

After finally graduating and marrying, I moved to Pennsylvania Dutch Country and the city of York because it has some of the best farms in the East. Although I knew absolutely no one there, I hung out a shingle. Almost all of the lawyers had been born there, descendants of old families that had been there for generations. It was extremely difficult to crack the market; besides I knew very little anyhow, not having any experience. The lawyers were all very nice, but they had no desire to share the practice. If I had been black, I could well have believed in a conspiracy.

But through a lot of hard work and taking the dregs that no one else wanted, we did prosper. After two years, I was elected to the autonomous School Board, which was responsible for 10,000 students and levied its own taxes. We were a microcosm for the entire country at that point. There was our city school district, there was a suburban district called York Suburban School District, and many country districts. Our city schools were excellent and contained many blacks. The blacks had exactly the same advantages as everyone else.

I was also made an adjunct Assistant Professor at Pennsylvania State University, working with lawyers and farmers, to help them better understand the problems of each other.

I was also chosen by the Sheriff of York County as his solicitor.

A Black Woman Was Always Chosen

While at Williams, I learned the blessings of civil service which protects government workers from politics. However, while at law school in Washington, D.C. I learned that what I had learned in the Ivy Tower was not accurate. The courts in Washington were a disaster. If you tried to find any document from any case, it was impossible. They were scattered in piles all over the floor, virtually useless. None of the employees cared because they could not be fired. In York, they still had the "spoils" system, whereby the Prothonotary (Clerk of Court) was elected. His employees were political people who worked for the party. If a Democrat won, the staff would be totally changed and the Democratic workers were rewarded with jobs. If a Republican won, their workers were rewarded. *But the*

FREEDOM WILL CONQUER RACISM (AND SEXISM)

office was an epitome of excellence. The employees were polite and efficient. If they weren't, the voters would elect a new Prothonotary the next term. The "spoils" system (which everyone condemned) worked!

And the only employee who stayed *no matter who won the election* was the head of the office, a black woman named Mattie Chapman. Everyone respected and liked her.

Courtrooms Are "War"

We've been told that a courtroom is a wonderful institution that always gives justice. That is not true. They sometimes give justice, and sometimes they don't.

We still had Justices of the Peace when I was practicing. They were usually well respected persons in the community, who would gather the parties together in their home office, with the following:

"Now, Bill, I've known you since you were born and your father too. And Tom here too. Why don't you two just shake hands and let's settle this. There's no reason for you two to be fighting like this."

They were *not* lawyers, just old farmers.

But somewhere the "elite" decided that this didn't work. These Justices of the Peace weren't lawyers; they didn't even understand the "Rules of Evidence," much less the "Rules of Civil Procedure." They were just a bunch of farmers who didn't know anything So it came down from "on-high" somewhere that these Justices of the Peace were to be replaced by real judges with real courtrooms.

But now, thirty years or more later, the big rage in legal circles is "arbitration" and "mediation." We've suddenly discovered that what we destroyed had a lot of advantages (although most of the lawyers and judges don't realize that we are going back to the Old Days because they never saw the other system in operation). The rigid rules of evidence that must be used in a courtroom may be necessary, but these rules often get in the way of discovering the truth. I am not saying that the old system was perfect and didn't have its problems, but the autocratic, rigid system of lawyers is often not the best either.

We must remember this when we're talking about the Civil Rights Act. A lawsuit in a courtroom is an act of war, and the "good" person does not always win. And even if they do win, the emotional costs to the winner are seldom worth their victory.

More Boys to Die

When it became apparent that the liberal "elite" were once again drafting our teenage males, this time to send them to die in Vietnam, I just could not believe my ears.

WHO WROTE THIS BOOK?

At the beginning of the Vietnam War in 1964, Lyndon Johnson had just won the presidential race against Barry Goldwater by painting him as 1) a "racist" (for voting against the Civil Rights Act) and 2) a "warmonger." The "official" biographer of Johnson said that he ran on "peace, harmony and prosperity."[1] It was one of the dirtiest campaigns in American history, even running television spots showing a little girl sitting among the falling bombs that would occur if Goldwater were elected. I was never an avid supporter of Goldwater, but this was nasty stuff. It was conceived by a member of the "elite," Bill Moyers, who now runs around on PBS with a halo around his head while making millions of dollars off of us.

When I had been with the Army in Korea in 1954, the French were driven out of Vietnam, and the rumor was that we would be sent there to save that country. But Eisenhower had more sense than to enter a land war in Asia. Certainly, we were on the correct side of the controversy in Vietnam, but was it *our* fight? (If anyone doubts that we were on the right side of that struggle, read the book by a young doctor who went to Laos in the 1950's and died of disease while trying to help those people. *The Edge of Tomorrow*, and other books by Thomas A. Dooley, M.D.)

Even worse, when the liberal leadership of America decided later that Vietnam was too tough a fight for them to continue, either personally or politically, they began to blame our teenage boys for being there. As if it had been those teenagers' idea to go there and die.

Jane Fonda went to North Vietnam and mocked our teenage boys who had been drafted out of their homes and sent there by her liberal "elite" friends. *If she wanted to protest the war, that was fine* (I would even have helped her), but to give help to those people who were killing American teenagers and South Vietnamese was shameful. There was another woman in World War II, Tokyo Rose, who did the same thing for the Japanese. She served many years in jail. But Jane Fonda is still lionized in America by the "elite," and many other women buy her exercise tapes without any thought as to what she did.

After interfering in Vietnam, we abandoned all of the people there who had trusted us and left millions of them to die at the hands of the Communists.

When our teenage boys came home, they were greeted with contempt by the liberal "elite" who had sent them there.

Life As A Single Parent

A long cherished goal was finally achieved in 1965 by buying an excellent farm only five miles from the center of York. The schools in that white area were not as good. One of the proudest boasts of those School Directors was that they had the lowest cost per pupil of any district in the

FREEDOM WILL CONQUER RACISM (AND SEXISM)

county. That was not my goal, but I did not believe I could impose my beliefs on them. They were happy. They did not have all of the same goals in life that I did. They would rather spend their money on snowmobiles and motorcycles. But they were honest, decent people and they were not stupid.

During this time, I began teaching a 2-day course in Estate Planning for Penn State. As a part of it, I had a professor from the life insurance department talk to the class. I could not believe what I was hearing. Farm families were being advised to spend $2000-$3000/year in life insurance. This was money they did not have and could not afford. So I began to do a little research, and I found out about the difference between "term" life insurance and "permanent" life insurance. As a result, I wrote a book titled, "How to Avoid Being Overcharged by Your Life Insurance Salesman." It received excellent reviews in the *Wall Street Journal's* weekly edition and the *Christian Science Monitor*, but the insurance industry did not appreciate the attack.

Shortly after this time, I became a single parent and moved to Massachusetts with my children, who were 4, 6, 8, and 10. I could no longer practice law so I began a legal newspaper, which I could operate largely from my rented house. As a result, I have a pretty good idea of what it is like to raise children by oneself. No matter how hard a single parent tries, he or she can never replace a traditional home. However, I must have done something right, because my oldest daughter has a Ph.D. in Clinical Psychology, my son is a professional photographer, my next daughter is a lawyer, and my youngest daughter is in sales.

How They Treat Blacks

The Boston suburban area has a program for both public and private schools where volunteers are bussed out from the city to attend better suburban schools. I enrolled my four-year-old daughter in a cooperative nursery school. Some of these black children came to our nursery school. When I was taking my stint as a volunteer one day, I opened the door to the shop which was always to remain open. I was accosted by a little four-year-old boy with a screwdriver who told me, "Get out of here, man, or I'll cut you up." That boy obviously did not say that just to me. He needed some tough love. I was told by teachers that they could not discipline the black children. But how could that help those children? They were begging for love and discipline. I often wonder what happened to them. I knew others of them who came to eat and sleep over with us, and one of my other daughters went to sleep at their homes. So I know that the program did good. But I often think about that tough little boy who the "elite" were afraid to discipline.

WHO WROTE THIS BOOK?

I Find Out About Discrimination Laws

I first learned about the discrimination laws soon after I started my business in 1972. After a few years we had to move from our suburban office to the center of Boston. Since the excellent secretary and bookkeeper did not wish to work in Boston, I had to find people to replace those two women. Another employee suggested that I hire a friend of his. Within two weeks this employee had:

- Paid Xerox $600 for one bill when it should have been $2, and paid the telephone company twice in one month for the same bill.
- Overdrawn our checking account at the bank. I did not know about it until the bank called me and asked if we were having financial problems.
- Was unable to balance the checkbook and wrote in a "correction factor" to make it balance.
- Made a total mess of our subscription records. We had to mail our newspapers weekly and we were the official reporter for the weekly copies of the opinions of the Supreme Court of Massachusetts. It took weeks to get our records back in order after she left with lawyers and judges complaining constantly about not receiving their copies.

She filed a complaint with the state Commission Against Discrimination, which dismissed it after an investigation. But it took me over a week to answer all of their questions and fill out their forms. It was a week I did not have, particularly since I had to straighten out the mess she had made in our accounting books. In addition, an investigator asked me if I had given her any training. Training!? In keeping a check book?!

It was a good thing I had experience as a lawyer in negotiating and that I was not tired, or I would have blown the whole thing right there.

Years later, another new hire was performing poorly, but we kept hoping that she would change her attitude and improve. Then she became pregnant. I was told that no one could ever fire a pregnant woman. I did not believe our country had come to that point, but I found out they were correct. Actually, the investigator who was in charge of the claim was agreeing with us that we did not discriminate ... except for one thing. A few years earlier, we had helped out another female employee who had been with us for some time. She had personal problems and in order to help her out, I had continued her pay beyond the normal period. This pregnant woman complained that since I had assisted another employee with a medical problem and since I had failed to do so for her also, I was discriminating against a pregnant female. She was right, the lawyers told me. I should not have been kind to the other employee This meant in the future I could never help a longtime, loyal employee who was suffering with a medical problem unless I did exactly the same for every employee. Of course, this

FREEDOM WILL CONQUER RACISM (AND SEXISM)

meant that I could not help *anyone* in the future. We had to make a settlement in this case of the pregnant woman.

A few years ago we hired a sales person who was about 50-years-old for a branch office. After about 8 months, it became obvious that she was not doing well and it was not working. So we closed down the office and terminated her. She complained to the EEOC that we discriminated against her because of age. It was difficult even for the EEOC to determine how we could be guilty of discriminating against her because of her age when we had hired her only 8 months previously. That case was dismissed, but again we had many pages of Interrogatories to complete and many hours of lawyer fees to pay.

I learned it's not any fun being *constantly* second-guessed every time you make a hire, promotion or termination.

Respect for The People

I have much more respect for "The People" as a result of my experiences than do the "elite." The people will solve their problems if they are given a little leadership. However, the "elite" believe that the problems will be solved only if the "elite" take full charge of everything. But we have learned that we can not run everything from one point in Washington. If we try, we will surely lose our freedom and liberty.

Endnotes

SECTION I
Chapter 1

1. An excellent history of the legislative debate is found in Whelan, *The Longest Debate, A Legislative History of the 1964 Civil Rights Act*. This citation is found at pp. xvii and 16.
2. Id., p. 172.
3. *Time*, June 19, 1964, p.17.
4. Whelan, p. 229.
5. Id., p. xvii.
6. Id., pp. 8 and 105.
7. *Time*, May 10, 1963, p. 19.
8. Hugh Davis Graham, *The Civil Rights Era: Origins of National Policy, 1960-1972* (New York: Oxford University Press, 1990), p. 74.
9. Id., April 19, 1963, p. 30.
10. Arthur M. Schlesinger, *A Thousand Days* (Boston: Houghton Mifflin, 1965), p. 958.
11. *Time*, April 19, 1963, p. 31.
12. Alonzo Hamby, *Liberalism and Its Challengers: FDR to Reagan* (New York: Oxford University Press, 1985), pp. 163-64.
13. Whelan, p. 17.
14. Id., p. xxi.
15. Id., p. xxi.
16. Carl Brauer, *John F. Kennedy and the Second Reconstruction* (New York: Columbia University Press, 1977), p. 267.
17. *Time*, June 14, 1963, p. 23.
18. Schlesinger, p. 966.
19. Id., p. 976.
20. *Time*, June 21, 1963, p. 16.
21. Id., June 7, 1963, p. 17.
22. Id., August 2, 1963, p. 9.
23. Id., June 7, 1963, p. 17.
24. Id., July 19, 1963, p. 18.
25. Id., June 21, 1963, p. 17; July 5, 1963, p. 15.
26. Id., September 13, 1963, p. 26; September 27, 1963, p. 17.
27. Id., August 30, 1963, p. 9.
28. Id., July 12, 1963, p. 19.
29. Id., p. 19.
30. Schlesinger, p. 968.
31. *Time*, August 30, 1963, p. 13.
32. Schlesinger, p. 927.
33. *Time*, July 26, 1963, p. 12.
34. Id., June 14, 1963, p. 24.
35. Id., June 28, 1963, p. 17.
36. Id., June 14, 1963, p. 24.
37. Id., August 30, 1963, p. 14.
38. Id., January 3, 1964, p. 13.
39. Whelan pp. 20 and 24; Schlesinger p. 969.
40. *Time*, September 6, 1963, p. 14.

41 Whelan, p. 63.
42 Id., p. 63.
43 Id., pp. 27 and 28.
44 Id., p. 54.
45 Id., p. 54.
46 Id., p. 68.
47 Id., pp. 16 and 70.
48 Id., p. 70.

Chapter 2

1 Whelan, p. 80.
2 Doris Kearns [Goodwin], *Lyndon Johnson & the American Dream* (New York: Harper & Row, 1976), p. 191.
3 Whelan, p. 91.
4 Id., p. 91.
5 Id., p. 166.
6 110 Cong. Rec. 1518 (1964).
7 Whelan, p. 115.
8 110 Cong. Rec. 5092.
9 Id., p. 6549.
10 *Time*, April 10, 1964, p. 22.
11 110 Cong. Rec. 7213.
12 Id., p. 7246.
13 Id., p. 7246.
14 Id., p. 7218.
15 Id., p. 7418.
16 Id., p. 7420.
17 *New York Times*, April 24, 1964, p.23.
18 Time, April 24, 1964, p.17
19 Id., June 12, 1964, p. 38.
20 Id., April 24, 1964, p. 17.
21 Id., April 24, 1964, p. 17.
22 Id., April 24, 1964, p. 17.
23 110 Cong. Rec. 11848.
24 42 U.S.C. s. 2000e - 2(j).
25 110 Cong. Rec. 12723.
26 Id., p. 12723.
27 Id., p. 15876.
28 Id., p.15893.
29 *New York Times*, July 15, 1964, p. 34.
30 Id., July 16, 1964, p. 30.
31 *New York Times*, July 3, 1964, p. 9.

Chapter 3

1 Whelan, p. 231.
2 Id., p. 92.
3 Congressional Record 110 part 2, p.2574, February 8, 1964.
4 Id., p. 2584.
5 Id., p. 2577.
6 Id., p. 2578.
7 Id., p. 2578.
8 Id., p. 2578.
9 Id., p. 2578.
10 Id., p. 2580.
11 Id., p. 2581.
12 Id., p. 2581.
13 Id., p. 2584.
14 Id., p. 2583 by Mr. Andrews of Alabama.
15 Id., p. 2583 by Mr. Rivers of South Carolina.
16 *Time*, February 21, 1964, p. 21.
17 *New York Times*, February 11, 1964, p. 33.

SECTION II

1 The Supreme Court said that a law *must* "define the criminal offense with sufficient definiteness that ordinary people can understand what conduct is prohibited and in a manner that does not encourage arbitrary and discriminatory enforcement....Where the legislature fails to provide such minimal guidelines, a criminal statute may permit 'a standard less sweeping [that] allows policemen, prosecutors, and juries to pursue their personal predilections.'"
2 *Kolender v. Lawson,* 103 S.Ct. 1855 (1983).
3 Civil Rights Act of 1964, s. 703(a)(1).
4 *New York Times*, April 24, 1964, p.23.

Chapter 4

1 *Fortune*, March 1973, p. 162.
2 Prof. Herman Belz, *Affirmative Action from Kennedy to Reagan*, (Washington DC: Washington Legal Foundation, 1984), p. 4.
3 Id., p. 5.
4 Id., p. 5.
5 Id., p. 5.
6 Id., p. 5.
7 Id., p. 5.
8 *Fortune,* April 19, 1972, p. 156.
9 Id., p.156.
10 42 U.S.C. s. 2000e-12. "The Commission shall have authority from time to time to issue, amend or rescind suitable *procedural* regulations...". [emphasis added]

ENDNOTES

11 *EEOC Guidelines on Employment Selection Procedures*, 29 C.F.R. s. 1607, 35 Fed. Reg. 12333 (Aug. 1, 1970).
12 For example, see 110 Cong. Rec. 7246 and 13082.
13 Id., p. 7213.
14 Civil Rights Act of 1964, s. 703(h); 42 U.S.C. 2000e-2(h).
15 *Griggs v. Duke Power Company*, 401 U.S. 424 (1971).

Chapter 5

1 Congressional Record, June 4, 1964, p. 12723.
2 *Griggs v. Duke Power Company*, 401 U.S. 424, 431 (1971).
3 2000e-5(g)(1).
4 *Duke Power*, 401 U.S. at 434.
5 Id., at 426.
6 Lex K. Larson, *Employment Discrimination*, (New York: Matthew Bender), s. 49.50.
7 *Duke Power*, 401 U.S. at 430.
8 Id., at 430.
9 Larson, s. 75.20.
10 *Duke Power*, 401 U.S. at 433.
11 110 Cong. Rec. 7213.
12 Id., at 431.
13 110 Cong. Rec. 7213.
14 Id., p. 7218.

Chapter 6

1 The Equal Opportunity Employment Act of 1972, s. 706.
2 *New York Times*, February 23, 1972, p. 1.
3 Id., February 27, 1972, Sec. IV p. 3.
4 Belz, p. 7.
5 *Duns*, June 1974, p. 85.
6 Id., p. 3.
7 D.L. Rose, Memorandum for the Deputy Attorney General from David L. Rose, Chief, Employment Section, Civil Rights Division, U.S. Department of Justice, July 19, 1976, 122 Cong. Rec. 22590.
8 *Duns*, p. 82.
9 *Business Week*, January 27, 1975, p. 94.
10 *Duns*, p. 83.
11 Id., p. 85.
12 Id., p. 84.
13 Id., p. 85.
14 Id., p. 84.
15 *United Steelworkers of America, AFL-CIO-CLC v. Weber*, 443 U.S. 193 (1979).
16 16 Id. at 194.
17 Congressional Record, June 4, 1964, p. 12723.
18 *United Steelworkers*, at 207.
19 Belz, p. 18.
20 Id., p. 16.
21 *Public Opinion*, August/September 1985, p. 41.
22 *Bangor Daily News*, August 16, 1985, p. 6.
23 *Newsweek*, June 24, 1996, p. 39.

Chapter 7

1 At his press conference, Time, August 30, 1963.
2 *New York Times*, June 30, 1988, p. A19.
3 *Watson v. Fort Worth Bank & Trust*, 487 U.S. 977 (1988).
4 Id., at 983.
5 *New York Times*, June 30, 1988, p. A19.
6 *Watson* at 996.
7 *New York Times*, June 30, 1988, p. A19.
8 *Wards Cove Packing Co., Inc. v. Atonio*, 490 U.S. 642 (1989).

Chapter 8

1 *Brown v. Board of Education*, 347 U.S. 483 (1954).
2 Paul D. Moreno, *From Direct Action to Affirmative Action* (Baton Rouge: Louisiana State University Press, 1997), p. 137.
3 *Brown v. Board of Education*, 349 U.S. 294 (1955).
4 Paul D. Moreno, *From Direct Action to Affirmative Action* (Baton Rouge: Louisiana State University Press, 1997), p. 136.
5 Id., p. 145.
6 Id., p. 140.

SECTION III
Chapter 9

1 As quoted from footnote 13 in Henderson H. Donald, *The Negro Freedman* (New York: Henry Schuman, 1952), p. 2.
2 Robert Higgs, *Competition and Coercion* (Chicago: The University of Chicago Press, 1980), p. 53.

3 Id., p.78.
4 Id., p.117.
5 Id., p. 48.
6 Id., p. 48.
7 Id., p. 49.
8 Id., p. 119.
9 Id., p. 120.
10 Thomas Sowell, *Preferential Policies*, p. 21.
11 John Sibley Butler, *Entrepreneurship and Self-Help Among Black Americans* (Albany: State University of New York Press, 1991), p. 171.
12 Robert Higgs, *Competition and Coercion* (Chicago: The University of Chicago Press, 1980), p. 86.
13 Id., p. 86.
14 Id., p. 66.
15 Id., p. 87.
16 Id., p. 88.
17 John Sibley Butler, *Entrepreneurship and Self-Help Among Black Americans* (Albany: State University of New York Press, 1991), p. 69.
18 Id., p. 76.
19 *Business History Review*, August 1986, p. 345.
20 Id., p. 350.
21 John Sibley Butler, *Entrepreneurship and Self-Help Among Black Americans* (Albany: State University of New York Press, 1991), p. 47.
22 Id., p. 324.

Chapter 10

1 Smith and Welch, *Closing the Gap, Forty Years of Economic Progress for Blacks* (Santa Monica: Rand Corporation, 1986), p. xxviii.
2 Id., p. xvi.
3 Id., p. viii.
4 Id., p .xxiii.
5 Id., p. xxiii.
6 Id., p. 12.
7 Id., p. 12.
8 Id., p. ix.
9 Id., p. xxix.
10 Id., p. xxix.
11 Id., p. xxvi.
12 Id., p. xxvi.
13 Charles Murray, *Losing Ground* (New York: Basic Books, Inc., 1984), p. 70.
14 Id., p. 70.
15 *Collected Bulletins by Johnson O'Connor*, Human Engineering Laboratory, 381 Beacon St., Boston, MA, at p. 46.
16 *An Objective Approach to Group-Influencing Fields,* Human Engineering Laboratory, p. 52.
17 Id., p. 52.
18 *Collected Bulletins by Johnson O'Connor*, Human Engineering Laboratory, at p. 46.
19 Jon J. Durkin, *Aptitudes, Knowledge and Black Children,* Human Engineering Laboratory, Bulletin #107.
20 Thomas Sowell, *Preferential Policies* (New York: William Morrow and Company, 1991), p. 174.
21 Smith and Welch, p. 104.
22 Murray, p. 245.
23 Id., p. 245.
24 Smith and Welch, p. xxv.
25 Id., p. xxiv.
26 Id., p. 105.
27 Murray, p. 159.
28 Id., p. 161.
29 Id., p. 161.
30 Murray, p. 162.
31 Id., p.127.
32 Id., p. 127.
33 Prof. Mark Rosenzweig, University of Pennsylvania. Paper presented at National Academy of Sciences, April 1996, as reported in *The American Enterprise*, July/August 1996.
34 Michael Tanner, Stephen Moore, and David Hartman. *The Work vs. Welfare Trade-Off,* Cato Institute, as reported in *The American Enterprise,* July/August 1996.
35 Murray, p. 98.
36 Id., p. 98.
37 Id., p. 195.
38 Edward S. Shibadeh and Nicole Flynn, *Segregation and Crime: The Effect of Black Social Isolation on the Rates of Black Urban Violence,* Social Forces 74 [1996] 1325.
39 *American Spectator,* June 1995, p. 24.
40 Thomas Sowell, "Presuppositions of 'Affirmative Action,'" 26 *Wayne Law Review* 1319.

ENDNOTES

41 R. Freeman, *Black Elite*, ch.4, as cited by Sowell.
42 Sowell, p. 1319.
43 Id, p. 1319.
44 William Raspberry, *Washington Post*, March 4, 1988.
45 Walter E. Williams, *The State Against Blacks* (New York: New Press, 1982), frontispiece.

Chapter 11

1 *Public Opinion*, August/September 1985, p. 42.
2 The NAACP, Urban League, Southern Christian Leadership Conference, Operation PUSH, the National Conference of Black Mayors, and the Congressional Black Caucus.
3 *Public Opinion*, p. 42.
4 Much of this section is from an essay by Marvin Olasky, *Booker T. Washington, Freedom Through Faith and Labor*, published by the Capital Research Center, 727 15th St., NW, Washington, DC 20005.
5 John Sibley Butler, *Entrepreneurship and Self-Help Among Black Americans* (Albany: State University of New York Press, 1991), p. 66.
6 As quoted in *Booker T. Washington, Freedom Through Faith and Labor*, published by the Capital Research Center, 727 15th St NW, Washington, DC 20005.
7 Capital Research Center, 727 15th St NW, Washington, DC 20005.
8 *The American Enterprise*, March/April 1997, p. 15.
9 *The Washington Times*, February 17, 1997, p. 6.
10 Id., February 18, 1997, p. 12.
11 Austin M. Folk and Stuart B. Nolan, *#20 Patterns of Corporate Philanthropy*, Capital Research Center, 727 15th St. NW, Washington, D.C. 20005.
12 *The American Spectator*, July 1996, p. 40.
13 Id., July 1996, p. 39.
14 Clint Bolick, *In Whose Name*, p. 39.
15 Id., p. 25.

Chapter 12

1 Epstein, p. 92.
2 Id., p. 125.
3 Id., p. 46.
4 Id., p. 125.
5 Id., p. 98.
6 *Plessy v. Ferguson*, 163 U.S. 537 (1896).
7 *Berea College v. Kentucky*, 211 U.S. 45 (1908).
8 Epstein, p. 16.
9 Id., p. 59.
10 Id., p. 68.
11 Id., p. 72.
12 Id., p. 93.
13 Bruce Bartlett, Senior Fellow with the National Center for Policy Analysis, *The Washington Times*, February 16, 1997, p. B3. Mr. Bartlett recommends two sources which tell of black advancement. Prof. Juliet Walker of the U. of Illinois tells of black success even before the Civil War (some of whom were very wealthy) in *Business History Review*, Autumn 1996. Prof. John Sibley Butler of the U. of Texas has a book about black entrepreneurship since the Civil War, *Entrepreneurship and Self-Help Among Black Americans* (State University of New York Press, 1991).
14 Epstein, p. 254.
15 Walter Williams, *The State Against Blacks*, p. 35.
16 *New York Times*, by Robert D. Hershey, Jr., July 9, 1996, retrieved from America Online.
17 *Washington Post*, July 6, 1988.
18 Walter Williams, p. 43.
19 *New York Times*, by Eric Schmitt, July 9, 1996, retrieved from America Online.
20 *Allgeyer v. Louisiana*, 165 U.S. 578 (1897).
21 Williams, p. 76.
22 Id., p. 92.
23 Id., p. 93.
24 *Local 28 of Sheet Metal Workers v. EEOC*, 106 S.Ct. 3019 (1986).
25 Williams, p. 45.
26 Id., p. 123.
27 Id., p. 145.

Chapter 13

1 Solomon Northrup, *Twelve Years A Slave*, p. 25.
2 Id., p. 139.
3 Id., p. 62.
4 Id., p. 221.
5 Id., p. 158.
6 Thomas Sowell, *Black Education, Myths and Tragedies*, p. 292.
7 *Human Events,* November 15, 1996, p. 20.
8 In an interview produced by the Hoover Institution at Stanford University and PBS. Quoted in the *Washington Times,* November 18, 1996, p. A8.
9 *The American Enterprise,* March/April 1997, p. 11.
10 Keith B. Richburg, *Out of Africa* (New York: Basic Books, 1997), pp. 247-248.
11 *Running Boston's Bureaucratic Marathon,* Institute for Justice, Washington, D.C.

SECTION IV

1 Betty Friedan, *The Feminine Mystique* (New York: Dell Publishing Co., 1963) p. 13.
2 Id., p. 173.
3 Id., p. 26.
4 Id., p. 11.
5 *New York Times Magazine,* March 10, 1968, p. 62.

Chapter 14

1 Friedan, p. 142.
2 Marcia Cohen, *The Sisterhood, The True Story of the Women Who Changed the World* (New York: Simon and Schuster, 1988), p. 33.

Chapter 15

1 Cohen, p. 139.
2 *New York Times Magazine,* March 10, 1968, p. 24.
3 Id., p. 24.
4 Id., p. 58.
5 Id., p.62.
6 Friedan, p. 27.
7 Id., p. 142.
8 Id., p. 142
9 Id., p. 347.
10 Cohen, p. 268.
11 Id., p. 275.
12 Id., p. 59.
13 Id., p. 58.
14 Id., p. 59.
15 Id., p. 59.
16 Friedan, p. 63.
17 Id., p. 63.
18 Cohen, p. 31.
19 Id., p. 29.
20 Id., p 36.
21 Id., p. 117.
22 Id., p. 34.
23 Id., p. 45.
24 Id., p. 50.
25 Id., p. 109.
26 Id., p. 78.
27 Friedan, p. 339.
28 Cohen, p. 35.
29 Id., p. 120.
30 Id., p. 125.
31 Id., p. 125.
32 Id., p. 257.
33 Id., p. 257.
34 Id., pp. 72-79, 232-254.
35 Cohen, p. 309.
36 *New York Times Magazine,* March 15, 1970, p. 128.
37 Id., March 10, 1968, p. 55.
38 Cohen, p. 167.
39 *New York Times Magazine,* March 15, 1970, p. 27.
40 Cohen, p. 204.
41 Id., p. 202.
42 *New York Times Magazine,* March 15, 1970, p. 128.
43 Cohen, p. 101.
44 Id., p. 334.
45 Id., p. 334.
46 Id., p. 332.
47 Id., p. 336.
48 Id., p. 350.
49 Id., p. 321.
50 Id., p. 321.
51 Id., p. 218.
52 Id., p. 114.
53 Id., p. 249.

ENDNOTES

54 Friedan, p. 266.
55 Id., p. 266.
56 Id., p. 266.
57 *New York Times*, Editorial, June 6, 1997.
58 *US Today*, Editorial, May 19, 1997.
59 *New York Times Magazine*, March 10, 1968, p. 58.

Chapter 16

1 110 Congressional Record, Part 2, February 8, 1964, p. 2580.
2 Id., p. 2580.
3 *Johnson v. Transportation Agency, Santa Clara County, California*, 480 U.S. 616 (1987).
4 Id., p. 642.
5 Id., p. 677.
6 *Equal Employment Opportunity Commission v. Sears, Roebuck & Co.*, 628 F.Supp. 1264, 1292 (N.D.Ill. 1986).
7 Id., p. 1292.
8 Id., p. 1292.
9 Id., p. 1264.
10 Id., pp. 1273, 1276.
11 Id., p. 1289.
12 Id., p. 1307.
13 Id., p. 1306.
14 Id., p. 1321.
15 Id., p. 1319.
16 Id., p. 1319.
17 Id., p. 1294.
18 Id., p. 1301.
19 Id., p. 1301.
20 *EEOC v. Libbey-Owens-Ford Company*, 692 F.Supp. 871 (July 29, 1988), and 482 F.Supp. 357 (1978), and 616 F.2d 278 (1980).
21 *New York Times*, May 27, 1967, p. 41.
22 *State Div. of Human Rights v. New York City Dept. of P. & R.*, 326 N.Y.S.2d 640 (1971).
23 *Gunther v. Iowa State Men's Reformatory*, 22 F.E.P. 1382 (8th Cir. 1980).
24 Associated Press reported in *The Washington Times*, June 20, 1997, p. A8.
25 *County of Alameda v. Fair Employment & Housing Comm'n*, 153 Cal. App. 3d 499 (1984).
26 *EEOC Dec. No. 80-25*, 26 F.E.P. 1808 (1980).
27 *Dolter v. Wahlert High School*, 21 F.E.P. 1413 (N.D.Iowa 1980).
28 *Lynch v. Freeman*, 817 F.2d 380 (6th Cir. 1987).
29 *Ryan v. Raytheon Data Sys. Co.*, 601 F.Supp 243 (D.Mass. 1984).
30 *Shore v. Federal Express Corp.*, 589 F.Supp. 662 (W.D.Tenn 1984), 777 F.2d 1155 (1985).
31 *Jackson v. Sargent*, 394 F.Supp 162 (D.Mass 1975), aff'd sub nom, *Jackson v. Dukakis*, 526 F.2d 64 (1st Cir. 1975).
32 *Gallup Opinion Index*, Rep.145, 23 (June, 1977).
33 Susan Manuel, *Women Say Court Erred on Hiring, USA Today*, March 31, 1987, p. 3A.

Chapter 17

1 Press release, March 29, 1996. "Radical Right Anti-Abortion Agenda Gets Boost; NOW Promises to Intensify Fight for Reproductive Rights."
2 Id.
3 Press Release, May 15, 1996. "Statement of NOW Action Vice- President Rosemary Dempsey on Hearings Held Today on Federal Anti-Marriage Bill."
4 Press Release, May 20, 1996. "NOW Leader Who Fought Colorado's Amendment Call Ruling On It 'Revolutionary'."
5 *Legislative Update*, July 15, 1996.
6 Id., July, 15, 1996.
7 "Whose Promises Are They Keeping" by Jena Recer, NOW Intern.
8 "The Wrongs of the So-Called 'Right,'" p. 1.
9 Friedan, p. 260.
10 Cohen, p. 175.
11 James Bovard, *The American Spectator*, July 1996, p. 40.

Chapter 18

1 *Vinson v. Taylor*, 23 Fair Empl.Prac.Cas. (BNA) 37, 42 (D.D.C.1980); 753 F.2d 142 (1985); *Meritor Sav. Bank, FSB v. Vinson*, 477 U.S. 57 (1986).

2. Most of the testimony of the trial was not transcribed. In addition to the facts cited in the District Court opinion, some of these were obtained from feature stories in the *Washington Post*, August 11 and 12, 1986 at p. C1.
3. The citations to the facts, unless otherwise cited are to the copy of the opinion that was in the transcript filed with the Court of Appeals. The Opinion of the United States District Court was filed February 26, 1980, and signed by Judge John Garrett Penn. p. 31a. See also an article in the *Washington Post*, August 12, 1986, p. C1.
4. *Washington Post*, August 12, 1986, pp. C1 and C4.
5. Opinion of Judge Penn, p. 31a.
6. *Washington Post*, August 12, 1986, p. C4, Opinion, p. 31a.
7. *Washington Post*, August 12, 1986, p. C4.
8. Opinion, p. 31a.
9. *Washington Post*, August 12, 1986, p. C4, Opinion, p. 32a.
10. Opinion, p. 32a.
11. Id., p. 32a.
12. Id., p. 31a.
13. Id., p. 32a.
14. Id., p. 33a.
15. *Washington Post*, August 11, 1986, p. C2.
16. Id.
17. Opinion, p. 43a.
18. Id.
19. Id., p. 42a.
20. 753 F.2d 142 (DC Circuit 1985).
21. See endnote 1.
22. *Variety*, July 1, 1996.
23. Amici Curiae of Women's Bar Association of Massachusetts, Minnesota Women Lawyers, Inc., Women Lawyers Association of Michigan, Colorado Women's Bar Association, at p. 10.
24. Id., p. 10.
25. By Jean Bethke Elshtain, Winter 1997.

Chapter 19

1. *Affirmative Action Reconsidered*, American Enterprise Institute, p. 28.

2. *Women's Figures: The Economic Progress of Women in America*, by Diana Furchtgott-Roth and Christine Solba. Independent Women's Forum, 2111 Wilson Blvd., Arlington, VA 22201. Tel: 800-224-6000.
3. *The Washington Times*, February 5, 1997, p. A14.
4. *Working Woman*, November 1986, p. 152.

Chapter 20

1. Friedan, p. 71.
2. *The Boston Globe*, January 30, 1997. A column by Diane White.
3. *New Man*, November-December 1997, p. 34.
4. Id., p. 37.
5. *Commentary*, February 1997, p. 25.
6. Id., p. 42.

SECTION V
Chapter 21

1. *Julia Prewitt Brown v. Trustees of Boston University*, 674 F.Supp. 393 (D.Mass. 1987), aff'd in part, 891 F.2d 337 (1st Cir. 1989).
2. *Citizenship Responsibility*, by John R. Silber, President of Boston University, delivered at the Citizenship Responsibility Symposium, Freedoms Foundation, Center for Responsible Citizenship, Washington, D.C., December 13, 1984.
3. Much of the factual information related hereafter is also summarized in the opinion of the First Circuit, 891 F.2d 337.
4. Any references to the trial may be found in the trial transcript.
5. *Newsweek*, March 27, 1978, p. 74.
6. See Silber's speech, endnote 2, *supra*.
7. Belsky, *Early Childhood Research Quarterly*, 1988 vol. 3, p. 265.
8. E.g. "Finesse in the Fight; Former BU Professor Proves She's No Lightweight", *Boston Globe*, August 7, 1987, p.77.

Chapter 22

1. Clint Bolick, *Changing Course* (New Brunswick: Transaction Books, 1988), p. 57.

ENDNOTES

2 Id., p. 5.
3 Id., p. 6.
4 Id., p. 9, quoting F.A. Hayek.
5 Id., p. 65.
6 Id., p. 65.
7 Harrington, p. 75.
8 Williams, p. 145.

Chapter 23

1 Nathan Glazer, *Affirmative Discrimination: Ethnic Inequality and Public Policy* (New York: Basic Books, Inc., 1975), p. 31.
2 Id., p. 32.
3 Id., p. 177.
4 Id., p. 177.
5 *Fullilove v. Klutznick*, 448 U.S. 448 (1980) at 535 fn. 5, in a dissent in a case in which the other judges upheld the constitutionality of a statute, Public Works Employment Act of 1977, which provided that at least 10% of federal funds granted for local public works projects must be awarded to minorities.
6 *Boston Globe*, December 7, 1985, p. 23.

SECTION VI
Chapter 24

1 Congressional Record, Volume 110, part II, p. 14485.
2 *Fortune*, April 19, 1982, p. 152.
3 Paul Johnson, *Modern Times, The World from the Twenties to the Eighties* (New York: Harper & Row, 1983) p. 663. U.S. share of World Exports of Manufactures was 25% in 1960, 22.5% in 1965, and has remained below 20% for most years since. U.S. Dept. of Commerce, International Trade Administration, Office of Trade and Investment Analysis, *Business America*, biweekly; *Market Share Reports*, annual. Output as a fraction of manufacturing capacity peaked at 90% in 1965 and has stayed below 80% for most years since. Board of Governors of the Federal Reserve System, *Capacity Utilization in Manufacturing, Mining, Utilities, and Industrial Materials*, G.3., monthly. Based on data from Federal Reserve Board, Commerce, U.S. Bureau of Labor Statistics, and McGraw Hill Information Systems, New York, NY.
4 *The Washington Times*, February 19, 1997. p. A12.
5 *Fortune*, March 1973, p. 166.
6 Id., March 1973, p. 167.
7 Belz, p. 14.
8 Id., p. 16.
9 U.S. Bureau of Labor Statistics, *Monthly Labor Review*, February 1995.
10 The value of the dollar dropped dramatically in the mid 1980s, as is evidenced by historical information on exchange rates. Board of Governors of the Federal Reserve System, *Federal Reserve Bulletin*, monthly.
11 The U.S. trade balance has been consistently negative since the early 1970's. It became worse in the early 1980's, became slightly better in the late 1980's due to booming exports, but it has worsened quickly in the 1990's. U.S. Bureau of the Census, 1970-88 *Highlights of U.S. Export and Import Trade*, FT990, monthly; beginning 1989, *U.S. Merchandise Trade; Export, General Imports, and Imports for Consumption*, series FT 925, monthly. The U.S. Direct Investment Position Abroad more than doubled between 1985 and 1992, from $230 billion to $486 billion. U.S. Bureau of Economic Analysis, *Survey of Current Business*, July 1993.
12 *Duke Power* at 433.
13 *U.S. v. Lee Way Motor Freight, Inc.*, 7 F.E.P. 710 (W.D. Okla. 1973).
14 *Jackson v. Sargent*, 394 F.Supp. 162 (D.Mass. 1975); aff'd sub nom, *Jackson v. Dukakis*, 526 F.2d 64 (1st Cir. 1975).
15 *Hill v. Nettleton*, 455 F.Supp. 514 (C.D. Co. 1978).
16 *Washam v. J.C. Penney Co.*, 519 F.Supp. 554 (D.Del. 1981).
17 EEOC Dec. No. 80-12, 26 F.E.P. 1794 (August 1, 1980).
18 EEOC Dec. No. 80-4, 26 F.E.P. 1785 (March 24, 1980).
19 *Bonilla v. Oakland Scavenger Co.*, 697 F.2d 1297 (9th Cir. 1983).
20 *Fisher v. Proctor & Gamble Manufacturing Company*, 613 F.2d 527 (5th Cir. 1980), cert. denied, 449 U.S. 115 (1981).

21 Id., p. 156.
22 *Business Week*, January 27, 1975, p. 94.
23 *U.S. News & World Report*, August 14, 1972, p. 68.
24 Id., p. 66.
25 *Business Week*, October 13, 1986, p. 66; *Newsweek*, October 6, 1986, p.35; *Wall Street Journal*, November 10, 1986, p. 23.
26 Id., January 27, 1975, p. 94.
27 *The Tab*, July 9, 1996, p. 7.
28 *The Women's Quarterly*, Autumn 1997, p. 12.

Chapter 25

1 For an excellent article on how the OFCCP is punishing business see an article by James Bovard in *The American Spectator*, July 1996, p. 36.
2 Daily Labor Report, Bureau of National Affairs, May 26, 1988, p. C-1.
3 Id., p. C-1.
4 Id., p. C-1.
5 Mark S. Pestal, *Deferring Frivolous Lawsuits, A Case Study*, Washington Legal Foundation.
6 *EEOC At A Glance*, U.S. Equal Opportunity Commission, 1974, p. 1.
7 *Fortune*, April 19, 1982, p. 148.
8 Id., p. 148.
9 *Missouri Lawyers Weekly*, July 21, 1997, p. 1.
10 *Human Events*, February 21, 1997, p. 12.
11 *Women's Figures: The Economic Progress of Women in America*, by Diana Furchtgott-Roth and Christine Solba. Independent Women's Forum, 2111 Wilson Blvd., Arlington, VA 22201. Tel: 800-224-6000.
12 *Nation's Business*, July 1982, p. 53.

SECTION VII

1 Thomas Sowell, *Preferential Policies, An International Perspective*, p. 15.

Chapter 27

1 Clarence Thomas, *Congress, The Bureaucracy, And The Enforcement of Civil Rights*, a paper presented at the Annual Meeting of the American Political Science Association, September 3, 1987, at p. 15.
2 Id., p. 16.
3 Id., p. 16.
4 Id., p. 18.
5 Id., p. 21.
6 Id., p. 21.
7 Donald Lambro, *Washington-City of Scandals*, p. 68.

Chapter 28

1 *Fortune*, March 1973, p. 191.
2 *The Washington Times*, October 12, 1996, p. A4.
3 *Newsday*, April 17, 1994, p. A94.
4 This anecdote is reported in *Boston Phoenix*, October 11, 1991, p. 14 and April 16, 1993, p. 18; GQ, August 1993, p. 144 (some of this article appears to be satire); and *The New Yorker*, May 3, 1993, p. 34.
5 *Boston Globe*, October 23, 1997, p. A25.
6 *Boston Globe*, November 3, 1997, p. A15.
7 *Human Events*, September 20, 1996.
8 Id., September 20, 1996.
9 *The Washington Times*, October 23, 1997, p. A9.

EPILOGUE

1 "The guilt of the accused was assumed, and he was treated as a sinner who was expected to seek salvation by unburdening his conscience and contritely accepting whatever penance might in mercy be imposed on him." Henry Charles Lea, *The Inquisition of Spain* (London: MacMillan Company, 1906), Vol. III p. 36.
2 *Duns*, June 1974, p. 85.

APPENDIX

1 Kearns, p.207